BRIAN HOGAN

D0891120

There's a Sheep in my Bathtub

Birth of a Mongolian Church
Planting Movement

Tenth Anniversary Edition

There's a Sheep in my Bathtub

Email: info@AsteroideaBooks.com. Web: www.AsteroideaBooks.com

If you love this book please review it on Amazon.com or Goodreads.com.

All scripture quotations in this publication are from the Contemporary English Version Copyright © 1991, 1992, 1995 by American Bible Society, Used by Permission.

All photographs property of the author, except page 74, property of Lance Reinhart and used with permission.

First Edition printed October 2007

10th Anniversary Edition published October 2017.

ISBN 978-0-9986111-1-2

Library of Congress Control #: 2017916313

DEDICATIONS

Jesus: The Team Captain of the only team that ever mattered. I was always the last one picked until that day in 1980 I heard you call out, "We want Brian!" Thank you!

Louise: There is absolutely no one I would rather be with on this Journey. I'm so glad I asked.

Our Apostolic Team: Magnus & Maria, Svetlana & Ruslan, Lance Reinhart, Mats Berbres. Without you this would have stayed a dream — and a whole lot less fun! *Ecclesia plantada*!

Our Mongol Disciples: Bayaraa, *Jesus' Assembly*'s first fourteen, all the others; Your joyful obedience to Jesus continues to make it all worth the price.

Contents

Map of Mongolia

FOREWORD

If you appreciate the adventures of pioneer missionaries, you will enjoy reading Brian Hogan's *There's a Sheep in my Bathtub.* Brian's workshops have inspired many with his dramatic and humorous style of teaching, and he brings that same stirring dynamic into this book. Many of us who have written about church planting movements have focused mainly on guidelines drawn from observations of field work and Scripture. Brian includes these but adds a plentiful and colorful variety of experiences from the human side, with their joys and pathos, laughter and tears. He relates how he, his wife Louise and their children overcame impossible obstacles with prayer and sheer endurance.

Their adventures include inadvertently crashing a party while searching desperately for a place to eat and being rewarded with a great banquet; on other occasions they had to eat things to survive that Westerners normally would feed only to a dog that they strongly dislike. They had to deal with clever con-artists, family tragedy, and other severe trials that tested their faith.

One of the challenges was to discover God's key to let the Good News of Jesus spread freely in a Buddhist society. The Mongolian people have a centuries-old world view that makes the truths of our faith incomprehensible and the usual Western presentation of the gospel sound like an alien invasion. They struggled to find a way to get entire families to embrace Christ and share to the new life with others. The breakthrough came in a way that men would not have planned, and included miraculous healings and other signs and wonders that confirmed the truth of the new message, liberating the Mongolians, young and old, from their spiritual bondage. Brian and his coworkers discovered how to train new leaders in the way that Jesus and His apostles did, and other New Testament guidelines.

I count it a privilege to be among those who have helped Brian develop his field strategies. He took seriously the New Testament guidelines that I taught while he coordinated the *Perspectives on the World Christian Movement* classes and later, in a YWAM School of Frontier Mission in the fall of 1992. I first learned to apply these principles in Honduran villages where traditional church planting methods were ineffective. Brian likewise learned to apply them in Mongolia, where God brought about a church planting movement under conditions that made Western methods impractical.

The most important of the New Testament guidelines that I helped Brian to apply, is that of building discipleship, church planting and ongoing ministry on the foundation of simple, loving, childlike obedience to Jesus' commands, as Jesus' Great Commission at the end of Matthew's gospel requires. Jesus said, 'If you love me, keep my commands.' Brian's love for Jesus and his resulting obedience to Jesus' commands simplified church planting in Mongolia. Many church planters follow such a long list of things to do to start a church that they fail to give top priority to the few essential activities, and end up doing so many things that the key, pivotal elements of church planting are buried in the plethora of work items. If you disciple others, plant churches or multiply cell groups, Sheep in the Bathtub will help you also to simplify the work by forming priorities that line up with Jesus' commands. Often the surest way to discern God's is simply by starting out doing what He orders us to do in the New Testament!

In an age when many missionaries limit their commitment to a short term, doing what they have set out to do, and no more, Brian and Louise went way beyond what they had expected. They stuck it out in spite of sub-zero weather, hostile authorities, deception from trusted friends and other obstacles that would have deterred the average missionary. They persevered to see a movement for Christ in Erdenet, Mongolia, develop through an inauspicious birth, growing pains and many trying setbacks, to finally become a mature, truly indigenous church planting movement that has served as a model for many new workers.

George Patterson

ONE

Iron Gates

The five of us were bundled up against the frigid winds blowing through Beijing as we unfolded ourselves from the taxi's cramped interior. We'd had our Hotel Dong Fang concierge order us a cab to get us here by the start of business this morning of February 22nd, 1993. Heavy black iron gates of the Mongolian Embassy to The People's Republic of China loomed before us. Behind those gates and inside the embassy were the visas we needed to enter Mongolia and follow God's call on our lives.

We couldn't help but notice a crowd of about 50 was encamped between us and the gates. Asking my wife, Louise, to wait at the curb with our three young daughters, I pushed through the milling collection of Chinese and Mongolians to the armed guard at the gate. I comforted myself with the idea that all these people probably had no legitimate business inside, and I would be quickly passed through. The unsmiling guard, however, failed to move aside or provide an explanation in English. I mimed I needed to speak to someone inside and he motioned me over to an intercom. This was good progress. We'd be inside, out of the cold, in just a few moments.

The speaker crackled to life in response to my buzz. "Yes, how may I help you?" an accented female voice queried. I explained my family needed to get in to secure our visas for Mongolia.

"That is impossible until Wednesday, sir. The Embassy is closed for our Mongolian national holiday."

I was stunned. We had, with some difficulty, purchased tickets to fly into Ulaanbaatar, Mongolia's capital, the next day. We couldn't afford to stay any longer than two nights at the Dong Fang, and we had no way of contacting our friends in Mongolia to tell them we would be arriving late. Stalling for time to sort out my thoughts, I blurted, "What national holiday?" She answered it was the weeklong winter festival called *Tsagaan Sar,* the Herdsmen's New Year. I held down the talk button and quickly maintained we couldn't wait for Wednesday, since we had non-exchangeable tickets on MIAT, the national airline.

"Sir, I am sorry but the ambassador is celebrating the holiday and will be indisposed until Wednesday. He cannot issue any visas until then."

I was crushed, but I really had no alternative, so I kept begging her to make an exception. I told this lady all about my three small daughters who, at seven, four and almost two years old, couldn't stand outside in this bitter cold (-6° C / 20° F). The girls' staccato complaints through chattering teeth in the background helped our case. I wished I could hold them up to a security camera and show her their frost-nipped cheeks and runny noses.

It worked! Asians have a wonderful soft heart toward children, and especially larger families.

"Okay, go back to your hotel and telephone at two o'clock in the afternoon. Perhaps the ambassador will be awake and able to help you then."

I thanked her profusely and pushed back out through the crowd to Louise and the girls. I was praising God for this new hope, but Louise was discouraged by the news, and the exhaustion and strain of moving a family of five into the unknown was clear on her face. I knew if we just went back and twiddled our thumbs in that small hotel room until two o'clock we'd all be ready for straitjackets. We had to get our minds off what we were facing. We prayed briefly and committed everything one more time to the Lord, and then caught another cab and went to Tiananmen Square to kill time.

Not one sign remained of the massacre that happened there just a few years before. We stood in the endlessly shuffling line to visit Mao's preserved corpse in his huge "Mao-soleum." There were constant warnings to be quiet and respectful. There was a very religious reverence both encouraged by the guards and observed by the thousands visiting. We were so nervous about the girls blurting something out, grabbing a flower, or goodness knows what. As we exited into the cold yet refreshing outside air, Melody said loudly, "That was just a dead guy!" We beat a hasty retreat from this shrine to the founder of Chinese Communism. Still, her seven-year-old wisdom was a graphic reminder of the risen Christ's superiority over the gods of men and their governments.

Back in our hotel room, when two o'clock finally came, I called the Mongolian Embassy and the same woman told me to call again in an hour. We decided I should go again in person and wait at the embassy, while Louise stayed behind with the girls and covered me with prayer.

A crowd of 20 was milling around at the gates when I arrived. I quickly determined we were all in the same boat. There was another American there who spoke Mandarin Chinese. He was an elderly missionary trying to transit through Mongolia to teach in Siberia. He had actually been brought up in China by missionary parents before the Communist Revolution expelled them. My new friend explained everyone had been told to wait in case the ambassador could be sobered up enough to grant visas. He had been busy observing the Tsagaan Sar custom of getting drunk on vodka and gorging on meat dumplings and staying that way for an entire week. Someone within had divulged that he was apparently just short of comatose from last night's revels, and the staff had been unable to rouse him.

As we waited, stomping around to prevent losing toes to frostbite, we experienced some strange crowd dynamics. A rumor would shoot through the growing group at the gates that the back gate was open and admitting people. Suddenly, like migrating wildebeests, without any discussion, all of us would go tearing around the large compound's perimeter. We'd arrive at the back gate, only to find it as closed and guarded as the front gate. We'd sheepishly wander back around to the front of the embassy until another rumor would start us off again. Every once in a while, a car would go in or out and the guard would hold us all back. His hand on his gun dispelled any thoughts of a run on the embassy.

After about an hour of this, it hit me that the physical reality of having the gates of Mongolia, represented by the embassy, closed against me was a picture of the same thing happening spiritually. I began to pray loudly and worship fiercely against those "gates," actually laying my hands on the iron gates and commanding them to open for the ambassador of the King of Kings and Khan of Khans. I sang out loud "Jesus Christ is Lord of Mongolia." My missionary friend moved away to the other side of the crowd, convinced the strain had fully unhinged me. Mongolians and Chinese gave me extra room and gazed on me in stunned amazement. Even the guard did nothing as I walked past him and grabbed the gates. They all thought I was a lunatic. I felt God in what I was doing and so I continued, telling him silently if He didn't move to open the gates I'd die of embarrassment. Either way my problem would be solved.

After about five minutes of verbal prayer warfare and worship that seemed like 50, I abruptly ran out of things to say. I just sputtered to a stop. At least 30 pairs of eyes were drilling into my back as I faced that gate. I was afraid to even look in the guard's direction.

"God . . .? Now what? I can't just stand here."

I had an urge to call inside on the intercom. Without asking the stunned guard, who was right next to it, I walked over and punched the buzzer. A male voice answered, "What?"

"This is Mr. Hogan. I was instructed to return at two o'clock to see the Ambassador. It is now half past three. You need to open this gate and let me in," I said with sudden confidence.

"Ummm . . . five minutes?" he sputtered in reply.

I could see his face in the window across the courtyard. I held up my wrist and pointed to my watch. "Five minutes," I repeated firmly. I saw him nod.

Exactly five minutes later, to the amazement of all those waiting, myself included, the gates swung open. You could have knocked the whole crowd over with a feather! Not one of us had been allowed inside that whole day!

I marched across the courtyard, conscious of the envious stares following me in, and entered the building. After hanging up my coat, I found myself in an elegant sitting room with two French diplomats and an American petrochemical executive. It turned out they were more comfortably engaged in the same thing the people outside were doing: waiting for the possible appearance of the ambassador. They had been informed when, and if, the staff could rouse him, we might be able to see him. To marshal more prayer, I called Louise at the hotel, filled her in and then waited.

After about a half hour, I started worrying about my more conservative missionary brother outside in the wind whipping across from Siberia. I went over to the Mongolian manning the desk who had buzzed me in.

"Do you see the old man out there?" I asked. He nodded. "Well, he is an American who was born in China many years ago. He has spent his life helping Asian people. If he becomes ill from this cold and dies, I think it will be a huge shame on your country for leaving this good and frail man outside."

"Please tell him to come inside!" he exclaimed with real concern and he hit the gate opener while I ran out front and waved him past the guard. He gratefully joined the little VIP group waiting inside.

At six o'clock, after a two and a half hour wait inside the Embassy, the Ambassador of Mongolia appeared through a doorway, supported by two friends equally hung over and pained. He took the seat at the desk vacated by the intercom guy. Our group quickly lined up to meet with him.

"Gentlemen, I am not feeling well and my head hurts from too much . . ."he rasped, clicking his forefinger against his throat in what was clearly sign language for drinking. He managed a smile both sly and wry. "You will please present your documents, invitation, and return airline tickets. I will issue you visas if all is in order. And please, talk quietly." His friends left the room. I noticed a boy of about 10, whom I assumed was his son, standing beside the Ambassador. This kid was doing all the stamping in the passports for his father.

I noticed everyone except me had availed themselves of the visa application forms stacked just out of eyeshot from the chair I had just vacated. I got out of the short line and frantically began filling in the five forms we needed. Juggling passports and transcribing numbers, dates, flight info, and remembering everyone's birth date was keeping me busy, but not too busy to realize I was in trouble. I had the passports and sufficient dollars for the visas, but I had neither return tickets nor letter of invitation or contract to work in Mongolia! I could hear him asking the older missionary to produce each of these items - and that just to transit through the country!

"Oh God," I breathed, "you haven't done all this and opened those gates out there just to have this man send us back. Please get me through this!"

I finished scribbling out the forms just as the line dwindled to only one in front of me. Soon I was the last one. I was still struggling to rubber cement the correct photo on each application when the Ambassador wearily reached out for my paperwork. As he scanned our applications, I was praying hard he would not ask me to see our return tickets or proof of a Mongolian hosting organization, as he had just requested everyone before me.

By some miracle, he didn't ask me to produce any tickets at all. He only wanted to know who was inviting us into Mongolia.

The truth was I didn't have any clear idea of this myself. My only hope was the two very-young Mongolian entrepreneurs I had been in contact with had actually been able to come up with something since we had left home. Aldar and Batjargal, who'd made a business out of helping missionaries, had been telexed instructions to fax the embassy with the details of any contract they could manage to arrange for us. We had never received any response, and indeed we doubted our telex had even reached them. The last contact we'd had with them had not been promising.

With sudden inspiration I replied, rather louder than he preferred, "It's written on our letter of invitation they telexed you. Why don't you get the telex and we can both look at it."

Strictly speaking, this was a possibility. If any contract for us to work in Mongolia was in existence, it was certainly here somewhere. I prayed he wouldn't even look.

The Ambassador shot me a disgusted look and said in a raspy voice, "That will not be necessary." He passed the five open passports to his boy and our blue Mongolian visas were stamped inside at six forty-five p.m.

We flew out for Mongolia early the next morning. God had been true to his word to us. The "door of steel" (the iron embassy gates) we'd encountered proved to be only "tinfoil" as we burst through. As exhilarating as these miracles were, Louise and I were both hoping we had faced our last barrier of this kind.

The Mongolian Embassy in Beijing with modernized gates (9/2017)

TWO

Jump Start

The path leading to that frigid day in Beijing had begun a decade earlier, during my second year at Cal Poly (California Polytechnic University) in San Luis Obispo. I was reading a magazine I'd found in the dormitory called, "In Other Words," a publication of Wycliffe Bible Translators, when the Holy Spirit fell on me and I began to sob uncontrollably. God poured into my spirit His passion for nations that had never heard. I knew immediately this was what people called a "call to missions;" I just had no clear idea what "missions" was. I spent the next five years figuring out what God wanted me to do with this call.

The first thing I did was to change my major, which had been Natural Resources Management. I reasoned that working in the forest, which had always been my dream, was definitely not what I was supposed to do now. Whatever "missions" meant, I was pretty sure it had something to do with people. So I switched to a major in English. Since I had no clear idea of what I was to be preparing for, a general education seemed the best way to go. Besides, English had been my favorite subject, next to History, so why torture myself with something I didn't enjoy?

It wasn't long before I began to think maybe the whole college thing was a distraction from what God wanted for me. I already had decided the main reason I was in college was so I could be a part of the church in San Luis Obispo. I began to think it might be simpler to just leave school and pursue my mission path. I was heedlessly about to do just that when I felt God telling me to submit the decision to my mother's approval. I knew that wasn't my thought. It sounded crazy—of course she'd say no.

Besides, I was almost 20! But the fact I knew it wasn't my idea led me to take it seriously. If God wanted me to drop out, I knew He could over-power my mom and make her tell me to go ahead with my plans.

I waited until she came up for a visit and took her on a walk through the incredible Sea Oak forest in nearby Los Osos. The chill coastal fog raised goose bumps on my arms as Mom and I made our way among the gnarled and twisted moss-hung trees in the preserve. It was the kind of place I imagine ancient druids collecting mistletoe and the aroma of damp oak and loam powerfully conjured that otherworldly vibe. Mom knew that something was up and when we stopped to relax on a trunk that followed the ground rather than reaching for the sky, she pressed me to "spill my guts" and end the mystery. Would she promise to really pray about something, even if she had strong feelings about it? When she agreed, I asked her to check with God and see if He wanted me to drop out of college. She was honest about her feelings against it, but she promised to get God's opinion on the matter. The rest of her visit we were both a bit subdued. True to her word, Mom really did seek God, and a few days later called and told me she felt I wasn't finished at Cal Poly. Since I had been telling God I would take whatever she said as guidance direct from Him, I was trapped. I stuck things out at college.

Actually, it was no great sacrifice. My studies didn't tax me very much. My grades were good. I was on track to finish in four years—quite a feat for Cal Poly. During my third year, I joined a special school that was being offered at the Vineyard Christian Fellowship, the church I'd been attending. It was a high intensity and commitment discipleship school that was supposed to be first priority before college or any other com-mitments. The "School of Discipleship" ran for nine months and com-bined intensive Bible study, relationships, and ministry opportunities. About 35 of us went through it. We all got extremely close and even more devoted to Jesus. One of the young women in the class, Louise Hugo, came to me several times and asked for a lift home, but thrifty and practical as always, I found someone who lived closer to her to take her home. I didn't have any idea she was attracted to me, and she even-tually told God He could have me back. She was content to remain a "single woman for Christ!"

At the end of the school year, we were all sharing our summer plans, and I was surprised to hear Louise was going to lifeguard in a summer camp just as I was planning to do. We talked a bit about this and then said our goodbyes along with everyone else. I didn't think any more about it until I received a postcard from Louise halfway through the summer. She had ended up moving to Santa Barbara to help our pastor, Jack Little, with a new Vineyard church plant there. She was also life-guarding, but at the YMCA. The main thing that caught my eye was her signature: "Love, Louise." I had a lot of time to think while I cleaned the pool all alone. I spent a lot of time thinking about Louise and kicking myself for never having noticed her much. She wrote "love" — I wondered how much.

Just after classes had started again, I drove down to a worship concert in Santa Barbara. It was in a large auditorium and as I was walking up the ramp to leave, I caught sight of Louise walking out ahead of me. I ran up behind her intending to strike up a conversation and surprise her. I put my arms around her from behind and said, "So when you going to marry me?" I couldn't believe what had just popped out of my mouth! Louise looked over her shoulder and saw me. "So, when are you going to ask?"

We were both a bit shocked by what had just happened and conversation lagged a bit as we walked out into the parking lot. We arranged to meet at a coffee shop where some friends were gathering after the event. We slid into the booth next to each other and about 10 others. At some point I leaned over and whispered, "About what you said earlier . . . I'm asking." With all the others sitting around us and suspecting nothing, we managed to decide we'd better pray about it. We discovered we both were called to missions work (whatever that meant!) We agreed to pray until we knew and then make plans accordingly. We said goodnight and headed back north in separate cars — without a kiss.

I prayed about marrying Louise until the next morning; by then I was sure. I called her and took her out to a Mexican restaurant built over the creek in front of the old Spanish Mission in San Luis Obispo — our first "date." I didn't waste any time in telling her I had heard from God and we were supposed to be married. She told me she hadn't gotten any word yet and she would need more time. That was okay. I knew God would tell her the same thing.

Ha! That was the longest week of my life. But at the end of a week, Louise Hugo shared my conviction that we were going to be man and wife. We made it official on October 8th, 1983, although we had to keep it a secret for several weeks so Louise could make a visit to her home in the Mojave Desert and break the news to her devout Catholic parents.

Just a week after we both graduated from Cal Poly, Louise and I were married. It was the 16th of June, 1984—just eight and a half months after I blurted out that surprising proposal. God had plans that were bigger than either of us could begin to imagine.

Our first year of marital bliss was anything but. After four months of slogging away in menial and uninspiring jobs, an opportunity to minister came our way. My Grandma Alice was suffering from Alzheimer's dementia. She and my grandfather needed help if they were to keep living in their own home in Las Vegas. My aunt was building an addition onto her home for them, but it would take time. Louise and I offered to move in with my grandparents until their new place was ready.

Making new friends in a strange city, while living in a single room of someone else's home, is not the easiest thing for newlyweds still struggling with their developing relationship. Caring for Grandma Alice was another challenge. She was losing the ability to carry out the simplest tasks, and Louise needed to take over many of them. Grandma would constantly put things away in odd places, causing us to engage in hour-long searches for car keys and wallets. She'd take a walk every day and buy a dozen eggs every time. We were giving eggs away every week, even while we struggled to buy other groceries on our small salaries. We both ended up life guarding and teaching at the YMCA pool, and we had agreed to pay for groceries in lieu of rent. To spare their dignity, my grandparents had been told they were helping us out.

At church one Sunday we were introduced to a group from a Christian boys home called the Mizpah House. We began to volunteer there and were eventually hired on as counselors. I loved working with these delinquent kids! Their main trouble seemed to be an excess of personality, and I found I enjoyed being around them. Within the structure of the group home program, real relationships and growth were happening all the time. It was exhilarating, and yet, it could be heart breaking at the same time. We often lost kids through running away or violating the law—both of which resulted in transport to youth prison. Connecting with a boy and hoping he would make it, and then having him run away and lose his place in the program brought grief. It hurt. The staff used to wryly joke: the ones you wish would run away never do. Eventually, although we loved the work, the emotional toll and the minimum wage were wearing us out. We had also discovered we were expecting a baby. I took grad classes and secured a substitute-teaching certificate. Eventually I was substituting almost daily and going by Mizpah only to visit. I had learned I loved working with troubled kids and I was gifted at it. We began thinking maybe our calling was to urban youth ministry.

Well before Louise and I had really figured out how to be a couple, we found ourselves a trio. Louise had been in labor as she walked me to work at a nearby elementary school a hot September day in 1985. At lunch I was called into the Principal's office with a note. He told me Louise was at the birthing center and asked me if I would mind finishing out the day in the class I was teaching. I informed him I was leaving immediately and advised him to call Sub Service and ask for a sub for the sub. There was no way I was going to risk missing the birth of my first child.

As it turned out, we had several hours together using the breathing exercises we had practiced. The midwife came into our room at the birthing center regularly to check on the progression of labor. Around four thirty p.m., Melody Grace entered the world. I used the phone in the room to call everyone we knew. By seven that evening, the three of us were back in our suddenly much roomier lodgings.

Just weeks before Melody joined us, Grandpa Jim and Grandma Alice had moved across town to my Aunt Dottie's—into their new semi-independent apartment. All of a sudden, for the first time in our year and a half of marriage, we had an entire house to ourselves. What bliss! Except now there wasn't much to keep us in Las Vegas. On an Easter visit back to San Luis Obispo we were both shocked by how green everything was. We had become so used to the desert we had forgotten how lovely growing things were. We both realized we didn't really like Las Vegas and if we stayed very long we might become stuck there. Besides, the air conditioning on our car went out about this time. We decided a summer in the blistering heat of Las Vegas, with temperatures over 100°F (38°C) daily, without air conditioning or many substituting gigs, was not an option. Within a month, after 20 months in Las Vegas, we loaded up our meager belongings hightailed back to Los Osos. We didn't know it then, but this was to be our third of 23 moves in 23 years of marriage.

Intent on pursuing what we thought God was calling us to do, I worked as a salesman while going back to school at Cal Poly as a Counseling grad student. Eventually, I landed a job starting a new boys' home for a company contracted with the state. I was the manager and worked long hours getting the home set up, staffed, and licensed. A couple of months after we opened for business, the owner of the company wanted a job for his daughter, and gave her mine. I was welcome to stay on as staff working for her, but the idea held no appeal for me. I had to find something else, and fast. I went to the career center on our old college campus to see what job listings they had there. Little did we know it, but this trip to job hunt at Cal Poly would finally open the door and eventually our minds to what God had been calling us to do all along.

THREE

Vision Quest

Back on the campus of our alma mater, only the tangy aroma of toner kept me awake as I searched their entire catalog of job listings for English and Counseling majors. Out of all the offerings, only one position held any attraction at all. I circled it and took the booklet home to Louise so she could follow up and get me an application. It was for a teaching post in a mission elementary school on the Navajo Reservation in Northeastern Arizona. An organization called Navajo Gospel Mission was offering to pay one-half of our support if we would come and teach Navajo fourth and fifth graders. We had no idea what they meant by "half support," but half of something was surely better than all of nothing.

When I returned home from work the next day, Louise was buzzing with excitement. She had called the number listed and spoken with a board member of the mission who lived in our county. He had told her that, while teachers were a need, the biggest need was for dorm parents for the boarding school boys. He thought we sounded perfect for that position and had the mission director in Flagstaff, Arizona call Louise immediately. Tom Dolaghan was an Irishman who's caring and love came right through the phone lines with his brogue. Tom was so excited about our joining the mission that his enthusiasm spread to Louise. The two of them had practically sealed the deal before Louise remembered she ought to involve me. This was what I walked in on. I was on the phone to Tom within a couple minutes. It didn't take long for me to join in the general euphoria. We were going to be missionaries!

It turned out Navajo Gospel Mission was a "faith mission" which meant all workers had to raise their own finances through family, friends, and churches. Because of the Navajo Gospel Academy's urgent need for staff and the short time available for support development before school started in less than four months, we were guaranteed at least one-half of the mandated support amounts by the board, no matter how much came in for us each month. We got the blessing of our church, the Los Osos Vineyard, visited three small groups to share the vision for the Navajo, and sent off a prayer letter to everyone we could think of. About a month and a half after I circled that listing, we were in Hardrock, Arizona, in the middle of the Navajo homeland for "Indian Missionary Candidate Training." Together with other new missionaries, we studied Navajo language and culture, the history and strategy of Navajo Gospel Mission (NGM), and spent a weekend living in a Navajo camp with a family—herding sheep and hanging out. We loved it!

We also fell in love with the other young missionaries we were training alongside. Some were heading for other postings among the Navajo, but several families were targeting the Tarahumara and Hupa tribes. We met one highly unusual family: Rick and Laura Leatherwood and their

Laura & Rick, Apostles to Mongolia

three young boys, were training to work with the Navajo, but all Rick could talk about was Mongolia. He explained God was calling them to the Mongolian people, but Mongolia was completely closed to missionary activity—even short visits were impossible. Rick and Laura believed God was going to open Mongolia to the Gospel and they wanted to be

Navajo hogan   **Mongolian ger**

ready. So, Rick studied the cultures of the world and had determined the Navajo were as close to Mongolians as he could get. Both semi-nomadic nations herded sheep, rode horses, and ate the same food prepared the same way. They even lived in strangely similar round homes: the wood and mud Navajo hogan and the felt-covered Mongolian ger.

The strong cultural connection was explained by the fact the Navajo were among the last to come over the land bridge from Mongolia and Asia, to the American continent. The Leatherwood family would live with and work among Navajos to prepare to penetrate Mongolia. Louise and I were puzzled and fascinated at the same time. God was planting a seed in our hearts that would take five years to bear fruit.

About a month later, in August '87, we three Hogans moved into the boys' dorm at Hardrock Station and prepared to "adopt" 10 Navajo boys ranging in age from 5 to 11. We would have these boys from Sunday evening through Friday afternoon, 20 hours every day. The only time we were "off-duty" was when all the boys were in class and at meal times when they were at the cafeteria. It was tiring but very rewarding. We had a ball, playing with and training these children. Every evening we shared devotions with them and tucked each one into bed. The youngest students were not used to speaking English, sleeping in beds, taking showers, or even spending much time indoors. Everything was a learning experience.

After school we'd explore the rocky hills and colorful canyons, play "Capture the Flag" with the girls' dorm, and talk about Jesus. When the boys were in class in the mornings, Louise, Melody, and I would visit their families in their encampments scattered all over the region. We were thrilled as relationships with these other young parents slowly began to form. The mission had been operating under a "mission-station strategy" in which the Navajo were expected to come to the mission compound for ministry, both practical and spiritual. The school was one device to influence these people. To our fresh point of view, this didn't seem to be working very well. The mission was not impacting many of the families in our area, not even those of our students. We felt we needed to go out and become a part of their world, not wait for them to join ours.

Our strategy was very successful with the Navajo, and they began to invite us off the compound and into their camps. This caused problems for us with the older missionaries—and everyone was older. There was no one our age on staff. Most were our parents' age or older. We were bucking tradition and the status quo in a big way. Dorm parents had never ministered off the compound before. In fact, the four kid-free hours we had each weekday were not considered time-off. It had always been used for working in maintenance, a task for which I am particularly unsuited. At any rate, we perceived that envy was at the root of the problems we were causing. Everyone working out there had originally wanted deep and satisfying relationships with Navajos, but the methodology of the mission-station had ensured those desired friendships would not happen. Now these first-term "kids" were being accepted by the locals in a way no one else really had been.

Our popularity with our coworkers decreased in direct relation to our acceptance by the Navajo families. It got to the point that we were always "in trouble" and it didn't seem right to involve our Navajo friends. The only people we could talk to were two missionary couples, Tom and Theresa Elkins and Mike and Cora Hendricks, who lived 20 dirt-road miles (32km) or so away from Hardrock. Tom and Theresa were with another mission and lived in the middle of nowhere with a Navajo family. They were our heroes and our friends. Mike and Cora ran the NGM station in Piñon, Arizona (Motto: Where the pavement ends and the Wild West begins) and were among the only non-Navajo in town. They were our only safe sounding-board. Together, these two families kept us sane.

We met with Tom Dolaghan at the end of the first school year. Linda, our direct supervisor in Hardrock, was sympathetic and supportive of us and had made Tom aware of what a hard time we were having with the other missionaries. His suggestion was for us to go home for the summer to raise support. (Actually, our support level was strong, at 90-100 percent every month. This was a miracle since we hadn't done much at all to raise support. Most of the staff at Hardrock lived on less than half their required support levels). We would also need to decide whether we wanted to complete the rest of our two year commitment. Tom told us he was praying we would return in September, but he would understand if we didn't.

We spent the summer speaking to groups and counseling with our pastor in Los Osos. He told us he could not think of any reason why we would want to go back, but it wasn't that simple for Louise and me. We missed our boys and Navajo friends deeply, and we really loved the work, but it was hard to see how relationships with our fellow missionaries were going to improve. We kept calling out to God to show us what to do. Finally He spoke to us very clearly. The Father told us we would never learn real commitment in the local church where we had the luxury of relating with only those we chose and with whom connecting was easy. We needed to go back and make the difficult relationships work, regardless of how painful that might be. So we did.

Brian, Louise and Melody with our Navajo boys
Navajo Christian Academy Boys' Dorm, 1988

Navajo Gospel Mission compound, Hardrock, AZ (captured from slide)

FOUR

Getting a Little Perspective

That second year in Hardrock, 1988–89, really set the course for the rest of our lives. We worked very hard on getting along with our coworkers and saw real openness and friendships develop. Apparently, our refusal to cut and run made an impact and caused many to re-evaluate us. Our ministry off-compound continued to blossom and as it looked increasingly like the school would be closing the following year for lack of teachers, we began to dream of a ministry solely among the Navajo camps, or possibly on an NGM team in another tribe. We felt like we had found our place and our calling and we were going to spend the rest of our lives working among Native Americans. Then something happened that changed everything.

Tim Brown brought a class called "Perspectives on the World Christian Movement" into NGM as he joined staff in our Flagstaff HQ. This 17 week college credit course on missions was going to be taught live in Flagstaff and brought out 108 miles (174 km) to Hardrock via the magic of videotape. We were all encouraged to take this class. To be honest, we were not very interested. We were already missionaries and couldn't really see the value of studying something we thought we were fairly expert in. Besides, Louise was due to deliver our second child during the second half of the class. We had contracted with a midwife in Flagstaff, but she felt we were too remote for a home birth and had suggested we get a nice hotel room in town when the time came. With our boys and Melody to care for and another baby on the way, we didn't feel the timing was right to take this class.

Tim was very persuasive. He told me, "Brian, you really need this course." When he finally convinced me—he wouldn't let me take it alone. Tim explained this class would impact my life and ministry so profoundly that Louise would be left behind and confused when the changes came. Eventually we both decided to take it. It was a lot of work! We put in many hours of reading and taking quizzes every week. We would gather in the dining hall with the other students, all missionaries, and listen to teachers like Don Richardson and Betty Sue Brewster call into question almost everything we were doing as a mission. It dismayed and invigorated us at the same time. A whole new world opened up for us. God took our breath away with His unchanging mission purpose that runs through the Bible from Genesis to Revelations. The historical lessons really captured my imagination by showing me how God pursued His passion for the nations across human history even after the close of Scripture. As we studied culture under the world's foremost missionary minds, the lights began to come on and we understood what we had been observing among the Navajo. But it was in the strategy section of Perspectives that Louise and I were arrested with a vision that would impact the rest of our lives and end up propelling our family out into the ends of the earth.

One of our seventeen Perspectives professors was an animated older man with a surplus of energy and passion named George Patterson. George and his wife, Denny, had served in Honduras, pioneering principles of church planting resulting in spontaneous multiplication of disciples and churches. I shouldn't say pioneering, rather rediscovering. The principles George taught us were straight from the New Testament. George had taken Jesus seriously in the Great Commission:

"Jesus came to them and said: I have been given all authority in heaven and on earth! Go to the people of all nations and make them my disciples. Baptize them in the name of the Father, the Son, and the Holy Spirit, and teach them to do everything I have told you. I will be with you always, even until the end of the world."   Matthew 28:18-20 (CEV)

George had begun training his disciples to immediately begin obeying the simple and clear commands of Christ in the New Testament.

Things like:

- loving God and other people
- repenting, believing, and receiving the Holy Spirit
- getting baptized and baptizing others
- celebrating the Lord's Supper
- praying
- giving generously
- making disciples.

This resulted in explosive growth not only in numbers of believers, but in daughter and grand-daughter congregations. This possibility captured our hearts. We longed to be a part of starting a church planting movement out among the completely unreached people groups we had been learning about.

Suddenly, the call we had been struggling to bring into focus, our calling to missions, was crystal clear. We had been created to plant churches where the name of Jesus was not even known. Like Paul put it, we were not to build on someone else's foundation (as we'd been doing in Hardrock), but where Christ had never been preached. Our future was clearer than it had ever been, and the next step was to finish our two-year commitment at Hardrock and head out for the unreached. The most accurate term for this job was the Bible's word for it: apostle. The original meaning of 'sent one" described perfectly what we were called to be as church planters.

Molly Anne joined our family on Election Day '88 in a "home birth" at the Quality Suites in Flagstaff. Louise didn't finish the work required to get her Perspectives certificate, but the "damage" had been done. We were both intent on getting to the field to work among people groups classified as completely unreached by the Gospel. The Navajo were 25 percent Christian. In fact, our friend Rick Leatherwood was working on mobilizing Navajo missionaries in hopes of eventually using them to penetrate Mongolia.

Other than falling off a 40 foot cliff and breaking my jaw, which required surgery and a week in the hospital, the rest of our time on the reservation was really fulfilling. Our Navajo boys adored "Baby Molly" and wanted to hold her almost constantly. One evening I went out to the TV room to fetch Molly back from the boys so Louise could nurse her. Louise noticed our new baby smelled like Doritos and asked me to tell the boys to be careful with food around Molly, as she was too young to eat anything yet. When I told them this they said, "Oh, don't worry Brian, we chewed the chips up good before we fed them to Molly!" So, Molly's first solid food was chewed up Doritos lovingly fed to her by her Navajo big brothers. I couldn't blame them. That was how they had seen baby siblings fed at home in the hogan.

Meanwhile, back in Hardrock, transition was in the air. Due to the closure of the Navajo Christian Academy, many on staff were looking for off-compound ministry opportunities. Our family didn't stick out as much as usual as we made plans to move again. We hoped to go straight into training with Youth With A Mission (YWAM), as we'd heard of a new school they had called the School of Frontier Mission (SOFM) that trained long-term church planters for the unreached. We were going to apply for one at their Pasadena, California base, right next to the United States Center for World Missions. We were familiar with the Center through the Leatherwoods, who used to be on staff there, and through Perspectives, which was created there. I figured we could stay with my mom and volunteer at the Center for a couple of weeks while we talked with the YWAM folks about our training.

As a new short-term volunteer, I was assigned to the Center's Mobilization Department, mainly working with churches around the country to encourage and motivate towards greater involvement in frontier missions. My supervisor was a young guy named Wes Tullis. One day over lunch with Wes I was discussing our plans to get out onto the field and he challenged me. He told me Louise and I should replace ourselves at home with at least 10 people each who would catch the same passion for missions we had already. I nodded politely, but inside was chaffing at even the thought of delaying at all to mobilize others in the States. I remember telling Louise about Wes' words that night and saying I knew that idea was not from God. As if God would want us to wait here while so many were perishing without Him elsewhere!

Yet, the YWAM door seemed closed when we were not accepted in time to make the Pasadena training. So, a bit confused, we moved back north to Los Osos and our home church to see what would happen next. A friend and former employer hired me for a sales position selling pagers. We were still very excited about all we had discovered and wanted to pass it along. We started up a small class in the church—a sort of mini-Perspectives. Twenty people signed up to take the 12 video-based lessons with us. We were amazed! The material had the same powerful impact on them that it had on us back in Hardrock. They begged us to offer the full Perspectives program in our county. They took up a collection and sent me to the Perspectives Coordinators' Workshop in Pasadena. When I came back home I planned the course, invited the biggest names in missions to speak, and they all agreed to come!

We ended up with over 100 students from all over San Luis Obispo County in that first Los Osos Perspectives class in 1991. About halfway through the class, on March 1st, Louise gave birth to our third daughter, Alice Marie. Once again, she had an excellent excuse for not finishing the readings and getting her certificate. We offered the class again the next year in northern San Luis Obispo County and had another 100 students. This time Louise finally got her certificate of completion. All told, rather than the 20 Wes had challenged us for; we had spread the vision to 220 disciples. I had to admit our wait probably was God's idea after all. At the end of our second course, we had all the students pray for us and send us out. We were on our way to Salem, Oregon where another YWAM base had accepted us as candidates for their SOFM. At long last, we were on our way.

In June of 1992, we sold everything we owned except our clothes and our Subaru wagon, and moved again, this time onto the campus of the

Battlecreek Mission, otherwise known as YWAM Salem. Over the summer we were students in a Crossroads Discipleship Training School.
These DTS courses fill the role of an application process in YWAM, en-
abling the mission and the candidate to get to know each other before
they commit to working together. There is no other way to enter
YWAM. We joined the DTS reluctantly, but in obedience. We were frustrated by the delay, but on the other hand, the frontier mission school
we had come to take didn't start until September anyway, so we were
free. It turned out to be one of the best things we ever did. The relationships formed with fellow students and the staff were life changing, as
was the teaching. The focus was on getting the messenger straightened
out before sending them with the Message. It turned out we had as
much junk inside as the next guy and the cleansing and empowering
was both astonishing and necessary.

We had been feeling more and more God was calling us to Mongolia,
which had opened up along with the rest of the Soviet world three years
earlier. We had never gotten it out of our hearts or minds since God had
used the Leatherwoods to plant the seed. We'd kept in touch with Rick
and had been thrilled as he took teams of Navajos into Mongolia, and in
'89 and '90 led the first three to Christ on Mongolian soil. (There were
scattered conversions among Mongolians studying in Eastern Europe
during the 80's, but these didn't return to their homeland for safety reasons. YWAMers Peter Iliyn and George Otis Jr. had secretly led a Mongol to Christ in an Ulaanbaatar Hotel room in 1982, but this man was
never heard from again. Lone sheep don't fare as well as lone wolves.)
We told everyone God was calling us to Asia, but between ourselves we
talked most about Mongolia. My wife was not thrilled at the prospect of
living in one of the world's coldest climates. Louise grew up in the blaz-
ing sands of the Mojave Desert and likes it hot. Even after I was convinced God had chosen Mongolia for us, Louise needed confirmation
after confirmation. I couldn't understand why God was willing to tell
her over and over. But He did confirm, in so many ways. We saw a Mongolian ger as we drove up to Salem. A total stranger walked up to Louise
in a grocery store and started telling her about his brother in the Peace
Corps in Mongolia! Everywhere we turned it was Mongolia, Mongolia,
and more Mongolia.

During the last week of our DTS, I went to Hong Kong to participate in YWAM's Strategic Conference on Mongolia. It was there I met a young Swedish couple who'd just finished an SOFM in The Netherlands and had gone to Mongolia for their outreach. Magnus told us he and Maria felt God's call to plant a church movement in Mongolia. As they shared their vision with me I realized we had been called to do the exact same thing using the same New Testament principles George Patterson had shared with us. It was like finding my heart beating in someone else's chest. We were all utterly committed to following the leading of the Holy Spirit as we used the New Testament as a filter for everything we did in birthing the Church into this virgin soil. We were convinced that the answers for seeing the Church multiply among Mongolians were in the New Testament, rather than the methods and strategies of the experts. I told them right then and there we wanted to be a part of their team.

From the consultation I flew to Beijing and on to Mongolia. I took advantage of already being in Asia to get my first look at our future home on a brief fact-finding trip. I managed to visit with most of the first missionaries to arrive in the country, and traveled with a team of Mongolian evangelists taking the newly completed Jesus film to several outlying towns, including the second largest city, Darhan. I was in Ulaanbaatar on the day the Leatherwood family moved into town (they would continue to serve there for eight years!). The opportunities I saw everywhere I went encouraged me. Young Mongolians in particular were very responsive and everyone was curious about what our team had to say. I returned home and rejoined my family with just a couple weeks to rest before our School of Frontier Missions training began.

Our SOFM was a wonderful opportunity to train more in depth in the missionary skills we had been exposed to through Perspectives. I ended up serving in a staff capacity. Since Perspectives was part of the SOFM curriculum and I was a Perspectives coordinator, I was most qualified to lead that portion of the training. Our fellow candidates were training to serve on the frontiers with YWAM in Albania, Uzbekistan, Russia, Morocco, and one young guy was even preparing for Mongolia, like us!

His name was Lance Reinhart, and he would prove to be a strong friend and teammate to our family in Mongolia.

As we plowed into learning how to do missions and church planting effectively, I realized the careful way the Father had been preparing us over the past 12 years for this task. He had led us to and through unparalleled experiential hands-on missionary training in the Vineyard, Jews for Jesus, inner-city work, small group leadership, the Mizpah Boys Home, Navajo Gospel Mission and the Hardrock compound, the Perspectives course, serving as mobilizers, Discipleship Training School, and now the School of Frontier Missions. The lessons we'd learned, both positive and negative, and the opportunity to learn missions by doing missions, had forged in both Louise and me a burning determination to do this work well without compromising New Testament principles. Looking back, we were awed by our Father's unseen hand that so accurately prepared us even as we seemed to be tripping and stumbling from one thing to another.

When our school finished in December '92, we stayed on at the YWAM base volunteering in the Frontier Missions office and making preparations for our biggest move ever. In February we had tickets and plans to move our family of five from Salem, Oregon to Ulaanbaatar, Mongolia. Louise and the kids had never even been outside the United States before. We were wrapped up in preparations; seeing doctors, assembling everything we'd need to live there, making banking arrangements, and calling and writing our support network. We finally discovered why Molly had always been such a fussy child when we took her to the doctor. Since early infancy she seemed to have a sour disposition and her digestion never seemed quite right. My mother, the nurse, insisted we run a stool test on Molly before we moved. We found she had a parasitic infection called giardia. We suspected she picked it up along with her first solid meal served on unwashed, but loving, little Navajo fingers. As soon as the treatment took effect, Molly's whole personality transformed.

As we pulled our move together, little did we imagine the spiritual warfare we'd have to engage in to even set foot in Mongolia.

FIVE

"It'd take a Miracle"

Miracle Max: Have fun storming the castle!
Valerie: Think it'll work?
Miracle Max: It'd take a miracle.

—Rob Reiner's film, *The Princess Bride*

'Impossible' is the strongest border guard.

—Mason Cooley

In January 1993 (exactly 200 years after William Carey, the "Father of Modern Missions" set sail for India) we were embarking on what turned out to be a veritable hurdle course toward Mongolia. The first sign things were not going to be as smooth as we had hoped came as we received several reports from inside Mongolia that the government there was tightening up on granting visas to foreigners lacking an economic reason to be there—namely. . . . us. Also at this time, Magnus and Maria, the young Swedish leaders of the church planting team we hoped to join, faxed us to relate that the Bible translator in Ulaanbaatar, who had promised us visas, had severed ties with our team. We began to pray fervently for another entry approach. We were sure God had called us to go to Mongolia and plant churches at this time, so He would open another door. We shared this need in an intercessory prayer group on the YWAM base, and several received words from God we were to go into Mongolia through a door we hadn't even considered. I was puzzled by this guidance. Time was running out to apply with someone else or form a relationship with a new organization. Youth With A Mission had no official status in Mongolia, and so wasn't an option. How could we go through a door we didn't know about?

Later that week Louise and I were considering our predicament and I remembered Jim Bond (pseudonym for security). I'd met Jim at the YWAM Consultation on Mongolia I had attended in Hong Kong. His company had placed many Christian workers in Asian "creative access" countries through their business and teaching contracts. I told Louise that Jim had recently placed several workers in Mongolia and maybe a call to him would give us some ideas on how to get in. Louise had an immediate and powerful sense we needed to telephone Jim right then. Within 10 minutes we were connected with him in Hong Kong and marveling at God's timing. It was late in Salem, Oregon, but business hours in Hong Kong, and we caught Jim right between trips to Mongolia and India. He had just secured six English teaching contracts in a Mongolian city called Erdenet. Magnus and Maria Alphonce, the Swedish couple

I'd met at the Consultation and whose church planting vision matched ours so exactly, were splitting one of the contracts. We could have another. This was the answer to our prayers for a church planting team that would live close enough to really function as a team. Magnus had mentioned in his fax Erdenet was a field "white unto harvest." The name was Mongolian for 'precious' or 'treasure' and we all had a sense that God was planning on pouring

Maria and Magnus Alphonce   out a precious treasure in Erdenet that would bless all of Mongolia and beyond. The transpacific phone line fairly hummed with the excitement that built as we put everything together with Jim. At the start of 1993 Erdenet was a completely unreached city with no fellowship of believers. Exactly what we had been praying for.

As we spoke with Jim, though, we noticed obstacles. Jim's organization, under which we would serve if we took their Erdenet contract, had scheduled a mandatory training in Hong Kong in the first part of February, and the contract was set to start right after training. The problem was that, months before, I had committed to teach in three Perspectives courses in Oregon and Washington. These obligations would keep us in stateside until February 17th; yet the English teaching contract for Erdenet started two days before we could even leave the USA. Louise made it clear she felt moving a family with three young children into one of the world's coldest climates in the dead of winter was crazy. Jim suggested we might want to wait until the next semester began in September. I certainly didn't want to just twiddle our thumbs in Salem for another nine months. We had no home and had sold everything to attend the schools. After we were no longer students, we had no place to stay in Salem. The excitement that had been building during the call quickly fizzled. Jim promised he and his board would pray about our situation and he'd let us know. As we trudged back to our dorm room, it seemed as if we'd found our door, only to have it slam shut in our faces.

Once again, it was obviously time to go back to God with this whole thing. As we prayed together, we felt we should lay out all these obstacles before God. If He wanted us to go in February, I would need to fulfill my teaching commitments in the Pacific Northwest, be excused from the mandatory training in Hong Kong, and have the Foreign Language Institute in Erdenet (FLI) agree to let us start teaching a week late. Louise agreed if all these came together, God was behind this "foolish" winter move.

A little over a week later, Jim returned from India and faxed us the board had accepted us for service even without the training, and FLI had agreed to let us delay our employment. We would have two days with Jim in Hong Kong for a personal orientation. We were going to Mongolia.

We booked four tickets for February 17th, the day after my final teaching engagement in Seattle, WA. One advantage this date had was it beat Alice's second birthday by 11 days, saving us from having to buy her a ticket. Our flights would take us from Seattle to Vancouver, BC, then on to Hong Kong for our two-day layover with Jim. From there we would head for Beijing, China, where we would need to get airline tickets into Mongolia and Mongolian visas. There were no travel agents who could sell tickets for MIAT, the national airline, and Mongolia had, as yet, no embassy in the US. We had no idea how long we'd have to stay in Beijing, but we were praying it would be only a few days at the most. A longer stay in that expensive city would quickly devour our small moving fund.

Purchasing the tickets seemed to trigger an avalanche of discouraging reports from Mongolia. Several missionary friends faxed to tell us of the horrible winter the country was facing. Temperatures of -34°C (-30°F) and municipal central heating equipment in danger of permanent malfunction were testing the resolve of even field-hardened workers in the capital city. The cold wouldn't be our most pressing problem, however. Mongolia was also in the grips of the worst food shortage ever. The harvest in 1992 had failed and Russian subsidies, once the mainstay of the Mongolian economy, had dried up. We were further warned housing was almost impossible to secure.

This bleak picture was not a huge worry for us. We encouraged ourselves with the story of the 10 spies with a bad report on the Promised Land and the opposite outlook of faith Joshua and Caleb maintained. Mongolia was the land God had promised us! Besides, we were going in as English teachers, and our contract would provide for food ration cards, an apartment, and of course . . . our visas. All was well, until . . . I received a call from Jim in Hong Kong. The contracts in Erdenet had fallen through for this semester. When Magnus had gone up to sign the contracts, the school had balked at the idea of finding food and housing for a family of five. They were willing to hire Magnus and Maria on the spot however. We would have to change plans and start out in Ulaanbaatar, the capital city. We were disappointed, but one expects many of these setbacks and last minute changes in pioneer mission enterprises. So, okay, Ulaanbaatar would be our temporary home. Contentedly we continued our preparations, until January 25th, when a fax from Hong Kong arrived informing us negotiations for our contract in Ulaanbaatar had fallen through as well. The reasons cited were, again, difficulty with rations and housing for a family of five. Jim's inside people who had been arranging things for us had to fly out to Hong Kong. We were told nothing further could be arranged until April. However, if we still wanted to try to come, it was risky, but Jim had no objection.

"I don't recommend you moving to Mongolia this winter with no arrangements in place," Jim told us when we called him in a panic. "However, you may just be standing on the shore of the Red Sea. If you are, then you had better step out and cross it." Our minds reeling, we said we would seek God about what to do.

What in the world was God doing? It felt like a punch in the stomach. A quick check confirmed our tickets were nonrefundable. Besides, we had heard so clearly from God about going in February. We called together friends and the students of the School of Intercession in session at the Salem YWAM center and went to prayer.

The same morning we'd received the fax, two significant things had already happened. The theme of that morning's worship time had been "When the Storm Comes I will not be Shaken, for by Your Hand I am Saved." After this time of worship, a friend had come up to me and shared a vision she'd just had. She saw our family running through a stainless steel door, which shredded as we crashed into it. She looked closer and observed the door was only aluminum foil. When the fax arrived a few hours later, we knew the form our storm and door of steel were taking.

It wasn't long before the answers to the prayers began coming in. The unanimous response from all those interceding confirmed God was asking us to trust Him and go in total faith—without any guarantees except His goodness and faithfulness and call. We had always admired Abraham, and the many missionary heroes who followed after him, for their faith to go, risking all on nothing but the promises of God. This had always seemed so exciting and romantic. Now we were facing the same thing, and to be honest, it was scary. But to follow the dictates of circumstance and prudence over the commands of God would give the lie to everything we stood for and hoped to accomplish. So, hard as it might seem, our course was set. We would trust God to lead us and fulfill His Word.

Not willing or able to be completely passive, I contacted one man I knew in Mongolia, Rick Leatherwood. Rick agreed to try to work out another contract for us, but discouraged getting our hopes up. He advised waiting for spring also. Human wisdom from those who were living there and familiar with the situation was 100 percent opposed to our trying a February entry. But the answers to concerted prayers were continuing to pour in at 100 percent Trust God and GO!

As February began, Rick faxed us. He had been unable to accomplish anything on our behalf. He urged us not to come. It was up to God alone now. Our last human means had failed. The very next day we received a telex from two Mongolian friends I'd made on my September trip.

DEAR BRIAN, GREETINGS IN THE NAME OF OUR LORD JESUS! MAY YOUR NEW YEAR BE FILLED WITH HIS LOVE PEACE AND WISDOM. SO SORRY FOR LATE RESPONDING FOR YOUR LETTER FROM 10/15/92. WE'VE BEEN BUSY. ALSO WE'VE BEEN TOLD THAT YOU HAVE CHANGED YOUR MIND TO NOT COMING TO MONGOLIA. WE WOULD SUGGEST IT IS BETTER NOT TO COME IN WINTER. ESPECIALLY THIS YEAR, BUT OF COURSE IT'S UP TO YOU REALLY. WE'RE READY TO HELP YOU AS BEFORE. JUST PLEASE LET US KNOW BY TELEX. WE'VE FOUND OUT THE WAY TO GET A VISA FOR YOU. JUST LET US KNOW FROM WHERE YOU ARE GOING TO COME IN. HERE IN ULAANBAATAR WE HAVE VERY COLD WEATHER AT PRESENT TIME. 30 DEGREES BELOW! BE PREPARED AND PRAY MUCH! BLESSINGS, ALDAR AND BATJARGAL

This initially encouraged both of us greatly, but there was a hitch. We needed to telex them when and where we would be coming in from, so if they secured a contract they could send the letter of invitation to the embassy granting our visas. Our many telexes were returned undelivered. And then it was time to go. I believe this kind of obedience that seems mad to all those around us must be sweetest to the Father. We certainly felt His strong pleasure as we said our good-byes and left YWAM Salem. After teaching two missions history lessons in the Seattle area Perspectives classes on our last two nights in the United States, we took the leap of faith.

Following tearful farewells with my parents at SeaTac airport, we caught a "puddle jumper" flight to Vancouver, BC. The biggest hurdle was just getting all our luggage and three children together and through customs. We didn't have long to wait until we were on a 747 bound for Hong Kong, still a British Crown Colony in 1993. A long and uneventful flight deposited us there 14 hours later. The only losses were a torn bag, a misrouted suitcase, and our daughters' sleep patterns. All three girls were up and raring to go at two a.m. We stayed at a hotel in Kowloon that was run by the Catholics. We managed to slip in two days of sightseeing during our three days in Hong Kong with friends from our hometown who managed a Christian bookstore in the city. As we rubbernecked from cabs and on foot, the throbbing breakneck metropolis assaulted our senses. Constant noise in our ears, exotic smells of Chinese street food, and the hyperkinetic pace of life there made us all feel an onset of Attention Deficit Disorder. The contrast of peace and calm and spectacular vistas from Victoria Peak was the cure. We felt above it all as we picnicked with our hosts on this lofty perch.

Our first miracle occurred on our second full day in the Colony. I was meeting with Jim at his offices downtown on Hong Kong Island, half way across the colony from Louise and the girls who were waiting in our hotel room on the mainland. Jim gave me the bad news. His organization specialized in placing Christian teachers and students in countries closed and hostile to missionary activity. This made it necessary for them to keep an extremely low profile. Their board had decided the church planting we planned to do after language and culture learning could jeopardize their other workers outside Mongolia. Jim had wanted so much to help, but we all saw the board's wisdom. So, very kindly and with much love, we were "emancipated." We were still with YWAM, of course, but YWAM had no legal status in Mongolia.

While we were talking, I happened to ask Jim if he was working on our visas into China. His face blanched. He had forgotten! Normally it took two days, but our plane to Beijing took off early Sunday morning. There was one place to get a next-day visa and it was right around the corner, but it closed in one hour. Did I have our passports? No, they were in the hotel safe in Kowloon, across Hong Kong and through the harbor tunnel at rush hour. Things looked grim and it appeared that we would miss our next two flights. Because of the cost involved we decided to attempt the impossible. We ran out and hailed a cab and told him to head for Kowloon and "step on it." We plunged into almost total gridlock in the tunnel under the bay. It took a little over half of our precious time, praying feverishly to reach our hotel and get the passports and photos. Then a frenzied return trip brought us to the China Resources building with four minutes to spare. We were just in time to throw our papers in front of the clerk. I then found I needed two photos of each girl. God gave me the courage to extract a promise I could meet them before opening the next morning (a non-visa granting day) to deliver the pictures and still get the visas. This chain of miracles proved to us God had chosen us to penetrate Mongolia at this time against all human advice and circumstances.

The trip to Beijing was pleasant, and we relaxed, knowing all we had to accomplish in our two days there was to secure our visas at the Mongolian Embassy. Even though nothing had been settled when we left the States, I was flying high on faith that all would be well. The five of us piled into the taxi that the Hotel Dong Fang's concierge had called for us. After all, I thought as we roared off toward Embassy Row, God had already delivered us from the worst opposition we would face back in Hong Kong. Surely the visas would be a breeze . . .

SIX

Home for the Holidays

My biggest worry, as our MIAT jet touched down at Buyant Ukhaa International Airport outside Ulaanbaatar, was not whether we would clear customs or cross the border, but whether I'd find a place to take my four exhausted ladies after leaving the airport. There was no one in Mongolia expecting us, no one who knew God had done the impossible in Beijing and we were arriving on this frigid February day.

I kept up an enthusiastic front for Louise and the girls. They were all weary of travel and happy to be off the crowded plane. We ended up last in the passport line, which gave us time to fill out the arrival cards and customs declarations. With multiple forms to fill out and passports to juggle, carryon luggage to push along, and three active girls to corral within this slow-moving line, I had plenty to occupy my mind and body. The North Korean wrestling team was ahead of us in line and they played with our kids as we inched forward. Even so, I couldn't stop thinking about where to take us once we finished at the airport, or even how. Not speaking the language was surely going to present a challenge. The only hotel I knew was way out of our price range and I couldn't direct a cab to anyone's address.

By the time we made it past the border police, our visas all in order, our luggage was waiting almost by itself in the baggage area. It looked pathetic and lonely sitting there on the metal ramp, and I couldn't help but feel we might be looking the same way in a few minutes, out in front of the airport. It didn't take long to gather up our bags. We only had eight suitcases. The airline luggage allotment said two bags apiece and we had assumed this was the maximum we could take with us. We didn't realize we could have taken extra bags and boxes as "over-baggage." At any rate, we had trouble moving with the heavy suitcases we had since Louise and I were the only ones who could lift them. The other airports had all provided carts, but not "Ulaanbaatar International." The entire arrivals area comprised of just two large rooms—one where we had been for the past 45 minutes, and another we were about to enter.

The sight of Lance Reinhart, waiting for us outside the heavy double doors, made our day. I breathed a big sigh of relief when I heard my name shouted and saw his smiling Oregonian face. We'd last seen Lance at the graduation "Love Feast" for our School of Frontier Missions in Salem. He had been in Mongolia for a week already, having come in after his training in Hong Kong with the rest of the team we had planned to be on. He was, as they say, "a sight for sore eyes." A young Mongolian named Amgalanbaatar had also been waiting for us, ready to help with translation and the luggage. As we hugged and recounted our adventures, Lance briefed us on the local situation and where we would be staying for the first few days. The national holiday that was going on was our biggest problem, he explained. His team consisted of three single ladies: Molly, Ruth, and Laura, who'd been in Mongolia for a year already and knew the ropes. Molly is an Oregonian, Ruth a German, and Laura is from Michigan. The new arrivals on the team: a family of five, and Lance, (all serving with Jim's company) had been eating in restaurants since the hotel rooms had no kitchens and the store shelves were bare. The problem was all the restaurants were closed for the Tsagaan Sar holiday. It was highly ironic. The chief danger of this Mongolian holiday is forced overeating to the point of bursting—like a Thanksgiving afternoon that goes on for a week—yet we were facing a three to four day fast. All of the feasting takes place in obligatory parties at homes of friends and family, both of which we lacked. There is no commercial food production in Mongolia during this New Year's bash—there is no need for any. At any rate, by the time we had "caught up" with Lance and been filled in, our overloaded cab was pulling up in front of our hotel.

Our initial impression of our first "home" in Mongolia was not good. However, since the second and third impressions and those thereafter that first week were progressively worse, I remember having the warmest feelings I was ever to have for the "Builders' Hotel." This was the translation for the (for me) unpronounceable Mongolian name. I would never be able to tell a cab driver where we were staying. (I ended up memorizing how to direct them from a famous monument I could get my tongue around, and then using about a quarter of my vast Mongolian vocabulary: "Zuun gar tish" and "Baruun gar tish" - turn left, turn right). The hotel building seemed about average. It was concrete — gray and crumbling. At least we had a place to put our stuff, beds to sleep in, and a large tub to soak away the travel.

Lance introduced us to the other family who'd just come in with Jim's company. Bruce and Terrie and their three children had been YWAM leaders in Hong Kong for many years. They had flown in from Hong Kong the day after Lance, and were fulfilling a ministry dream by coming to Mongolia.

Tired as we were, getting some dinner was a priority. So, the hunt for dinner was on—Talley Ho! So we bundled the girls and ourselves back up into the layers of clothing necessary for survival at -20° to -30°C (-4° to -22°F), unknowingly beginning a ritual activity that would dominate our lives for four Mongolian winters.

Amgalanbaatar turned up as we were leaving the hotel. He seemed happy to guide 11 hungry Westerners to dinner. As we picked our way carefully over the broken sidewalks, he chattered away in much better English than you'd expect in a 19 year old with no formal language study. He informed us his "Christian name" was Adam. We walked to the first restaurant, the Ulaanbaatar Hotel, only to find its cavernous dining room closed for Tsagaan Sar holidays. Adam hailed cars enough to cram all of us into, and off we went to the next possibility. We eventually drove to four restaurants and found every one shut up tight for Tsagaan Sar. This holiday is the equivalent of American Thanksgiving— everywhere around us apartments were filled with people having huge banquets—straining the limits of how many *boodz* (steamed meat dumplings) the human body can consume—and we could not find a bite to eat. We now had driven all over the capital city and had six cranky and

a very modest pile of *boodz*

very hungry children beginning to "lose it." Adam was getting desperate. We had just failed again at a Chinese restaurant near the State Circus, when Adam saw a woman hurrying down the other side of the street. He ran across the road and accosted her. We assumed he either knew her or was hoping she knew of yet another dining establishment we could waste our time going to. Then he came running back and told us to come along—he'd found food. We followed this woman on foot for several blocks before she turned into a small ger district. This was the first area we had seen where the buildings were not concrete. Mostly we could see yellow and green fences, but where a gate was open we saw the neighborhood was a collection of fenced yards with one or two homes inside each fence. The houses were either the traditional Mongolian felt tents or small two room frame affairs covered in plaster.

The woman turned into one of these yards. As we followed her inside the gate, we saw two gers with light pouring out from the door and smoke-hole "skylight." She motioned for us to come inside. As the others were ducking carefully one-by-one through the door, taking great care not to step on the threshold (a taboo equivalent to stepping on the homeowner's neck); I pulled Adam aside and asked him what we were doing here.

"This family will feed you," he said, glowing with pride in a job well done.

"Is this woman your friend?" I was eager to know how this had been arranged.

"No. I went to school with her."

I was stunned. I looked, and half of my family was already inside the ger. "What? You do know this family, don't you?" He didn't. He had just asked the woman, whom he knew was heading to her family feast, to include 14 of us into her dinner plans. And she did!

I was uncomfortable with this arrangement, but since everyone else had completed the greetings ritual and been seated in the cramped tent, I had little choice but to follow them in. The others all assumed we were meeting Adam's family or at least close friends. The knowledge that these were almost perfect strangers whose party we were crashing I kept to myself throughout the evening. My knowledge made me all the more amazed at their incredible hospitality. The patriarch grasped each of us by both arms and sniffed each cheek in the traditional Tsagaan Sar greeting. We made our attempts to stumble through the traditional Mongolian responses to his questions ("Are you well? Are your animals well? Are you wintering well? Are you getting fat? . . .) while those who hadn't memorized any smiled and nodded mutely. Somehow they managed to seat all of us around the brightly painted orange table piled high with food. The entire roasted back and the grapefruit-sized tail of a fat-tailed sheep formed the centerpiece, along with a cake-like tower of stacked hard sweet rolls, and mounds of rice, potato salad, and coleslaw.

The family immediately shoveled more food than any of our hungry children would ever eat onto their plates and the kids dug in. For us adults there was one preliminary to eating to get out of the way. On my exploratory trip into Mongolia the year before, I'd learned the hard and fast rule of Mongolian hospitality—you must drink the three shot glasses of vodka the host pours for you. You have never experienced persuasion until you have tried to avoid the obligatory vodka. Women can get away with merely touching the glass to their lips three times and the host ritually splashes a refill into the glass each time, even though nothing was consumed. However, men do not get off so easily. So we three men; Lance, Bruce, and I, gamely choked down our firewater and then were able to "dig in."

What an incredible meal! They pushed food on us until we could not eat another bite. Hunger makes everything taste wonderful—well almost everything. To honor us they gave each adult a slab of pure white fat, carved from the sheep's tail. To the Mongolian palate this is the best part, but it was all I could do to bite off pieces and swallow them whole, without retching. I felt like when I was a little boy, being forced to eat my beets, except this time the reward was less tangible than apple crisp for dessert—it was cultural sensitivity. Every one of us was determined to learn and adopt Mongolian ways, even if it killed us. As the vodka and mutton fat lay congealing in my gut, I wondered if it just might.

After we'd finished eating a quantity of boodz, the girl Adam claimed to know from school came out and laid a dishtowel on the table and then returned to the kitchen. I picked up the dishtowel, thinking it was provided to wipe the gobs of grease off our hands, and proceeded to do so. Just as I laid it back on the table she returned with a stack of bowls. To my horror, she took up the dishtowel and wiped all of the bowls. We then graciously received the bowls which she then filled with milk tea, all the while nearly biting our lips off to keep from bursting out in laughter.

The food was never cleared, but when we could cram in no more, we moved into the singing and sharing portion of the evening's festivities.

A small gift was given to each of our children (whom I knew to be un-invited and unexpected guests) and each adult was expected to sing a song. I sang "Home on the Range" which I introduced through Adam as an American song about Mongolia. Then we shared back and forth about who we were and where we were from with Adam gamely trans-lating. All of us had a good time with our hosts, but finally the children were coming apart and we had to leave to get them into bed. We shared warm good-byes and bundled up and left the warm and glowing tent for the cold starry darkness outside. We little dreamed we would never see this family again. But none of us ever managed to retrace our steps to that particular neighborhood.

It took us half an hour to get a couple of cars to pack everyone into for the ride back to our lodgings. The children all fell asleep and had to be carried through the lobby and upstairs to bed. As Louise and I finally settled into our own bed I told her about how our dinner had been ar-ranged. We laughed at the strangeness of it all and then lay there filled with awe at the thought of going to bed in a place more foreign than we had ever imagined. We really were at the ends of the earth.

Lenin keeps his lonely Post-Communist vigil outside the Ulaanbaatar Hotel, the main watering hole for expats.

Our Mongol Parents, Ragchaa and Oyuun,
with their Tsagaan Sar spread

Visiting a ger. "Don't forget to duck."

SEVEN

Among the Horde for the Lord

Through restrictions on rental of state-owned apartments, the government had managed to keep almost the entire foreign community living in one small district towards the eastern outskirts of Ulaanbaatar. The name of this missionary ghetto was Sansar, Mongolian for "outer space." Manipulation of housing was a legacy from the days of Communism and one very effective bureaucratic tool for keeping foreigners from infecting the ideological purity of their citizens, and for enforcing apartheid between the messengers of the Good News and those who needed it so badly. At the time of my first trip into Mongolia, they had actually managed to limit all of the missionaries to one building in Sansar. Now, a mass eviction notice had been served on this missionary ghetto, which was to be privatized into an all-Mongolian apartment building. Yet the Sansar district remained the only place in vast and sprawling Ulaanbaatar where missionaries were finding anything for rent.

As determined as the government seemed to be on forcing us in with other foreigners, Louise and I were even more insistent on living among Mongolians. We'd already done time in a fenced "missionary compound" during our Navajo days. We had seen the barriers these expatriate subcultures erected against knowing and being known by the locals. Learning the Mongolian language and the culture required greater vulnerability on our part. So we intentionally searched for apartments everywhere in the city, except in Sansar and the adjacent Russian district. After our first three nights in the loud and boisterous "Builders' Hotel" we had moved into a somewhat nicer place, the Zuul Hotel, where we were willing to stay until we found an apartment in a Mongolian building, but we prayed it would be quick.

Our "Realtor," the young Amgalanbaatar, or Adam, as he preferred to be called, had been involved in one of the churches for just over a year, and had just begun studying in the new Ulaanbaatar Bible School. He was eager to help us and improve his English. We had been a little hesitant to accept Adam's constant companionship and assistance, but he was so helpful and we were quite helpless. We had been warned during our training those nationals who seek you out at the beginning when you know nothing of the language and culture are usually those who are eager for cultural change and material gain, infatuated with anything foreign. We were supposed to seek to relate to those content with being Mongolians and who would later make good leaders for the church. But when Adam proved to be the only way to find food that first week in the country, I guess we were hooked. He was with us almost constantly from the day we arrived. He helped with shopping, changing currency, getting police residence permits, finding things we needed, guarding our things when we were out-of-town, translation, language learning, and finding an apartment.

In hindsight, it should have been a clue that nothing ever seemed to work out quite the way Adam explained it. Exchange rates and fees rose between the time he left with our dollars and when he returned with our tugriks (Mongolian currency). Phrases he taught me to memorize turned out to be strangely worded, as if Adam didn't understand our goal of learning to speak naturally. Other Mongolians didn't seem to respect, or even like him. But when he found us a nice furnished apartment in a Mongolian building for a very reasonable rent from his relative, we overlooked the discrepancies. After half a week at the "Builders' Hotel" and two weeks in the "Zuul Hotel," we were overjoyed to have our own place. Even later, when it became apparent our landlord was not related to Adam and did seem to be connected to the mafia, we accepted Adam's excuse that we had misunderstood him. The fact Adam was active in his church reassured us he was everything he claimed.

Our 1st apartment was in the back bldg, our 2nd to the right.

Our long-term visa was secured when I signed with a Mongolian firm to be their English instructor. Aldar, our young entrepreneurial friend had continued to work on our invitation even after we had made it into the country. His father-in-law was an architect with the first privately owned Mongolian company, called 'MONAR' for Mongolian Architecture. When Aldar brought me in for an interview, the boss, a Mr. Orgil, hired me on the spot. I questioned him about hours and he told me they were very busy and could give me no more than three hours a week to teach the staff to speak English. I was delighted with this arrangement. I only had to work two evenings for an hour and a half and in return I was to be given a salary and a work visa. I would have plenty of time to care for my family's needs and learn Mongolian as well. Many other missionaries were teaching 20 or more hours a week and were really struggling to do much else.

Our first apartment in Ulaanbaatar had a balcony that overlooked the nearby Tuul River to the mountains beyond. Five stories straight down was the entrance to the "Broken Bones and Stab Wounds Hospital." At least that's the name as Adam translated it, and observation bore it out.

Everyone seemed to leave on crutches or with fresh amputations and bloody bandages. It was quite an initiation to the wild side of city life, but there was more to come.

By the beginning of April, the thaw had come and the river outside our windows had begun to break up and flow. One nippy morning I was visiting the ger of Adam's mother, when his brother, a policeman, rushed in and told us of the discovery of a body in the field next to the American Embassy, just a couple hundred meters away. Adam and I quickly joined the crowd milling outside the police barrier. The body was left as it had been found. The victim had been stabbed; his head, legs and arms had been chopped off. No blanket covered the grisly sight. The killer had used a baby carriage, still lying there, to transport the corpse. Detectives arrived as we watched. I realized with a shudder our apartment was less than half a block away. The fact Ulaanbaatar was 1992's murder capital of the world was becoming more than just a statistic. The police station downtown had a bulletin board out in front with grisly photos of severed heads. I laboriously translated the notice beneath the photos of the six decapitation victims. "Are these men known to you?"

I wrote home: "It breaks our hearts to hear about, and now see, murders and senseless deaths among Mongolian people who have had no access to the Gospel. Souls are literally plunging into eternity here. I want to be able to share the way to eternal life with them, and my inability to communicate at even a two-year-old level is so frustrating. Just as you begin to lose heart for the seemingly impossible language learning, something like this happens to spur you on."

Theft was so common it hardly raised an eyebrow, even in Ulaanbaatar's foreign community. I had my daypack and my jacket pocket slashed open with razors while in a crowded bus and market. This was the method of choice for the many thieves. They would slash an opening and then grope inside for anything worth stealing. From the very beginning things began to disappear. On our fourth day in the country, a suitcase loaded with schoolbooks and language learning supplies was lifted while we transferred between hotels. Later, money and possessions from our apartment disappeared. At first we suspected our many curious visitors, but later we were crushed to discover Adam was the thief. I had to sort through my feelings of anger and betrayal before I even dared to confront him. When I sat him down on our couch and shared the evidence he starting crying. Adam sobbed out a confession and seemed quite repentant, so I made sure he understood my forgiveness before I prayed with him. In the weeks that followed, amazement grew and mercy faltered as he continued to steal from us—even the girls' toys and Louise's perfume were lifted by his sticky fingers. We repeated our ritual of tearful repentance and reconciliation, but it began to get old.

He was no criminal genius. Our camera had gone missing with circumstantial evidence pointing to Adam as chief suspect. We shared our suspicious with him and he vehemently denied taking it. Just a day later we found it behind our couch. We felt terrible for having accused Adam. However, when the prints came back, the photos of our girls were all double exposed with images of Adam and his friends. Even the hapless Inspector Clouseau could have solved this one.

There were other hazards. Our friend Bruce, carrying his three-year-old son on his shoulders, stepped into one of the many open manholes and dropped completely beneath the sidewalk, but by a miracle of God, he and the child escaped with minor abrasions. Our own family began to experience an onslaught of senseless and painful accidents.

A favorite activity of young Mongolian boys is throwing rocks. This "game" usually seems to be without intent to harm, but during those heady days of 1993, with the Russians pulling out of Mongolia after seven decades of domination, their aim was often directed against Russian children. One Russian boy was reportedly stoned to death on a playground in Ulaanbaatar. To Mongolians, all Westerners looked Russian. Melody, our seven year old, was a frequent recipient of their missiles. One spring afternoon she and the Leatherwood boys were playing in an unfinished concrete building, and a local boy chucked a rock at them. Melody fell with a blow to the temple. This bled quite a bit, but, except for a star-shaped scar, caused no damage. We know the prayers of those back home and the Lord's tender mercies kept this rock from her eye, less than a centimeter away.

Molly, our four-year-old, was hit on the top of the head and knocked down by a glass pop bottle dropped or thrown from a balcony. Missionary kids must have extra angels. Molly's plastic headband took the blow and broke with the impact. Her head was sore for only a few days.

I was walking home at night in pitch darkness and tripped over a foot-high iron fence, severely cutting my shin. As I flew forward and landed on my face, my laptop and the printer I had just borrowed went flying in different directions. The printer was broken and I had to pay for it.

In our own apartment, Alice ran into the cement wall and badly bruised her nose. She then burned her hand on the stove in a ger we were visiting (unwittingly duplicating Melody's experience in a Navajo hogan at the same age).

All these "accidents" took place in a fairly short period not long after we had moved into our first apartment. We should have been prepared for furious spiritual attack as we established a beachhead among the people and off the "missionary reservation." We finally recognized these strange mishaps as a spiritual attack and prayed against it. The incidents completely stopped.

**Boys' sports had two seasons: Rock Throwing and Ice Sliding.
The best thing about winter—the stones were frozen to the ground.**

EIGHT

Shop 'til You Drop

While Louise and I struggled to learn the Mongolian language, we still had to keep house and put food on the table. Meal preparation took far longer in Mongolia than in the States. As spring progressed, food slowly became easier to find, but you still needed to search shops all over town on a daily basis to survive. Then when you had found it, you had to buy it. This was not as easy as it sounds due to a peculiar and convoluted system leftover from Communism in which the ladies selling products often seemed to be guarding them from consumers.

She sells sheep skulls in a cheap shop.

Maintaining a household in a nation just creeping out of Communism is no easy task. All the missionary wives agreed they had all the tasks they had back home, only here everything was at least 400 percent more difficult and time-consuming.

Take meal preparation for example. Nothing comes ready to cook. Meat starts out as a huge hunk of flesh, bone, fat, and gristle that's been hacked off the carcass of a cow or horse with an ax. It takes hours to finish butchering it into small enough pieces to eat. Most meat is so tough our girls called it "bubblegum meat."

Mutton makes for easier chewing, so on one occasion I bought an entire skinned sheep carcass and lugged it home and up the stairs to our apartment. The only place I could easily butcher such a large piece of flesh was our bathtub. I got down on my knees and went at it with the butcher knife until the entire sheep was reduced to chunks sized from leg o'lamb on down. I used the shower head to wash away all the blood and removed the waste to the garbage. I thought the tub looked pretty decent. In the evening Louise drew a hot bath in her daily ritual to try to thaw herself back to somewhere in the neighborhood of almost comfortable. When she slid into the water she noticed that the tub felt really greasy. From the aroma of mutton fat she deduced where the sheep had been processed. At first she was grossed out and angry, but then she figured that the lanolin now in her bath might be good for her sore dry skin, so she relaxed into her Mongolian spa treatment. She told me later her skin felt better than ever after that soak.

Most missionary families hired a household helper. Early on, Adam found us a student named Amaraa. Aside from help with shopping and housework Amaraa was a good Mongolian language tutor for Louise, who shot ahead of me in her learning. The only thing Amaraa didn't seem to do well was childcare. She tried to ignore our kids completely.

Amaraa disappeared from our lives the same day I finally had a showdown with Adam. His thefts and deceits had continued and accelerated. I finally met him in a park and confronted him with everything. This time, instead of tears, there was a hint of violence. I was glad I had taken a missionary friend along as backup. We never saw Adam or Amaraa again. We found another helper—this time on our own. Her name translated to "Happy Flower" and this described her perfectly. She literally bubbled joyfully about everything, especially Jesus. She was wonderful with the girls and hopeless with housework. She spread water on the carpets and tried to vacuum it up, blowing up our new vacuum cleaner in the process. She meticulously scrubbed the black Teflon coating right off all of our pans until they were shiny silver. It was always something, but we found it impossible to be angry with her. She adopted Louise as her older sister and spent hours teaching her worship choruses in Mongolian.

The language was tough, but we slogged ahead. We would go out every day and use our memorized phrases with as many people as we could—the goal was 50 usages per day. Our progress seemed slow to us but pleased our Mongolian friends enormously. The Russians had never even attempted to learn Mongolian, so Mongolians saw our struggles as an act of love.

Our planned move to Erdenet was looking very good. One weekend our entire family visited the city of 65,000 and began to check things out. We traveled by overnight train in sleeper berths. Our Swedish YWAM teammates, Maria and Magnus Alphonce, met us at the train station, and we had a great weekend together. Louise and the girls were meeting them for the first time; I was relieved to see everyone seem to click. One of the highlights was Saturday dinner. They cooked pizza for us. You cannot imagine how starved our taste buds were for this familiar food. The cheese wasn't mozzarella, but Russian cheese substituted nicely. Sometimes the kingdom of heaven is in your mouth.

Maria and Magnus had begun pioneering the work in Erdenet in the fall of '92. After tagging along with a Mongolian evangelistic team from *Eternal Light* in July 1992, the church they attended in Ulaanbaatar, they'd made weekly trips to Erdenet to visit the teen girls who'd responded. They had asked these believers to confirm their repentance with baptism, and 14 had agreed. The girls met around a two by three meter sauna plunge pool at the Erdenet Carpet Factory, and on Sunday, the 17th of January, 1993, Magnus, together with two young leaders from Eternal Light, had baptized them. This small beginning was one of the first beachheads of God's Kingdom outside the capital city.

As soon as the girls rose from the pool and everyone prayed, Magnus shared the vision of a newly born church. He laid out the three goals he and Maria had heard from God: to reach all the families of Erdenet with the Gospel, to plant a daughter church in Bulgan (capital of the neighboring province), and to reach other unreached peoples of the world. The young believers, blissfully clueless, responded enthusiastically.

Magnus and Maria moved from Ulaanbaatar to Erdenet just after our family arrived in Mongolia. They had challenged Bayaraa to come with

Erdenebayar or "Bayaraa"

them, and after hearing from God, she soon joined them. She became their language tutor and they, in this total immersion, surged ahead with the Mongolian language. Magnus, Maria and Bayaraa divided up the new believers into three initial house churches. The team called these gatherings "cell groups." (Much later we realized that the term "cell" had a distinct meaning in the outside world that didn't accurately reflect the fellowships in Erdenet. I have chosen to use the more accurate term, even though we didn't use it at the time.) The groups meet weekly, in the afternoons, to accommodate the students' schedules. As the believers won their friends to Christ, and the groups grew, the team multiplied each group into two every time it reached fifteen baptized regular attendees. Even though Magnus and Bayaraa led the first groups, they couldn't keep up with the multiplication, so they began to train leaders for the house churches. The groups began meeting on Sunday, and the leaders met for training at the Alphonce's apartment on Monday nights. Things were kept ultra-simple. All a leader needed was pencil and notebook to jot down the week's teaching.

Magnus and Maria took care to model the church they felt God was calling them to plant. Keeping things small and simple was a big challenge. The girls wanted what the believers in Ulaanbaatar had—loud, weekly "Song and Lecture Clubs." Maria and Magnus insisted on home-based gatherings and introduced a monthly celebration to bring the groups together. The girls wanted to be like the other churches, but Bayaraa convinced them by saying, "These differences must be very important because Magnus and Maria are so obstinate about them!"

Magnus also held the line against a sound system and praise choruses in English. Rather than copying other congregations, he wanted them to hear from God for themselves. He challenged them to ask God for a goal to reach by their first anniversary as a church. Excitedly they realized that three of them heard the number 120. The church prayed and adopted this goal. The night before the first anniversary, the church baptized its 121st believer.

The young and inexperienced church planting couple faced challenges from within and without. Very early, lying surfaced as an issue with the Mongolians, who saw nothing wrong with it. Meanwhile Magnus found confrontation—even though Biblically mandated—incredibly difficult because of his own Swedish upbringing. Both sides had to adjust. Visitors from Ulaanbaatar also brought a challenge. One missionary was so shocked at the responsibility he saw being given to "unready" Mongolians that he took over the meeting he was visiting. He said that he couldn't sit by and let Communion be served by new believers. Then he forbade their use of store-bought bread for Holy Communion. His visit and others by Mongolian believers from older churches in Ulaanbaatar brought confusion to the new believers in Erdenet. These visitors accused Magnus and Maria of putting into leadership young believers who would "make mistakes." "Of course they will!" Magnus responded. "That's how we learn." The new leaders did make many mistakes, but they accepted correction, gaining confidence and skill. They benefited from Maria and Magnus' trust and became competent leaders. As the girls took over the leadership of the house churches, Magnus shifted his focus to training them. Both Maria and Magnus invested much time with the first two "elders-to-be": Bayaraa and Odgerel, the first male believer. In its first year, the Church in Erdenet had come a long way.

Their approach to church planting was based around gathering the believers into small simple home fellowships, or house churches. The believers would gather in an apartment and "do church"; sharing the Lord's Supper, fellowshipping, worshiping together (not necessarily in song), praying, giving, ministering to each other, and interacting with God's Word. Magnus and Bayaraa prepared Bible teachings together. They focused on New Testament stories and simple obedience to Jesus' commands. On Monday night the leaders dutifully wrote down every word of the new lesson. These emerging leaders would then use exactly the same lesson during the week in their house church. Empty grocery shelves in Erdenet meant that having the groups share a meal would have hindered reproduction, so they saved that for special occasions. It was this strategy that began bearing fruit.

We didn't visit the house groups. The presence of a Westerner caused new believers to clam up and stifled interaction and worship. Our teammates wisely banned any foreigners, except those who moved to Erdenet and got to know the believers. This was our goal, and we hoped to pull it off by September of 1993. Getting out of Ulaanbaatar was as vital to our success as making sure we didn't end up living in the Sansar Missionary Ghetto. We had observed firsthand how working in an environment crowded with other missionaries prevents bonding with the locals while we were living in Hardrock, Arizona. We needed to do more than flee Sansar, we needed out of the capital city where the mission community was constantly enlarging.

Russians built Erdenet as a mining town in 1976. The mine generated over 70 percent of Mongolia's hard currency, and with the Russians leaving, and the ore threatening to run out, the bad old days looked better and better. We still saw far more Russian faces on the streets of

Erdenet than in Ulaanbaatar, and we were mistaken for Russians far more readily there. However, when we dressed Alice up in the Mongolian national dress, a dehl, the people of Erdenet really reacted. Everyone began to smile. Strangers picked her up and kissed her and

shopkeepers gave candy to all three girls. We'd stumbled onto a dynamite way of fitting in. The Russians never smiled, never spoke Mongolian, and never dressed their children in Mongolian clothing. They were also extremely unpopular former colonial masters. By smiling a lot, attempting to greet scowling locals in Mongolian, and dressing in dehls, we defused the resentment mistaken nationality brings.

Alice, Melody and Mollyanne rock the dehl.

On the train back to Ulaanbaatar, I met Byambaa (translation: Saturday) in the dining car. He'd been playing cards and drinking vodka with his friends, but we'd managed to strike up a friendship. He'd given me his photo and home address in Erdenet. I hoped this invitation to visit his family could be a breakthrough contact for work with men in Erdenet. We longed to see the church there burst out into the rest of the populace with entire families following Christ—so even a 17 year old boy was an important key.

On my next opportunity to get away from Ulaanbaatar, Lance and I traveled to Erdenet together. We'd been meeting with Magnus and Maria for several days, and had tried repeatedly to visit Byambaa, but he was never home. On our way out of town, we tried one last time. His sister got involved and forced Byambaa's best friend to lead us to another apartment where we woke him up. While he dressed, he insisted we go back to his family's apartment with him for a big meal, our third since noon. We were cutting it close on our train departure, but determined Mongolian hosts are almost impossible to refuse. They served up a bowl of flour noodles and beef, and then put a small ceramic teapot on the table. I began to pour myself a cup of dark black liquid, when the elderly patriarch told me: "Beesh, beesh." We'd learned by then that this meant "No, no." So I stopped pouring and stared at the half cup of unknown elixir. I had no idea what it was. I took off the lid and began to pour it back into the pot. Again he Beesh-ed me, but offered no constructive advice as to what to do with it. I let it set for a moment; sure I was missing some important cultural clue. Then he pointed to his noodles. How could I have mistaken the soy sauce for tea? I dutifully poured it over my dinner, relieved I could empty my cup of the embarrassing faux pas. At this, our hosts dissolved into gales of laughter that continued until they were crying. I was completely puzzled and my face was beet-red with embarrassment. Coming to my rescue, Byambaa's mother put a little of the dark liquid into my cup and filled the cup with boiling water. It turns out the mysterious black stuff was concentrated coffee. I couldn't sleep for hours after eating those noodles, even though I was exhausted from laughing at myself. Cultural adaptation teaches humility better than anything I have ever experienced. It sure is hard to be "puffed up" when four year old urchins can speak and behave much better than you can—college degree notwithstanding. At least Byambaa's family smiled a lot and insisted we stay with them on all future trips to Erdenet. Byambaa even hailed us a car so we made it to our train on time.

NINE

Left Bank Theatre of the Absurd

Even as we prepared to join Magnus and Maria in Erdenet, I was on the lookout for places where the gospel had never been preached, targets for the future teams of Mongolian church planters we'd be training and sending out. When we finally felt more settled and confident, and with the advent of long summer days, my feet were itchy to explore beyond Ulaanbaatar.

It wasn't hard to convince Lance to join me in a trip to Zuunhara. We both had time off during Naadam (national sport festival held every July), a midsummer Mongolian Olympics. Zuunhara was perfect. It lay along the railroad line and the Hara River, smack dab in the middle of the most gorgeous countryside on the planet. This was a town we had passed through often on our way to Erdenet. The train would stop in Zuunhara at ten p.m., just as the last light of the Mongolian summer sunset was failing. These last images out the train window each trip imbued Zuunhara with a certain mystique. Rather than remain perpetual faces pressed to the window, Lance and I wanted to actually get off the train there.

Standing on the platform at Zuunhara's Galt Teregnii Buudal (train station, literally: fire wagon's stop), watching our train pull away to the North, we realized it was too late for second thoughts. Night was falling, and we had no idea where we were going to stay. We didn't even know if Zuunhara had a hotel; our only contact was not a name or an address, but a Ham radio "handle." There was really nothing to do but hoist our packs and set out in the direction the other passengers had taken. We passed under a large monument to Sputnik, the first satellite, and laughed about the fact we had nothing to fear in such a modern metropolis. It didn't seem reasonable to go around asking where the Ham radio guy (whose name we didn't know) was, so as we walked, we asked for directions to the hotel. Most shrugged and told us they didn't know of any. A few questioned others passing by and started little discussion groups on the subject. Enough gestured in one general direction that eventually we ended up in front of a small, single-storied, plastered building with a wooden sign on the door announcing it to be a Zochid Buudal—Mongolian for "hotel" that translated literally to "guest stop."

The young woman who answered our knocks turned out to be the proprietor, and she quickly made it clear we were the first foreigners ever to honor her establishment. We were shown to the hotel's only room, which was furnished with two beds, four chairs, and a small table—all antiques. I'd barely put my pack down when a group of rough looking guys pushed into the room and stared at us as if we were extra-terrestrials. After all the greetings, during which we learned the leader of the pack was the hotel's handyman, they all sat down on the available chairs and beds. They proceeded to question us about every detail of our lives and what we wanted to do and see in their town. I guess this worked up a powerful thirst in them, because they, without waiting for invitation, opened and drank every bottle of pop we had brought to help us avoid uncertain water. When they finally left around midnight, we were left with all the empties.

The hotel lady came back in to introduce her seven-year-old son. This longhaired kid displayed none of the customary shyness around foreigners, perhaps because we were his first. Then she told us to sleep well and tied us in for the night. Literally. To our surprise we noticed the door had a gaping hole where the lock should have been. There was a rope in a corresponding hole in the doorframe and for security this was tied shut each night from the outside. Too tired to argue, or think of an alternative, we let it go. We undressed and fell into our beds and slept— until three thirty a.m.

I was awakened by the sound of our door being untied. Because nocturnal robberies were not unknown in Mongolian hotels, I was instantly awake with adrenaline pumping. I noticed Lance was ready too. Even in the dark we were surprised to see the slight figure of the hotel lady, rather than a burly brigand, come in through the door. She turned on the light and motioned to us to go back to sleep. I was flabbergasted. We watched speechless as she pulled a chair into the middle of the room, directly under our room's sole naked light bulb. Next she grabbed a stool from the hallway and placed it on the seat of the chair. Climbing cautiously up on top of this shaky tower, she began carefully wiping the glowing bulb with a rag—all the while studying us in our beds as surreptitiously as she could. It was an astounding balancing act, worthy of any circus. After an intensive cleaning, she clambered down and put the furniture back. She motioned again for us to go back to sleep, turned off the light, and tied us into our room again. I was at a complete loss for words, but Lance grinned and quipped: "Motel Six. We'll dust the light off for you." Our laughter must have woken anyone else asleep in the building and probably the neighbors too.

The next morning we were "untied" and had sausage and bread from our packs for breakfast. We would have been forced to swallow it dry had not the hotel lady brought in cups of steaming tsai. She never mentioned her cleaning of four hours earlier. We figured it was just a case of overwhelming curiosity: What do Americans look like while sleeping anyway? I did ask her where I could get a haircut—mainly because I thought I could avoid the long wait that always seemed to accompany trips to barbers back in the capital. She said she was a barber and I could have one later that day.

It was the first day of Naadam, and the whole town seemed to be walking or riding toward the outdoor stadium across the river. We joined the crowd, and after a two kilometer walk (about a mile), found ourselves at the center of the festivities. Many families had camped out at the site, and their many tents brightened the grounds. The largest was the Judges Tent right next to the competition field. Today's event was wrestling, the most popular of Mongolia's three national sports. Horse racing and archery were each scheduled on other days during the festival.

Our white skin placed us at the center of attention wherever we wandered. It wasn't long before the officials had half-invited, half-compelled us into seats of honor at the long Judges Table, under the shade of the Judges Tent. This was great because the day quickly heated up. As we watched the wrestling eliminations and the "eagle dance" every victor performed, I struck up a conversation with the doctor they'd seated next to us because he was the only guy in town (with the exception of the Ham radio contact we never found) who spoke any English at all. He was clearly nervous, as if the honor of the whole region depended on his mostly forgotten English from medical school days.

The contestants ranged from the rookie, a lanky, wiry boy just completing his military service, to the towering veteran heavyweight with legs the size of tree trunks and enormous belly hanging over his bikini briefs. All wore only leather briefs and a colorful long-sleeved vest that barely covered their upper back, and was completely open in the chest—apart from a cord pulled from the sides to hold it on. On their feet all wore gutal, cumbersome and ornately embroidered knee-high leather boots with upswept toes like the tips of skis.

I had heard this outfit had originally been designed to keep the "Manly Sport" of wrestling, well …manly. Apparently, at some point in the far distant past, a woman had entered the contest "in drag" and had beaten all comers. The shame of this, once revealed, had been enough to cause officials to change the uniform to one that left very little to the imagination.

There were pairs of wrestlers standing all over the grassy field, and all matches started simultaneously. Some faced each other in a crouched stance poised for either offense or defense. Others leaning heavily against each other with legs braced widely to each side, holding each other firmly by their scanty wrestling costumes.

As Lance and I watched the tournament, we noticed each of the individual matches followed a set form. The two wrestlers each had a PR guy or manager in full traditional Mongolian regalia: long dehl, "onion dome" hat, and the same boots the wrestlers wore. This guy would hold the wrestler's hat and dehl, shout their praises before each match, and generally be "in their corner." Some competitors were eliminated before they started, when their opponent turned them on their head almost as if it were a formality. If any contest lagged for too long, the manager would encourage his man by giving a slap to his rear. Real championship matches could continue for more than an hour. Imagine watching a pair of sweating giants locked together motionlessly each awaiting the opportune split second in which one would slam the other to the ground with lightning force. All that had to happen was for either opponent to hit the ground with more than his feet. Then it was over, and the winner would majestically and ceremonially mimic an eagle in flight; slowly flapping his arms as he lifts his knees high while "soaring" around a stand of poles adorned with something resembling a wig, the historic standard of the Mongolian Horde. Some of the victors would come to the Judges' Table for a bowl of *airag* - fermented mare's milk.

Our great seats in the Judges Tent with their close-up view of the action would have had any sports fan in ecstasy, but I was conversing with the doctor and eating from the plates of food lining the tables. Other than the fatty slices of mutton, in which the flies were a bit too interested, the best item on the deli plates was the *byaslag* - a Mongolian take on cheese. It is very mild with a soft rubbery texture on the inside and a tough rubbery rind. (In experiments at home we'd discovered it refuses to melt. It just sweats and eventually bursts into flame. Tragically this stuff has no properties conducive to pizza.) Anyway, the meager breakfast and the walk out to the field had induced an appetite, and I was on my sixth or seventh piece of byaslag when our doctor friend motioned for me to stop. This was the first time a Mongolian had ever tried to get me to stop eating anything. Usually they were forcing things down my throat in the name of hospitality. He tried to explain, but all I could understand was it wasn't safe. I questioned him further, and he used a Mongolian word I'd never heard. He could see I wasn't getting it and he tried very hard to come up with an English word from his rusty vocabulary.

He brightened and declared, "Feca."

"Feca? What is that?"

He pointed to the cheese and repeated, "Fee-caa."

I still looked puzzled, so he said, "English word. Feca."

"I've never heard it. Is the byaslag feca?"

He nodded and smiled. I decided to get Lance involved. He, too, had no idea what this guy was talking about in Mongolian or English. The doctor just kept saying: "Feca."

Finally, we both looked so puzzled he got up and began to act it out. Lance and I made quiet jokes about charades.

The doctor pointed to the plate of cheese and then squatted and mimed an outhouse activity. I began to feel queasy.

"Fecal? Is that what you're saying? Fecal?"

"Yes! Yes, that's it, fecal." he said, overjoyed at my understanding.

"The byaslag is fecal?" I demanded with a sinking feeling. He agreed happily. I had lost all my appetite and was wondering how hard it would be to self-induce vomiting. I turned to Lance.

"This is so gross."

"Why, what's 'fecal' mean?" demanded Lance.

"It's medical jargon for human or animal waste."

"Yuck!" The expression on Lance's face matched the retch in my gut.

I never did get ill from that cheese, although we didn't find out what the doctor had really been trying to warn me until our return to Ulaanbaatar. That's one of the problems in learning a new language. If no one nearby speaks your tongue, checking your conclusions can get sticky. There was nothing wrong with the byaslag. The doctor was just letting me know it tends to affect one like prunes do and can be inconvenient if one eats too much too far from the *bie zasax gazar* (toilet, literally: 'body repair place'). I was belatedly quite relieved, so to speak.

That evening the hotel lady, true to her word, gave me a haircut. Word had leaked and a small crowd had gathered to watch. She did a fairly good job, considering the pressure of having an audience for her first attempt at curly hair. Afterwards, a good part of the male populace followed me into our room for conversation in broken Mongolian. We soon discovered everyone in town was a "professional photographer." At least that's what each told us as soon as he'd caught sight of Lance's camera. It was strangely ironic so many photographers lived in the same town and none of them had a camera. The most outgoing of these guys actually got us to agree to let him guide us into the countryside the next day. As I ushered our last guest to the door, the hotel lady's son ran by — completely bald. Apparently I'd created a monster with clippers.

The next morning we went exploring with the "photographer." We walked several miles to a place on the river away from all human habitation. As I crossed a creek, the branch I was using as a bridge snapped and my jeans were soaked to the thighs. It was such a perfect summer day that the obvious solution, out there in the middle of nowhere, was to hang up the pants in a tree and let them dry while I fished with the drop line I'd found in a shop on our way out of town. We spent several hours at this bend in the Hara River nestled under a huge rock hill. Our guide insisted on taking a picture of Lance and me with the hill as the backdrop, so Lance gave him the camera and we posed. He began to snap pictures as rapidly as he could. We began shouting and gesturing he should quit. He'd snapped off 12 shots before we wrestled the camera away from him. Again he assured us this is what he did for a living.

On the long hike back to Zuunhara our guide insisted on stopping at every ger we passed to show us off. Mongolian hospitality requires hosts to serve a meal to all guests, so the time we left the fifth ger, we'd been overfed with mutton, dumpling soup, noodles, byaslag, yogurt, candy, bread, and endless dairy products, until we were in serious pain. Anyone who has ever encountered a determined Mongolian host or hostess will tell you that saying "No, I'm full" will get you nowhere. They force it on you anyway. We finally flat out refused to be introduced to any more of our guide's vast circle of friends along our route. When at last we reached town he insisted we go into this restaurant where his friend worked with him. He made it clear they wouldn't try to feed us since it was closed for Naadam and wasn't a home.

How do you stop a "professional photographer?"

Inside the restaurant (a guanz - the local version of the "greasy spoon") we found his friend, a burly woman wielding a large butcher knife, busy carving up an enormous hog back in the kitchen. A cigarette with a long drooping ash hung from the corner of her mouth as she mumbled. We sat near her at a table and talked while she worked. I was amazed at how much pure white fat fit on this pig. She was cutting off whole slabs, which she then cubed. After about 10 minutes we started making our good-byes and getting up from the table. The woman gestured with her knife, making it clear we were not free to go yet. To our complete dismay she served us each a plate of rice with barely steamed cubes of pig fat all over it. I told our guide to explain we couldn't possibly eat this now, but thanks all the same. He just shrugged. I tried to explain this to the lady, but she said something back I didn't catch, although her meaning was clear by her expression and the way she pointed her knife. We'd clean our plates or else.

At the "Pig Fat Cafe" moments before being "served"

When I want an image of Hell, I think of this meal. I know Hell is much worse: I just can't imagine how. Somehow I was finally able to choke down every last piece of fat while our determined hostess stood over me to make sure I received her hospitality. When we escaped outside at last, our guide was still in the restaurant making his good-byes. I asked Lance if that wasn't the worst experience of his entire life. He said, "That wasn't bad at all." I looked at him incredulously as he emptied his pockets of wads of money. He had dropped each piece of fat onto a one, three, or five tugrik note in his lap, and then surreptitiously twisted them into little bundles and pocketed them. He had eaten none of the fat, unobserved as the woman had glowered at me. A five tugrik bill was only worth about one cent, so it hadn't cost him much. Lance then gave his portion of the unfortunate pig a decent burial by treading it into a nearby mud hole before our guide stepped out.

As soon as we escaped into our hotel room we collapsed into our beds. We had both been overfed into a stupor and walked to exhaustion. I was drifting off to sleep in the gentle breeze coming through the open window next to my bed, when someone screamed. I screamed in response and shot straight up into the air. This startled Lance so he did the same thing. When I recovered, I found the hotel's handyman rolling around in the garden under my window, holding his sides and laughing uncontrollably. After we had each gotten our hearts to stop trying to jump from our chests, Lance explained what had happened.

Lance had seen the handyman tiptoeing along outside our room toward my window. Guessing the guy intended either to spy on our naps or scare me, Lance had pretended to sleep while keeping an eye on the action. When the guy had leapt up and screamed right next to me, my violent reaction had frightened Lance as well. We had ended up providing a show I am sure was the talk of Zuunhara for week to come. The handyman came into our room to recount it and act it out several times, laughing hysterically the entire time. I felt like a surprise guest on Zuunhara's hit game show: Westerners do the Darnedest Things.

After he'd gone Lance asked me, "When our guide was snapping all those pictures of us today, had you already put your pants back on or were you still in your underwear?" Neither of us could recall. We laughed until we were sore. I made him promise not to show the pictures to anyone until I saw what developed. (As it turned out I had been dressed for the photo shoot. We still have a fistful of photos in which Lance and I, trying to get his camera back, advance toward the camera, ever closer to the photographer in each shot.)

I had mixed emotions as we caught the train out of Zuunhara at ten o'clock that night. As we rumbled north to Mongolia's second largest city, Darhan, I already missed the quirky small town where odd, rural Mongolians had so quickly become friends. This was just one of hundreds with absolutely no Christian witness. I resolved to send as many Mongolian church planters as I could out into these unreached villages.

'At any rate I'll never go there again!' said Alice as she picked her way
through the wood. 'It's the stupidest tea-party I ever was at in all my life!'
                    Alice's Adventures in Wonderland by Lewis Carroll

Zuunhara today is home to a growing church planted by Mongolian workers trained at Erdenet's Mongolian Mission Center.

TEN

Vacation of Ill Repute

Once summer finally came that first year, we were more than ready to get out of Ulaanbaatar. Even a glance at a map of Mongolia, shaded with its yellow and brown tones, draws the eye to a blue jewel in the center of the country's remote north. This large deep pristine lake is one of the country's most distinctive features. Huvsgul, mirroring its much-larger sister Lake Baikal across the Russian border, drew us like a magnet.

We decided a vacation to Lake Huvsgul was the perfect thing to refresh our weary city-dweller souls. Apparently I'd already earned a month-long vacation. The architecture firm I worked for shut down every August so employees could "hudoo yavax." This phrase meant "go to the countryside," but functioned in society as a universal excuse for shortages, absences, inefficiencies, for almost everything. As I talked the trip through with my coworkers, it became clear travel on our own in Mongolia would be very difficult. Fortunately, one of the architects had a sister living in Möron, the town where our plane would land, and another relative living in Hatgal, a town 40 miles north of Möron at the southern end of the lake. He wrote me a letter of introduction to his sister and sent it with us, insisting we ask for her immediately upon arrival in Möron.

We planned to fly from Ulaanbaatar to Möron, to stay in Möron a couple days visiting other missionaries, and hire a jeep to take us north to Lake Huvsgul. In Hatgal, we planned to stay with my coworker's relatives while we enjoyed what that beautiful locale had to offer. Our main problem would be food since the farther you got from the capital city, the

scarcer were the food supplies. We decided to bring what we could ourselves and trust in the usual hospitality of the Mongolian people we'd
meet along the way.

When the big day finally arrived and it was time to board a plane for the
central regions of Mongolia, we discovered domestic air travel in Mongolia is a completely different matter from travel to other countries. Our
plane was old, intended mostly for cargo, and dangerously overcrowded. There was no assigned seating; a ticket merely gave you the
right to struggle for a place to sit. We didn't each get a seat of our own,
but with God's help, Louise and I got all three girls onto the plane.

Möron is a sort of county seat for the large surrounding area. Even so, it
had only one hotel. So, we hailed a car. In Mongolia, any car is a potential cab, and one need only waggle a hand at it to get a ride. We went
straight to the hotel, hoping to get a room. It turned out to be no problem—the only other guests were several long-haul truck drivers. We
showed the innkeeper our letter of introduction and she sent a messenger to tell this woman to come to the hotel. Naraa arrived within an
hour, very excited to meet someone sent by her relative in Ulaanbaatar.
She was very gracious and took us off to her house to feed us and introduce us to the other relatives. Then while she was at work, we were able
to explore the town of Möron on our own, taking in the museum and
former zoo. Apparently the animals had all been eaten during the food
shortages of the previous year. The zoo was now a sad weed-filled place.

Our hostess arranged for a car to take us to the lake. Somewhere near
the appointed time this Russian jeep (a ubiquitous model called a Sixty-
nine) pulled up to our hotel and we piled in. We then began a long journey over some of the worst roads we have ever traveled. Our driver
raced over the rocks and potholes in such a reckless manner we feared
for life and limb. Our daughter Melody gets carsick, and I lost count of
how many times we had to yell "Zoks!" (stop) and let her out to heave
into the bushes. When we finally arrived in the tiny town of Hatgal, we
were sore, tired, dusty, rattled, and thankful the trip was over.

As we were leaving Möron, our hostess had given us a second letter of introduction to their relatives at the lake. After asking just one person, our driver was able to take us directly to their house. This couple, Hotbot and Enkhee, and their young son and niece lived in a log cabin with a big yard, surrounded by a fence, right on the shore of Lake Huvsgul. The locale was stunning; mountains, forest, and lake surrounded us. My eyes, like famished prisoners, drank in the deep green and sparkling azure beauty after six months of the gray ugliness of Ulaanbaatar. The pain of thousands of needles pricking as my legs returned to life just made everything outside that horrible vehicular torture rack seem all the sweeter.

The family, who had no idea who we were, received us with the same enthusiasm with which they'd receive their own long-lost relatives. They actually slaughtered a sheep for us and we feasted on freshly boiled mutton that evening. They had never heard a word of English, and though communication was painstaking and frustrating, our stay with them was the best time of language learning we'd ever had. We ate

Getting out into the countryside simplifies meal preparation. The goat is being dispatched in the traditional manner. They make a cut and reach inside to open an artery. Seems like a peaceful way to go—except for the cutting and sticking a hand inside part.

together and struggled to ask (and answer) each other's questions. As the long summer day came to a close, we were wondering where we were going to sleep. The one-room cabin the family lived in was clearly not big enough to accommodate all of us. The solution came as the mother led us to the next house over, for which she was caretaker during the owners' absence. She opened up this larger two-roomed cabin and made sure we were all settled in for the night before leaving. (This time no one tied us in.)

Everything went fine until about two o'clock in the morning. We woke up to a loud truck pulling up outside. Then the front door opened, and in came the rather large family whose house we were sleeping in. We felt rather like Goldilocks when the bears came home. These people did not even blink when they saw strangers sleeping in their beds. Apologetic, we began to get up and out, but they wouldn't hear of it and insisted we stay put. Somehow they communicated they would just cook some food and then go somewhere else to spend the night. We were aghast. There was no way we were going to put them out of their home. American manners came up against Mongolian hospitality and were completely routed. We stayed in bed while they cooked a meal, Grandma hacked away with her rasping tubercular cough, and everybody laughed and talked. At four a.m. they piled back into their truck and roared off. Needless to say we never got back to sleep.

We felt so bad about taking their house from them, even though they didn't see it that way, the next morning we told our hosts we'd feel better staying in the local hotel. I had noticed a large wooden hotel in Hatgal the day before and had made a mental note a room there would be far more comfortable than the floor of the one-room cabin. However, when we brought up the idea of transferring to the hotel, our hosts were horrified. We tried to assure them we would still eat all our meals with them and partake of their wonderful hospitality, and we only wanted to free up the house for the family that actually lived there. From the reaction we got, it seemed they understood us to say we were going to drown ourselves in the lake—not simply check-in at a hotel. Finally, through sheer perseverance, we were able to gather up our things and walk the four blocks to Hatgal's only hotel.

It was an expansive wooden edifice that had originally provided lodging for Communist bigwigs visiting the Young Pioneers' camp and barracks next door. Since the fall of Communism, the camp had closed and now seemed like a ghost town. The hotel, however, was clinging to life, and the current owners were trying to make a go of this strange new market economy. We were surprised to find, upon checking in, these owners were three young women. Among them they had several infants and small children, but all three appeared to be single working mothers. They were quite happy to see a large American family show up and ask for a room. As we walked the entire length of the hotel, I noticed most of the rooms we passed were bare. At the end of the hallway, there was a sitting room with four suites opening off of it. All of these were furnished I was relieved to see.

The young woman who walked us back opened one of the rooms and gave us the key. The girls were tired, so we quickly got them tucked into the beds and down for a nap. Louise and I set about unpacking our things and putting them into the tastefully antique wooden dressers. We had just finished when an insistent tapping began at our door. Mongolians don't knock and then wait for an answer, they tap constantly and steadily until the door is answered or they get bored. I found the girl who had checked us in at the door. She told us we had to move to the room next door. I tried to explain it was too late. The girls were sleeping, we were comfortable and already moved in, and we liked the room. She insisted we move, growing a bit frantic at my resistance. I pointed out we were the only guests in the entire hotel, so leaving us in this room could hardly be a problem. She pushed past me and began to gather our things and move them herself. I decided this had to be another of those inexplicable things that happen with great regularity in the foreigner's experience. It is easier to go along than to resist. Determined Mongolians have a lot in common with Star Trek's Borg: "Resistance is futile." We gave in and began carrying sleeping children to beds in the next room.

All we could figure out was that the hospitality imperative must have compelled our inexperienced hostesses to upgrade us to a better room. The view was much better from our new room. It was on the corner and had two walls with windows overlooking Hatgal and the mountains.

When the girls woke from their nap, we explored the town a bit, found a wonderful antique traditional copper kettle in a shop for next to nothing, and wound up at our host family's place on the lake for dinner. They seemed surprised we were happy about the hotel and had no horrors to report. We didn't bring up the room snafu. Just a little after dark, Hotbot walked us back to our hotel. Tired, we went to bed.

Around eleven that night we were awakened by loud laughter coming from the room next to us, the one we had so briefly occupied. As we listened to the growing din, we realized a large party was going on right on the other side of our wall. It actually sounded like girls were being tickled in there. Neither Louise nor I could sleep, and we were worried the girls would wake at any moment, so I got up and dressed to go ask them to quiet down.

I knocked on the door several times before anyone inside heard me. When the door finally swung open I wished it hadn't. The scene inside was not easy to erase from my mind. An orgy was in progress. Filled with shame and embarrassment for those within, I averted my eyes down the hall and, in my halting Mongolian, told the man at the door, "My children sleeping. Don't make loud . . . umm . . . please stop . . . laughing." He laughed at this request and told the others. As they all laughed louder, I heard a couple girls trying to shush them. I assume the hotel girls were trying to do both their jobs at once. I went back into our room and told Louise, "Now I know why they didn't want us to stay here. Our hostesses seem to have embraced Capitalism. They really are working girls. This is the town bordello." As we tried to figure out why they had to use the room next door to us out of the entire hotel, we came up with a theory we never had the nerve to check out. That was a bit deeper into culture study then we wanted to go. We decided the "House of Ill Repute" was having a sale. The advertisements must have said come to this certain room at ten o'clock on this night. That explained their panic when they had put us in the best room and then realized what night it was. We were grateful they had moved us after all.

Our hostesses did manage to finally quiet things down and the party seemed to dwindle away within another hour or so. The next morning all three of the hotel girls showed up at our door with mutton stew, hot water for our in-room sink (without plumbing), towels, and a very contrite, anxious to please and make amends, way about them. They even said sorry several times, without mentioning what they were apologizing for. They were certainly hard to stay angry at. As a pastor of ours used to tell us, "You can't demand righteousness of a people who have no access to it." Until the Gospel could penetrate such remote locations as Hatgal, the people would have no idea about the One who gives us His righteousness.

The rest of the vacation went much smoother. We took a small motorboat trip up the lake, and spent a couple nights in an old fire brigade camp hoping to become a tourist resort. We didn't see much hope unless they imported something beyond sticky noodles to feed their guests. The quaint custom of putting the bill into negotiation before allowing visitors to leave was also discouraging. Still, Huvsgul's eye popping grandeur of steep mountainsides dropping sharply into azure waters was unforgettable.

When we were about to board the plane going back to Ulaanbaatar from Möron, our hostess presented us with gifts. She insisted we take a large plastic bowl brimming over with berry jam and a whole fried chicken in a mesh bag. How practical! These would have been difficult items to travel with on any airline, but this particular MIAT flight was even worse than our flight out. When the plane pulled to a stop, the crowd wanting to go to the capital rushed the runway and struggled to get past the deplaning passengers. Imagine an entire rugby scrum climbing up a ladder. We shoved the bowl of jam into a plastic bag and entered the fray with luggage, girls and gifts in tow. Mongolians took pity on us and lifted the girls out of our hands and into the plane. Louise and I were not at all sure we would be joining them on this flight. In the end, God smiled on us. The entire family made it safely back home. Even the jam didn't spill very much. Ever since, whenever I refer to this trip as our "vacation" or "break," Louise stares daggers at me.

Just over two years later an identical plane, perhaps the same one, crashed near Möron, leaving 40 dead and a lone survivor. One probable reason for the accident was the added weight of unregistered passengers (known as "rabbits") bribing their way on board. The wreckage and remains were strewn across a densely wooded slope. The destruction and mingling of human remains meant a final death count was never known.

Melody and lakeside cowboys

ELEVEN

Language Acquisition Made Pitiful

The famed linguist Betty Sue Brewster had trained us to learn language in context—in community—the way children do. Betty Sue and her late husband Tom had called this style of language learning "Language Acquisition Made Practical" or LAMP. Our Perspectives class had introduced LAMP, and later Betty Sue and her son Jed had taught for a week of our School of Frontier Missions. We had bought-in to the LAMP method for our assault on the Mongolian language. I agreed with Betty Sue that we would best learn both language and culture not through study and research, but rather through being with people. The small amount of material available on Mongolian language and culture made formal study in the States an exercise in futility anyway, and we'd already learned from the Navajo that the difference between the books and the reality was enough to make or break a missionary.

It was with this understanding that we excitedly hit the streets of Ulaanbaatar with little more than Betty Sue's injunction of "learn a little and use it a lot" ringing in our ears. Our daily goal was to speak a few memorized lines to 50 individuals. This often resulted in more than just the usual hilarity . . .

The Dreaded Hat Mongers

The zakh was Ulaanbaatar's swarming sanctuary of burgeoning Capitalism—free markets at their most freewheeling. The actual English equivalent of *zakh* is bazaar, or outdoor market, but everyone I knew called it the "Black Market." It wasn't actually illegal, like a proper black

market, but after 70 years of Communism any expression of private en-
terprise and profit was viewed with a mixture of anxiety and longing.
Mongolians were at a crossroad and deeply conflicted about quickly
changing standards of public morality. "Business" was still a bad word
and a businessman was commonly described as being unemployed. Yet
the most popular pastime was hatching schemes for enterprises that
would open the floodgates of wealth. The only people getting rich in the
new economy were the businessmen, while most people were still stuck
on the idea that private property and profits were theft. This left most
Mongolians scheming how best to embark on what they still saw as a
life of crime.

Into this gap between the real and the ideal grew the zakh—a large, flat
area nestled in the hills on the north side of Ulaanbaatar, filled to overflowing with people buying and selling. It first appears as complete and
utter swirling chaos, an undulating sea of black hair. Thousands and
thousands of Mongolians along with their wares jam into this limited
space—creating one of the most densely populated spots on earth in the
middle of the world's least densely populated country. There are vague
sections where goods of a certain type are to be found; a shoe section,
hardware, rugs, precious metals and antiques, pets, even a "food court."
Sellers would stand with their items held out for viewing or spread out
on a blanket at their feet. The variety of wares was ever-changing and
endlessly fascinating, at least to me. I loved to visit the zakh even though
it meant a taxi ride to get out there and back. If I bought furniture or
anything too big to carry, I would have to hire a horse cart to transport
it back to our apartment. Once, Lance and I were sitting on a couch I just
purchased, perched upon a cart behind the horse and driver. We were
joking about doing the royal parade wave to the crowds we were passing through. Suddenly the cart hit a massive pothole and we flew into
the air. Both of us came back down hard onto my new Mongolian-made
couch and, with a loud crack the frame snapped in two. When we
reached home the driver helped us get the poor couch up five flights of
stairs and into the apartment. Lance and I turned it over and figured out
what was required to fix and strengthen the broken frame—another trip
to the zakh of course, to get the required hardware.

The zakh was a language learner's dream. Our strategy for learning Mongolian was LAMP, which holds as its main premise that language learning is not an academic exercise, but a social one. The best way to learn is to get out and talk with native speakers. The LAMP watchword is: "Learn a little, use it a lot!" I would memorize a short script in Mongolian and then go out into the streets and markets and practice it on 50 people.

"Sain bain uu? Minee nerig Brian gedig. Bi Mongol hel sorch bain. Bi baag zereg yerdag. Ta nadad tuslax uu? Bayartai. ("Hello. My name is Brian. I am learning Mongolian. I don't speak much yet. Will you help me? Goodbye.")

I'd note people's responses, so I could discuss them with my language helper, Monkho. Then I would learn and add a new phrase like: "I am an American" to my spiel. The next day I'd go out and do it all again. There was no better place in all of Asia for meeting 50 people quickly than the Ulaanbaatar zakh.

One crisp spring day of around -10°C (14°F), I was slowly moving through the masses at the zakh—not really shopping for anything, just learning. I inadvertently wandered into the section occupied by the "dreaded hat sellers." This particular group of merchants was best avoided completely, and I generally gave their area a wide berth. Their product was fur hats—immense fluffy fur hats no local would be caught dead wearing. These hats looked like a blow-dried longhaired cat had crawled onto your head and died there, and only tourists were ever seen underneath one. Perhaps because of the near universal distaste for their product, the hat sellers were renowned for pursuing their quarry and refusing to accept a simple "No, I'm not interested." In their piranha-like zeal, it was common to find them surrounding you, shouting as they moved along with you as a pack, thrusting huge fur balls into your face for inspection. Even locals tried to steer clear.

However, I hadn't been paying sufficient attention to where I was in the vast marketplace, and two ladies on the fringe of the pack, armed with a box of hats, caught me. Quickly I launched into my memorized Mongolian phrases as I frantically pretended to examine their hats, hoping against hope they wouldn't start yelling their sales pitch ("Malgaa awarai!" "Take this hat!"), and draw the pack's attention onto me. Their box of furry hats really looked just like a box of dead cats. This gave me an idea for some fun. While I talked, I worked my hand down to the bottom of the hats and got inside of one. Just as I came to the end of my little speech—and before they could launch into obnoxious selling—I quickly pulled up the hat and made a sound like a frightened cat. MEEROOWOOW! The results startled even me. Both women shrieked

Fitting-In in my dehl

and fell backward into the crowd throwing the box of hats up into the air. I jumped too. One lady ended up sitting on the ground. The hats were everywhere. In seconds the shock turned into laughter, the ladies laughing loudest of all as the people nearby and I helped gather the scattered hats back into the box. We had to reenact the joke several times to the continued glee of all concerned. This was my first experience with the physical nature of Mongolian humor. To the Mongolian mind, one can never have too much slapstick comedy. The Three Stooges could have taken over the country without a shot.

Making Friends on the Bunny Slopes

One day during our second winter, I was returning home from a successful trip to the zakh laden down with treasures, the largest of which was a huge electric wok in a box. It was a bit of a struggle even to see out from behind the stack of packages, as I carefully picked my way across the vacant lot next to our apartment complex. This field was all steep hillocks of dirt and broken concrete, punctuated with protrusions of iron rebar. Some care was needed when crossing it at any time, but covered in fresh snow, as it was that Saturday afternoon, required the circumspection of a cat.

I reached the summit of the mound nearest our building and noticed an old woman cleaning her winter dehl at the bottom of the slope in front of me. I assumed that was what she was doing. I'd never seen anyone rub snow into the sheep fleece that lined the oostei dehl (fur-lined dress), before, but I had noticed dozens of folks doing an identical thing to their carpets after each fresh snow. Fields would fill with children vigorously rubbing snow into the large carpets that lay on every Mongolian living room floor, then shaking and beating it out with sticks. Apparently the dirt went with the snow. Shortly after a fresh pristine snow, every vacant lot would be covered with these squares of soiled snow—resembling a dirty gray quilt.

At any rate, this grandmother looked up the hill from her task at the huge foreigner, loaded with packages, towering up above her. She appeared at little startled and dropped the dehl she was just finishing into the snow at her feet. To take the edge off her shock, I called out a Mongolian greeting: "Sain bain uu?" ("Are you well?") Unfortunately, at the very moment of meeting between two alien cultures, my size 13 boots (European size 47) turned into downhill skis. I began to slide down the hillock—straight for the terror-stricken woman.

Showing a remarkable agility for one so advanced in years, she shrieked and leapt sideways at least a meter. This cleared the way for me to fall flat and face-first onto her freshly cleaned dehl, as my boxes went flying in every direction. Immediately, her winter dehl started moving, and the added momentum of a fairly hefty American turned it into a sheepskin sled. Fortunately the ride came to a halt after a few meters. Silence descended.

I was trying to figure out how to get up, collect my things, and escape without showing my face any further, when I heard the laughter start. I looked over for the source of this mirth and saw the old woman, sitting on the snow where she had landed, holding her sides and laughing her head off. Even though I was mortified, it was one of those embarrassing moments so extreme that laughter is the only possible response short of committing hara-kiri. I began to laugh too. When she was able to gasp out a word she yelled, "Sain bain uu?" in a fairly good imitation of my accented Mongolian. This convulsed both of us. It was hard to breathe, lying there in the snow, dissolved in hilarity with that woman. We lay there for five minutes, helplessly laughing our fool heads off, every once in a while barking out, "Sain bain uu?" Finally, I was able to stagger to my feet, and I helped her to hers. Together, still laughing, we gathered my things, including the badly dented wok (which caused even more mirth). I said "Bayartai" and headed off to my stairwell entrance, her laughs following me the whole way. I toyed with the idea of pretending to live somewhere else, but realized that she, and everyone else, already knew exactly who I, the foreigner, was and where I lived.

They tell you when you haven't mastered a language, it is almost impossible to tell a truly funny joke in that language. On the other hand, I found that humor of Jerry Lewis' type translates very well. It may be hard to tell a joke, but one may become a joke without any effort at all. For weeks thereafter, every time I would walk by the groups of old women sitting outside our building I would overhear the words: Amerikhoon (American), tsas (snow), and "Sain bain uu?" followed by giggles and stifled laughter. There's really nothing like language learning to build humility into the Man of God.

Killing 'em at the Funeral

Soon after moving in to our first apartment in Ulaanbaatar, we met the retired couple next door. We wondered how we would be received as the first non-Mongolians ever to live in their building. This couples' friendliness, in spite of the language barrier, was heartening. One of our local friends told us the man next door was Mongolian KGB. This worried me a bit. Had we been permitted into this exact apartment so we could be watched? Louise and I resolved not to worry about it or to be covert in our actions. God had done such incredible miracles to get our family into the country; He could certainly keep us here. We would not be expelled unless God determined we were finished with what He'd sent us to do. So, we continued to develop a pleasant non-verbal relationship with our neighbors.

Because not many Mongolians had phones in their apartments, those who were blessed to have a phone line allowed neighbors to come in and place calls. We had a line and we had a fairly regular stream of visitors using it. Sometimes people would even receive calls on our phone. I would have to figure out the apartment number being shouted into the other end and then go out into the hall and up or down a flight of stairs or two to find the person wanted. Since we didn't know much language yet, we were always telling callers we were American in an attempt to determine if they had the right number. Then there were international calls. Usually the phone would ring in one long drawn out wail to let us know it was a call from overseas. We would run to get it and find silence. The connections must have been very tricky because it often took three tries or more to connect. Then you had to yell out words, and be careful not to talk over each other because all sound would cut out if you did. When we got a very early morning call from a Sunday school class in Salem, Oregon, so the children (all gathered around a speaker phone) could interview a missionary, we began to have second thoughts about phone ownership. My mind was complete mush. I must have sounded the complete idiot as I stumbled through their questions. One child asked me what my children were doing "right now." When I said they were sleeping because it was the middle of the night in Mongolia, their very embarrassed teacher quickly terminated that call.

Late one night there was an insistent steady knocking on our door. When I answered it, I found our next-door neighbor lady appearing very distressed. For several minutes she tried to get me to understand something, but my vocabulary just couldn't handle it. Finally she pushed past me to get to the phone. While she was on the phone I looked up the term she had been repeating about her husband: "nas barsan." I knew the first word was the word for "age" and the second meant "lost." I suddenly understood when the dictionary revealed the word pair meant "death." She was calling 911 (or the local equivalent). Her husband had just died. After she finished her call I tried to comfort her. Usually it is hard to know what to say at these times, but I didn't even know how to say anything. It was so frustrating, especially as I was feeling really bad for keeping her from the phone for so long when she first knocked.

Apparently the impression of love and caring somehow made it through all my linguistic bumbling. Our neighbor lady invited Louise and I to the funeral reception. A ger was erected for a cookhouse in the courtyard five stories below our apartments. Since friends and relatives would be crowding in from all over, the apartment kitchen was not up to the task of cooking enough food. People would spend the whole day sitting and talking and eating in our neighbor's apartment. I went over to spend an hour or so in the afternoon. The small apartment was filled with people. Conversation was muted and somber, but the food and drink was being consumed at a healthy rate. I sat for a while, feeling kind of unconnected, until a young boy came and sat next to me. I decided to try out my Mongolian language skills on him.

Me: "How are you? My name is Brian. What is your name?"

Boy: (stares at me and remains utterly silent)

Me: (undeterred) "How old are you?

Boy: (not a peep)

I paused a bit at this point, trying to think of something he might respond to, even by gesture. Other conversations had trailed off as most were very curious about this American trying to converse in Mongolian. There were a few glares at the boy for being so unresponsive and rude. Then it occurred to me that if he could point his dad out to me, I could ask him my questions about his son. I would get to change the pronouns—a good substitution drill for language learning. "What is his name? etc. So I turned to the boy again and asked:

"Which one is your father?"

There were several shocked gasps around the room, and the boy's eyes went really wide. After a long moment of stunned silence, someone let out a loud laugh, and then the entire assembly erupted into gales of laughter. Everyone, except for the boy and me, was practically rolling on the floor with glee. I ended up joining the fun although I had no idea what they found so funny. Whatever had occurred, I was now "in," and when I left everyone shook my hand and several kissed me on the cheek.

The next day I recounted the incident to Monkho, my language tutor. I ran through the whole thing in English. He asked me to repeat exactly what I had said to the boy in Mongolian. When I came to the line that brought down the house, Monkho went pale. I asked him what the problem could be with a simple question of who the kid's dad was. Monkho

My language helper, Monkho, with daughter Temudjin

explained I had used the wrong word for "which." I protested he had just taught me this word a week before. Unfortunately, it turned out he had neglected to mention it was never used for people, only things. What I had actually said was "What kind of a father do you have?" which is just about the worst insult in Mongolian. It is a direct challenge to the person's legitimacy. When I told Monkho how the shock had given way to laughter, he said everyone had realized I was a foreigner and could not have meant to be so vulgar. He also figured most of them thought the boy was being inexcusably bad-mannered and had it coming. My face was hot and scarlet with delayed embarrassment. Once again I'm "the life of the party."

Another One Rides the Bus

Public transportation in Ulaanbaatar has got to be one of Mongolia's unique attractions. It should be televised as an "extreme sport."

During our first year in Mongolia, we would often get around the city by riding the bus network. There were several reasons for this. Tickets were incredibly cheap, the equivalent of about two and a half cents. We also worried that riding around in cabs might separate us from the people, making us look rich or elitist. The overcrowded buses were perfect for practicing our language scripts and for keeping warm, even in winter.

It is hard to describe just how crowded these buses were. The closest Western equivalent would be Volkswagen or phone booth stuffing. The sensation is one of pushing your way into a solid, writhing mass of heavily clothed and padded humanity . . . standing there feeling crushed, pushed and pulled this way and that by irresistible tidal forces of the crowd . . . wondering how you will know when the bus has reached your stop since the windows are thickly frosted with condensed and frozen human breath . . . realizing that even if you do guess correctly where to get off, actually extricating yourself from the pungent mass will take superhuman force. Amazingly, one incredible being seems to be able to make her way through this mob like a hot knife through butter: the ticket seller. This lady manages somehow to force her way through the bus to each passenger and collect his or her fare, make change, and tear them off a tiny paper ticket. If some deadbeat resisted coughing up his pittance, this conductor would get fierce. I watched one ticket lady forcibly propel a man twice her size off the bus because he sullenly refused to pay. These scenes were rare because most were properly intimidated by the obvious powers of someone who could actually move like that inside the bus.

It took a while, but we eventually learned the hard way what every Mongolian instinctively knew. When carrying cash, take a taxi. Theft was rampant on the bus. On several occasions, caught in the crush of bodies, I actually felt the pickpocket's hands in my back pockets. Since

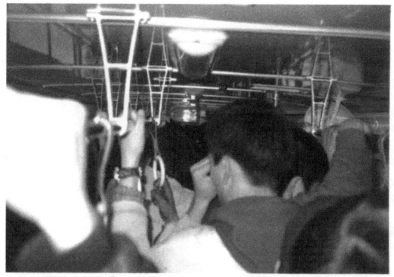

Bus in the world's least densely populated country.

my arms were immobilized, I was powerless to respond. I was glad I kept my money elsewhere. Many of the thieves were even more determined to get at hidden cash. They would use a razor blade to cut into pockets or bags, and the victim would know nothing until they moved off the bus and felt a breeze or found their belongings tumbling out through the new hole. I had my jacket pockets slashed open on several occasions. Louise sewed them back together each time and we called it "Frankenstein's Coat." After losing significant wads of bills for the third time, we finally decided when we were "loaded" we would hail a cab. When I told Monkho of our decision, he laughed, "Mongolians never ride buses when they have much cash." He also taught me the word for "thief." Monkho explained if you yelled, "HOLGAICH!" on a bus, the driver was compelled by law to lock down the doors and drive everyone to the nearest police station for a thorough search. I thought I just might try this the next time I was robbed on the bus. At our next tutoring session I practiced on Monkho. He roared with laughter. He let me know I was unlikely to achieve the desired result by shouting, "Refrigerator!" (horgogch) on a crowded bus. The differences in Mongolian vowel sounds are subtle, and I obviously needed more practice before hitting the streets as a crime fighting superhero.

Drinking *airag* (fermented mares' milk). An acquired taste - a blend of champagne and buttermilk.

Most language learning happens while hanging out.

TWELVE

The "Mother of All Moves"

During that first year of learning language in Ulaanbaatar, we experienced the adventure and frustration of trying to raise three children, maintain a household, attend language school, build relationships with Mongolian neighbors and fellow missionaries, teach English to architects, and do it all in a post-Communist country whose basic infrastructure was collapsing. During the final part of '93, the biggest worry facing the missionaries and fledgling church in Mongolia was the threat to end religious liberty through a constitutional amendment. A massive amount of prayer and some diplomatic pressure by the U.S. led to the failure of this measure, but the Buddhist lamas (priests) and Communist politicians continued in an unholy alliance to do anything they could to stop the Gospel. Things were tense.

But for us personally, creating a home in this strange land proceeded apace. One thing that helped us to bond with the people was our Mongolian names. Our Mongolian friends had renamed every member of our family. This turned out to be a big help in speaking a language that adds countless suffixes to the end of names. Our English names just didn't work in Mongolian. My name was changed to Byambaa (Saturday); Louise was Tsetsgee (Flower); Melody translates directly as Uyanga; Alice became Tuya (Ray or Beam) and Molly got the prettiest name of all, Sarangerel (Moonlight). When we used these names the locals would just melt. They were an instant door opener.

Our plans to join Magnus and Maria in Erdenet by September fizzled. I had signed a one-year contract to teach for 'MONAR' Company, and our relationship with our mission agency changed. YWAM had joined an umbrella mission called Joint Christian Services International (JCS) for its work in Mongolia. We had tried to work within this twelve-mission partnership, but we ran into snags in defining our ministry. The director felt very strongly about limiting the scope of ministry to relief and development work, at least for the first five years. He kept pressuring us to abandon our plan to plant churches in Erdenet and to take up one of the JCS mercy ministry projects in the Gobi Desert, instead. We reached an impasse and, after hours of prayer and soul-searching, decided not to continue under JCS auspices. Like a shoe that doesn't fit, JCS was just not right for us. Almost immediately after making this decision, we ran into Rick Leatherwood on the street. He invited us to join his mission, Mongolian Enterprises International, and promised to send us to Erdenet. We agreed to join the formal language school for one semester in order to better master the grammatical structures of Mongolian. This, and the contract with 'MONAR,' seemed to point to February as a more likely date for our move.

God seemed to be putting everything together for us to join Magnus and Maria Alphonce in Erdenet on our first anniversary in Mongolia: February 22nd, 1994. Magnus and Maria had done a terrific job of pioneering the church there. There were now five large house churches and more believers being baptized all the time. Magnus and Bayaraa taught the Word to Mongolian leaders in his home every week, and then each would pass on what she had learned in the house church she led. There were finally several young men and a few older women, but the bulk of new work needed to focus on breakthroughs into new groups. Our focus, as we joined the work, would continue to be on learning language (which accelerates when one is away from Ulaanbaatar's large expatriate community and can immerse in the language without constant temptation to function in English) and cultural adaptation. We were all praying an older family like ourselves might be the key to appealing to someone beyond the teen girls who made up almost the entire congregation. We all knew something had to change the makeup of the group if a healthy, enduring, and reproducing church movement was to emerge.

Yet in the midst of this concern, there were so many signs of health among the believers in Erdenet. Magnus, Maria and Bayaraa had carefully discipled the first believers and taught them to pass on to their own disciples how to obey Jesus' commands. In fact, every facet of a walk with God was modeled for the Mongolians. First the missionary would do something while the believers observed. Then they would assist the church planter, doing the same thing together. Finally the missionary would watch while the believer took over the task on her own. Many of those first believers became house church leaders, and Bayaraa and Magnus modeled how to lead these discipling groups. They met as leaders to share how the churches were doing and to learn from the Word insights to pass on in their groups. Over time we developed a prayer guide to help the fellowships pray for the people groups of the former Soviet empire. Every week each house church would intercede for an unreached group in this booklet complete with maps, pictures, and stories in Mongolian. From the very beginning the disciples were steeped in God's heart for the nations.

Moving anywhere outside Ulaanbaatar was quite an undertaking. We needed housing, supplies, furniture, and a convincing reason to be there. Our strategy for entering Erdenet was business. I pitched a plan to my employer, 'MONAR' Co., Ltd., to move our family to Erdenet to provide business consultation, to develop materials for learning language, and to provide private tuition from English classes. They were excited about the potential profits of an expansion in that direction (the fact that they were an architectural firm seemed inconsequential. They already had honey-making and ger production ventures, in addition to running a boutique and cafe), and eagerly contracted me for another year.

Now that we had a Mongolian company behind us, Louise and I made another trip up to Erdenet to meet with the mayor and explore business and housing possibilities. I returned to secure our housing in January. Maria had a Mongolian friend Zagdaa, whose sister found us an apartment. Although foreigners could not buy apartments, we were able to purchase the right to rent it from the widowed herdsman who had been awarded the apartment when his wife died. He couldn't live in town and keep his sheep alive in the countryside, so he took the local cash equivalent of $1000 we offered and vacated the two-bedroom apartment on the ground floor. The location was perfect—right on the main road and just a few buildings away from our teammates. We were actually going to make it to Erdenet at last.

Baby Church on her first birthday -- already 120 souls. We moved to Erdenet a month later.

Louise is fond of citing that we have moved 30 times in 33 years of marriage. In spite of this statistic, moving our household is an activity we both loathe. Even moving across town in the States is full of stress and altogether too much work. Moving from one city to another in Mongolia is extremely involved, frustrating, and arduous. Here's how our frigid February three-day move from Ulaanbaatar to Erdenet played out:

Day One (February 17th): Inside the apartment, Louise packed our things into boxes. I went out to pick up our passports and train tickets. New visas and police stamps in each passport were required for the move, so I once again needed the services of Aldar and Batjargal, young Christian businessmen "fixers" for foreigners. When I reached their office, I discovered they had slipped up and purchased our passenger tickets on the train to Erdenet for that very evening, but the cargo wagon

carrying our stuff was not going until the following day. We had 14 people planning to go to Erdenet on Friday, and Aldar had bought Thurs-
day tickets. (Rick and Laura Leatherwood and their four children, along
with Helen Richardson, their nanny, were helping us on the move, and
Magnus and Maria, the Swedish half of our church planting team, were
also traveling home with our troop.) I told Aldar the tickets must be
changed to Friday, but he said that was impossible. I insisted he at least
give it a try and trudged home to give Louise the bad news. We started
praying while we kept packing all day and almost finished. We had a
goodbye dinner with missionary friends and went to bed not knowing
whether we would be able to accompany our things to Erdenet the next
evening.

The next morning I went out early to the Russian Cultural Center to collect a Russian Army bunk bed I had bought for the girls for only 15 dollars (the Cold War "peace dividend"?). The Russian guy who'd sold me
the bed wasn't there until the fourth time I went by the office. Meanwhile, the truck I'd ordered never arrived, but my helpers did, so two
of us scrambled out to find a truck while everyone else began carrying
87 items, including large furnishings, down five flights of stairs with 10
narrow turns. These guys took great care not to damage the furniture.
Out at the field where trucks parked hoping for work, I hired a truck
and driver for the equivalent of $21. Back at the apartment building we
loaded everything up (except the still missing bunk bed and a desk my
company had promised) and raced to the train station. Porters wanting
to help for a fee surrounded us. They roughly trundled all our stuff off
the truck and into the Customs shed. These guys made that gorilla in
the '80s Samsonite commercials look gentle. Our furniture was never the
same. The Customs official decided he had better things to do than
weigh each item (rail freight charge was about half a dollar per kilo). He
estimated in our favor—500 kilograms. He told us to come back at five
o'clock to supervise loading it onto the train. So we went by 'MONAR'
Company's office to pick up my desk and then back once more to the
Russian Cultural Center to get the bunk bed. This time we were successful and so back across town we went to the train station to add these
items to our pile. While these were being weighed in, we met Aldar.
He'd done the impossible and changed our tickets that morning. Joy

flooded over me. I was praising God for averting the disaster that sending everything up to Erdenet unaccompanied would have been. We
paid off our truck driver and caught a taxi home. After a short wait, we
gathered up the girls and hailed a cab for the train station. Louise, Laura,
and Helen got the children, all seven of them, on board the train and
into the coupés (a compartment with four bunks that sleeps four—in
principle), while Rick and I kept a sharp eye out for thieves as the porters (for yet another fee) manhandled our stuff 20 meters into the cargo
car. Additional damage was inflicted as I watched. I wondered too late
if I could have paid more for "special handling." I was further dismayed
to see the only other cargo in this boxcar was coal. As they slid the cargo
door closed, the train began to move, and Rick and I had to run like
crazy alongside for several car lengths to reach the last passenger car
and jump into the moving train. Breathless, but onboard, we walked
through a half dozen crowded cars to reach our families. What a harrowing experience. As the kids noisily explored our car, we settled in
for the long overnight trip.

In Mongolia, the trains do a curious thing. They all meet up in Darhan,
the second largest city, in the middle of the night, so passengers can
transfer between the three major routes Siberia, China, and Erdenet. For
three hours the Erdenet train sits next to the other two while vendors
yell out their wares outside the windows. Normally accepted practice is
to try vainly to ignore the hubbub outside and continue sleeping, but I
was worried our belongings would switch trains and head to Irkutsk or
Beijing, so I ran back down the train to guard the cargo car the whole
time they had the door open. I watch them shovel out some coal, but
nothing else left that car while I was on duty. When they locked it up
again I headed sleepily back to my berth.

On the clear and chilly morning (only -10°C / 14°F) of the 19th of February, at eight forty in the morning, we arrived in Erdenet and I quickly
hopped off the train and ran back to guard the cargo car again. But it
had vanished. I panicked and ran back and forth until I found it again
on the other end of the train. The engineer had reversed direction in
Darhan in the middle of the night. That was standard, but I'd never before had occasion to notice. Willing myself to stop hyperventilating and

freezing my lungs, I noticed some believers from the church had lined up a truck and helpers. They all ran down to where I was climbing up into the doors of the train car. We carefully unloaded the cargo while the women and children caught the bus into town. Then the helpers piled onto our stuff in the back of the truck and left for our new apartment. Rick, Magnus, and I caught the last vehicle into town, which is about seven miles from the train station. The reason Erdenet's train station is so far out of town is Communist paranoia. The Soviet Union discovered and exploited the copper deposit in Erdenet, and military policy dictated that danger always loomed in the form of invasion by train. The Soviets therefore laid different gauge rail than China (to slow down the invading armies while they changed the axles) and protected their precious asset in Erdenet by putting the station in the middle of nowhere.

When we finally arrived at our apartment we found most of our things already inside. Other than damaged wood finish and cabinet doors knocked off their hinges, we had only a single causality: a broken coffee mug. We took our friends around town sightseeing and got them settled into the hotel, and later that day unpacked our boxes.

Our new apartment (ground floor to left of door. Iron bars on windows kept out drunks leaving bars closing elsewhere.

We had just barely begun to recover from the adventure of moving our family when we discovered it was going to be growing. A week after our arrival in Erdenet, Louise announced we would be having a baby around the beginning of November.

THIRTEEN

Power Encounter

The Living God was preparing to visit Erdenet, but this was hardly going to pass unchallenged by the "Prince of the Power of the Air." We hadn't thought Satan was much threatened by our family's presence in town. We were wrong.

About two months after we'd moved up from Ulaanbaatar, a man came to our door late one Sunday night and demanded money for our power bill. He looked really disreputable and offered no ID. We told him we'd ask our Mongolian friend about it and sent him away. We thought it just another scam for vodka money. Then he came again the next Sunday night and tried to force his way in while Louise held the door and yelled. He retaliated by opening up our meter box on the landing outside the door and cutting off our power for three days. We found out, while all our food rotted and we ate meals at friends' houses, the power bill for our apartment was a year and six months in arrears. We learned that this man—whose name was Dawaa—had not been paid his salary by the power company. The Erdenet Power Company was close to bankruptcy, and so Dawaa figured he could squeeze the rich foreigners for cash. The confusion over his identity turned this somewhat nasty man into an implacable enemy.

Dawaa, now enraged, was on a roll. He called the Erdenet Housing Authority, the agency that owns and controls all apartments in town, and accused us of purchasing our apartment for dollars from Zagdaa, the Mongolian friend whose name we'd foolishly mentioned to him. Since none of the buildings in Erdenet had yet been privatized since the fall of

Communism, this was a fairly serious allegation, but it wasn't true. A widower with 12 children actually had the "right to rent" for our apartment. The flat had been awarded to him as a bereavement benefit. However, since he had herds that needed shepherding in the countryside, he had no use for a place in the city. Zagdaa, as a go-between, had worked out an arrangement where we leased the "right to rent" from the herdsman. The Housing Authority—without bothering to check Dawaa's facts—sent word to evict us and called the police to check our registration. Two officers came by to get our passports, telling us to appear at the Police Station to pick them up in two days.

When I went to get the passports, the lady in charge of approving "immigrants" into Erdenet screamed at me for not registering with her the day we moved into town. I explained we'd been told it was unnecessary; they would come to us to register us. She then slapped a 20,000 tugrik ($50) fine on me and said she would have us evicted. She immediately added that she would accept English lessons in lieu of the fine. That night Dawaa came and turned on our power. He came in to inspect and counted every power outlet, light, and appliance, pulled out a calculator and came up with a figure for the unpaid power. The meter had been broken, so he used an estimation method. I pointed out that half of the outlets were not functioning, but he didn't care. He then slapped us with a 57,000 tugrik ($120) fine. When we protested that we had only lived here two months and could hardly be responsible for the whole 18 months of payment due, he told us that rich Americans could afford to pay. Overwhelmed, we started to pray.

The next day I had just begun my English lesson inside "City Bank" where I had been teaching the tellers and other bank employees. Somehow our trials came up during the lesson and one of my students, an older woman whom I'd figured to be the cleaning lady, was more interested than the others. She kept asking for more details and names. Finally I asked my translator, Ganaa, why this woman was so interested in my problems. "I think she wants to help you," she replied. I found out to my surprise this woman, who came to our evening class in a housecoat, was the President of the bank. She said she had control over Dawaa's funds and he would cease this attack on her teacher. The next morning, she got my power fine dropped. She talked to the big boss at housing who said we were okay until June when it would be discussed again. But his underling, Sukhbat—the woman who'd ordered our

Melody with my translator Ganaa and her twins.
Erdenet's City Hall in background.

eviction—defied him and turned our case over to the court anyway. She then "went to the countryside" for two months. Meanwhile, Dawaa, thwarted by my student in his fundraising through fining, started calling the police and slandering and accusing us. He claimed we were running a bakery out of our kitchen and had Mongolian slaves baking and selling the bread. (The Mongolian-owned bakery Magnus had started for the church was across town. Our only connection was buying bread there). He then said we were Christian workers who weren't engaged in any business at all, which was obviously false. Luckily, when the police confronted me with these stories, a newly found engineer friend from the copper mine spiritedly and articulately defended me.

I went to see the Vice-Mayor about our apartment troubles, and he said he knew all about them. He lived in the stairwell next to ours. He said not to worry. He would fix everything. I guess he did because, when the old shepherd, our "landlord," came into town to appear at court with Zagdaa, the court decreed in our favor. Orgil, my boss at 'MONAR Company' in Ulaanbaatar called the police lady and smoothed things over. All that would be required for the return of our passports was a small "face-saving" fine, and Orgil picked that up.

We'd seen an unsettling glimpse of the system's underbelly and corruption. Greed and envy are powerful strongholds in Mongolia and throughout the former-Communist world. Years of the Marxist-Leninist "gospel" had convinced the people no one else should have anything they didn't have. Many had advised us a bribe would make everything go away, but we'd maintained our integrity and paid off no one. People had aided us out of friendship, compassion, and response to the vulnerable posture we chose to take. We'd seen God powerfully intervene on our behalf and the devil fail to thrust us out of Erdenet. It was clear once again our Father had put us there and no one could dislodge us without His leave. There is such a peace in knowing that. We never felt a need for secrecy about why we were in Mongolia. We knew God had called us there, and not even the government had the power to evict us until God had accomplished His plans through us.

FOURTEEN

April Showers

Our team, which was just our family and Magnus and Maria Alphonce at this time, had spent the first few months of 1994 crying out to God in prayer to give us some kind of breakthrough. We were concerned that the church would continue to grow as it had been, gathering only teen-aged girls. A huge church of mostly teenage girls was not what we had come to Mongolia for, nor was it what God wanted for the Mongolians. Our training had emphasized that we should seek to reach heads-of-households who would then be able to bring their families and friends into the Kingdom. It was painfully obvious to us that our teenaged disciples didn't fit the model. I wish we had been aware of another New Testament principle our training hadn't covered. Students of church planting movements have noticed that successful church planters "start working with whoever is responding to God" and "seek to join the Father in what He is doing." By these principles we were doing quite a bit better than it appeared to us at the time.

We searched for whatever might be holding back the older Mongolians from the gospel. Everywhere in the country the story was the same—except for the first batch of believers from right after Mongolia opened up, only teens had been embracing God's offer. We knew that there was nothing wrong with the gospel message itself. Could this trend have something to do with the translation?

In new mission fields people tend to reject the message when it's presented in alien cultural forms. We wondered if this wasn't happening for all our Mongolian friends over twenty.

The translator of the Mongolian New Testament had to choose a word for "God." Mongolians had a common word for god, but he rejected it for referring to the Almighty because the Tibetans had appropriated it when they brought Tibetan Buddhism into Mongolia in the early seventeenth century. The translator felt that the Mongolian word, Burkhan, was sullied irreparably by Buddhist use. In a musty, out-of-print dictionary he found a term he felt would work. It was a term no living Mongolian seemed ever to have heard. The translator, satisfied that he had solved any confusion that the name might bring, then used Yertontsiin Ezen, or "Lord of the Universe," exclusively throughout his Mongolian New Testament to refer to God. Through extensive interviews with non-teenaged Mongolians exposed to the gospel through the Jesus Film and other means, we began to realize that many reacted to Yertontsiin Ezen as if it were science fiction. It just didn't sound true or real to them and it made the God of the Bible seem like a foreign import rather than the God of all the earth. Burkhan, on the other hand, was the generic term for deity. It seemed to correspond to the English word "god" in being used for anything from small household idols to the Creator of Heaven and Earth. Surely this term was as redeemable for God terminology as our English word. Webster's New Collegiate Dictionary finds the origin of the word "god" from a Germanic word "gad," pronounced as "gohdt." The pagan ancient Germanic tribes got the word from Vedic Hindu roots. Since their missionaries had redeemed a local pagan term that we are all still using, we could see no problem in repeating the pattern in Mongolia so Mongolians could hear and understand God. Besides, in his excellent book Eternity in Their Hearts, Don Richardson pointed out that whenever someone speaks of the Uncreated Creator they are speaking of Him, since there can be only One.

Our team concluded that we had to change the term for God if we were going to see the broader response for which everyone was praying. For several months we had been moving the church family to use a more literal translation of the New Testament. An old Mongolian dialect version had recently been released at the end of a circuitous process. London Missionary Society missionaries among the Mongolian Buryat tribe across the Russian border in 1846 had translated the entire Bible, and the New Testament had been revised (as "Gunzel's Revision") and re-printed in the 1950's by Scandinavian Alliance missionaries. In 1994 the Witness Lee sect reprinted their work in modern Mongolian Cyrillic. (The sect didn't change the Word itself—just added advertisements for their services—which we happily tore out.) The believers found this red hardback Bible—with its old-fashioned dialect—tougher to read but loved how God's words spoke to their hearts. Not only was the transla-tion more accurate; the "Red Bible" employed the Mongolian term: Bur-khan. It allowed us gradually to shift to a more accurate terminology for other concepts: prayer, worship, sin, Satan, baptism, etc., rather than to use words from the other translation that never communicated Biblical ideas correctly.

Early in April, we realized that we were probably the only team in the nation that could get away with experimenting with God's name. We were too far in the sticks to attract the kind of backlash from other work-ers and churches that this move was sure to generate. We knew it would be controversial, but we counted on the two overnight train trips to act as a buffer for the rebukes this move would certainly trigger. We met with the leaders of the church in Erdenet and explained our thinking to them. They had been using both terms for a while within the Erdenet church but bravely agreed to start using Burkhan for all public preach-ing.

God was speaking to us in this, and we were confident we were praying according to God's will when we asked Him to help us reach other age groups and males. We just didn't know how to begin. We had relation-ships with professionals and families, but when these people met the church members, they pulled back from commitment. It just came across as a large and exciting "Girl's Club," and it turned others off before they were around enough to experience the life and joy there. We were acutely aware we needed God to do something to bump us out of the rut we'd inadvertently fallen into.

Finally, along with the spring thaw and new life we saw around us on the hills around Erdenet, we saw God's answer to our pleas. What began in April 1994 we would normally call "revival," but in a church little

over a year old, that term seems wrong. I started calling the intense outpouring we were experiencing "vival" — revival for the first time. Anyway, call it a burst of insight and growth or whatever, things suddenly
got extremely exciting.

It started with a video of the Church in South Korea praying. We lugged
our small combination TV/video player, the only one in the church, over
to Magnus and Maria's apartment to play the tape for the believers. We
assigned time slots and watched it in shifts. The sight of their Korean
brethren praying so fervently electrified each group of girls. They had
never seen anything like it. The results almost scared us. A deep spirit
of repentance came over all who watched, and low, racking sobs filled
the room. These young Mongolians spontaneously fell on their faces before God and wept. Then they began to pray as they'd never prayed
before. The same thing happened with each group. We were stunned.
God was at work here. It brought home that our participation is a privilege and a reward for obedience, not a prerequisite for the moving of
the Lord.

But this was just the warm-up for what was to come. What we had
prayed for had begun. The families of many of our young girls were
about to come to Jesus. Here's how.

Missionaries from Sweden had planted a cell group church in Abakan,
Siberia — a city just over the Russian border north and west of us. It had
grown to more than 70 cells and a Bible school. A team of second year
Russian Bible students, each a cell leader, felt led to do their outreach
helping Swedish missionaries in Mongolia. The Swedish missionary
running the Abakan church and school had pastored a church in the
same small Swedish village of Edsbyn, where Magnus and Maria had
lived and worked. He asked Magnus if this short-term team could come
and work under our direction. One of our prayers had been for the
planting of a church among Erdenet's Russian population. We knew it
would limit our effectiveness to focus on more than one ethnic group,
so we had asked God to send someone for the Russians. So it was an
easy call to make, and we faxed our acceptance of the Bible School outreach team.

Six women from the former Soviet Union arrived in April at the Erdenet train station. The most remarkable thing to us was how they all smiled. They were the first smiling Russians we, or any of the Mongolians, had ever seen. They shared in our house church gatherings and with the church's leadership. They prayed and people were filled with the Holy Spirit, freed from demonic oppression, healed, and saved.

The leaders of our church were affected in two big ways. They became really enthused about the small group church principles they'd been taught, because in the Russians' cell church growth they could see and experience an example of success that made sense to them. The other surprise was the way the Russian team brought a new experience of the Spirit. Right away, our provisional elders or "elders-to-be" as we called them; Bayaraa, Odgerel and Zorigoo, began speaking in tongues. For Bayaraa and Odgerel it was more of a re-ignition since they had experienced this gift the past summer but had not really continued in it. Now they were all extremely excited and eager to see this Holy Spirit baptism spread to the deacons and the rest of the believers. And as the team continued to meet and pray for believers, the Holy Spirit was poured out in a new way, and many, who had experienced only a trickle of His gifts before, started speaking in tongues and prophesying for the first time.

Our team was puzzled about this. We had prayed on many occasions that the Mongolian believers would speak in tongues, but nothing much had happened. Then, as soon as the Russian girls prayed, everybody started praising God in other tongues. Magnus and I took one of the house church leaders aside and asked her what the difference was between our prayers and theirs. She replied that until the Russians came, the Mongolian believers had no idea what tongues were, or what we had been talking about when we mentioned this gift. When we protested that we had prayed over her in tongues on several occasions, she looked surprised. "Oh," she exclaimed, "I thought you were just speaking fast in English or Swedish." Then it dawned on us. The Russians had modeled tongues for the Mongolians as we had, but their modeling had been received. All our believers spoke some Russian because it was required in school. When the Russian girls switched from praying in Russian to tongues, everyone heard the difference and understood at last what we had been teaching. That was all it took for them to let go and allow God's gift to flow through their mouths.

Without speaking any Mongolian, the Russian team was somewhat limited in their opportunities for effective ministry. Healing prayer for the sick seemed to be strong areas for them, so we sent them into the ger suburbs with a translator to look for sick people. Their first stop was the ger of Tuvshin's grandmother, who we knew was handicapped. Tuvshin and his wife, Zagdaa, had been Magnus and Maria's best friends in Erdenet for over a year. His grandparents were divorced, both remarried and living in different suburbs of Erdenet. His grandfather had recently believed and been attending our New Believers' class. The Russians started with his grandmother and her new husband. She was lame in one leg (it dragged while she crutched around), and he was almost completely deaf. Both of them were healed when the Russians prayed. She threw down her crutch and did a Mongolian dance with him. He no longer needed his hearing aid. The two overjoyed old folks then begged the team to go to another ger and pray for a grandson who was mute. The team thought it was a young child, so they were surprised to meet a young man of 20 who had lost the power of speech years before. When they prayed, the young man started speaking in tongues. An unbeliever in the crowd that had gathered said the Mongolian equivalent of: "Heck, he can't even speak Mongolian." The young man broke off his ecstatic praise and retorted, "Of course I can speak Mongolian!"

With each miracle the crowd grew larger. The Mongolian translator kept responding to questions from the multitude about who was doing these healings. For the first time they heard that Burkhan had come and was healing them. The Good News was making sense. Finally people were both hearing Mongolian terms that carried the Bible's meanings and seeing God's powerful seal of approval on His Word.

In fact, all I will talk about is how Christ let me speak and work, so that the Gentiles would obey him. Indeed, I will tell how Christ worked miracles and wonders by the power of the Holy Spirit. . . . But I have always tried to preach where people have never heard about Christ. . . . like a builder who doesn't build on anyone else's foundation.   Romans 15:18-20 (CEV)

In other dwellings, a girl with poor vision started seeing better and two children (one 11 years old) who had never walked took their first steps. A person who had scores of problems was delivered from demons while the Russians prayed. Tuvshin's grandfather heard reports about these miracles in his New Believers' class that evening and he called out that among those healed were his grandson and ex-wife. God had decided to get this family's attention.

One morning I took the Russian team on a tour of Erdenet. I saw a side of Mongolian men I'd never seen before. They really act like wolves toward young, pretty Russian girls; one reason for Russian frowns, I suspect. We ended up at the hilltop Russian-Mongolian Friendship monument overlooking the entire city from the east where two huge, angular hands

Erdenet's Friendship Monument

offer up a crown to Jesus, the King of Kings. Well . . . not exactly. The object in the hands was a gear and meant to symbolize industry and mining, but I believe God designed it, and the Soviets never realized it would become the symbol for the Church of Erdenet.

From this commanding vantage point, the Russians and I interceded in prayer for Erdenet and waged war against the strongholds of Satan in the city. God led me to pray for a house church to begin in District Two within two months. I explained to the Russians that this district and District One were the only two areas that had completely resisted the planting of any fellowships. They really went to work in prayer over each of these districts, each arrayed almost directly under our gaze.

Warfare waged over Erdenet

After our tour and spiritual warfare, the Russians came to our apartment to design a flyer on our computer. They wanted to announce an evangelistic meeting for Erdenet's Russian community, about 2500 people. They had planned dramas, songs, and sharing. They were also going to pray for the sick. We had a lot of fun designing the flyer in two languages and posting it all over the Russian district of Erdenet. The girls took some to the Russian Consulate and ended up preaching to the workers there.

When the big night came, it more than fulfilled our expectations. The rented hall was packed with Russians of all ages and young Mongolian believers. Mongolians and Russians, acting together, performed skits that presented the gospel. We were stunned to see these Russian people drinking in the Good News presented by Mongolians. By all strategic thinking this shouldn't have worked at all. The Mongolians had been the Russians' "younger brothers" for seven decades, and the two peoples didn't even speak with each other if they could avoid it. Also, the fact that the Mongolians had access to the gospel for only three years (in Erdenet only one), while Russia became a "Christian nation" in the Ninth Century, made this event even more astounding. God was doing an amazing thing before our eyes. The crowd applauded thunderously as "Jesus" rose from the dead in a skit; followed by impassioned preaching in Russian and an invitation. Over 40 Russians responded, wanting to make Jesus the Lord of their lives. Russian and Mongolian evangelists prayed with them and told them to stick around afterwards. Then the sick came forward. Some came forward for sick relatives who couldn't come themselves. They gave scarves to be prayed over and then taken home and laid on the sick relatives. It may sound strange, but it is Biblical (Acts 19:12) and it worked. People being healed began to testify. It was in Russian, so I only know the ones translated for me. One albino blind boy had his sight partially restored and another boy had his near-blind eyes opened. An older woman with spinal troubles was bending down and touching her toes for the first time in years. There were others: stomach, head pain, etc. but I missed out on the details. What I couldn't miss was how God was moving on the Russians of Erdenet. Those saved demanded another meeting the next night, which was right when the team would be leaving Erdenet. They had to bring their luggage and go straight to their train from the hall.

When the time came the new Russian believers brought friends who'd missed the first meeting. They were all baptized in the Holy Spirit and spoke in tongues. The Russian team managed to get three Russian apartments volunteered for hosting house churches. One of these new groups was in District Two and many of the newly saved Mongolians also turned out to be from this district. Talk about quickly answered prayer! Time ran out for the team of Russians. Their car arrived to take them to their train. On their way out the door, one of the new Russian believers called out, "Who will pastor us?" The leader of the team had pointed to Magnus, and Magnus pointed to me. After over a year of studying Mongolian, I found myself in the difficult position of leading a church where I didn't share a language in common with the congregation. Then the Russian team hopped into the car and raced to catch the Irkutsk train, making it just in time. On the ride to the station, Magnus asked them what we should do next, and they said, "We don't know. God will show you." So the new baby Russian church joined the Mongolian church at our celebration service (where the house churches gather for corporate worship) on May First. We found this highly ironic, since May Day was the big Soviet Communist holiday. I just know the Father enjoyed this joke. We were overwhelmed but grateful. Problems like unexpected church births are a joy to have.

Short, but warm, summers made river baptisms possible.

FIFTEEN

Downpour

We were in the middle of an outpouring. So much began to happen that I can't narrate all God was doing in Erdenet. Let me just open my journal at some spots to give you a picture:

Brian's Log; Sunday, May 1st, 1994

Yesterday the entire leadership of the church fasted and met for a day of prayer and teaching. All 24 were filled with the Holy Spirit, and all except two spoke in tongues, most of them for the first time. Other gifts experienced were prophecy, interpretation of tongues, and word of knowledge. Several leaders had visions, and two were set free from demons. Demonic oppression is widespread here. We are barely beginning to treat a huge spiritual wound.

Today is May Day. A few years back, everyone in Erdenet would celebrate the glory of eternal Communism on this holiday. Not so this year. This year the Living God led a celebration of His eternal Kingdom. During the celebration gathering Zorigoo taught on the Holy Spirit's power and around 30 responded to the message of salvation. Many were healed, including a nearly blind girl who started to see clearly. Kidney disease and headaches also had to flee at the name of Jesus. All 15 of the newly water baptized were baptized in the Spirit as we prayed for them on the stage. Many of them spoke in tongues and had visions and one prophesied. Some people have also been healed when church members have visited them in their homes. God's Spirit obviously didn't leave on the train with the Russian team.

Sunday, May 8th, 1994

Today in house church the teaching was on God's Holy Spirit. Then during the prayer time, He showed up. The first group all fell to the ground under His power. I taught a little about the various workings of God and warned against "putting Him in a box." Then we had a second group of five get prayer. I was told the boy I was praying over was partially blind. I asked him what he wanted from God and he replied "My sight." So that's what I prayed. I really sensed the Lord's love for this boy, and I just confessed to God without Him showing up nothing could happen. After praying, I asked the boy about his sight and he looked about, grinned, and declared it healed. The church was very encouraged, as everyone knew this boy and his problem.

In the third group to receive prayer there was a young woman in a yellow jacket. I noticed nothing was happening as we prayed for her. I asked God why and I received "slavery" in reply. As I pondered this, it came to me she was wearing a necklace charm from an idol. I looked at her neck and could see nothing. I asked Ganaa, who speaks English, to ask if anyone had such a thing on their neck. I didn't want to embarrass this girl, in case I proved to have heard wrong. As soon as the announcement was made, this girl, who'd already sat down, stood up and pulled out her necklace. It was a small leather pouch containing fetishes prescribed by the lamas. The church cheered. They were applauding God for knowing such secret things. We decided to pray for her again and had her stomp on the fetish while we prayed for complete freedom. After the group finished praying, several leaders assisted her in burning the necklace.

Wednesday, May 17th, 1994

Today I will teach the first lesson to the leaders of the first Russian home group. On Sunday we met with the Russian believers to divide them into house churches. Enough attended our meeting for two small gatherings, but they preferred to meet as one at first and divide as necessary. There is a nervousness left over from Soviet days that has left them apprehensive about small groups and being labeled a "sect." While there were about 50 who claimed interest in being part of the church, only 14 attended the organizational meeting. So today I will meet with four helpers (future leaders) and teach (through Ganaa, a Mongolian-English-Russian translator) a simple lesson on obedience to Jesus' seven basic commands. We needed to baptize the Russian believers quickly because it has been our practice to serve the Lord's Supper to baptized believers only. In the beginning, lacking Russian worship songs, it is best to center our worship service on Communion. It is so easy to feel overwhelmed at this new and unexpected responsibility, but God is giving me strength. Magnus is so busy with the Mongolian church and preparing to leave for Sweden for the whole summer that the Russians are pretty much all mine at this point. Over the summer I will be overseeing and assisting both churches, Russian and Mongolian. I praise God He has raised up wonderful godly elders-to-be for the Mongolian church. In Mongolian we use a really common word for these leaders, achlach, which just means "older brothers" with connotations of leadership—a close match to what Paul called his church leaders—and without 17 centuries of ecclesiastical baggage piled on top.

Our last baptism ceremony was memorable. Our middle daughter Molly Anne was baptized. She told Louise one morning she wanted to get saved and follow Jesus. Louise asked her what that meant and she said: "I'll praise God and do what He says!" Amen! Molly is the first Westerner baptized into the Mongolian Church. In Erdenet, we continue to baptize in bathtubs. It's not easy—the bathrooms are miniscule—but what can we do? This isn't the first time we've had "sheep" in our bathtub! The authorities won't even consider our requests to rent the municipal pool, and only Russians are allowed to use the spa and plunge pool at the mine. So, we gather all those desiring baptism into an apartment, along with their house groups and leaders. We worship in the living room while first women, then men, line up in the hall. An elder-to-be and the house church leader whose member is receiving baptism stand next to the tub in the tiny bathroom. The person sits down in the full bathtub and is first laid back down into the water by one leader, then the other pushes the baptizee's knees under water—which acts as a spring lever—causing the person's upper body to rise up out of the water. Then they get out and change clothes in the bedroom while the next in line enters the Family of God. The tub is drained and refilled after every third or fourth person. All the while, the church worships in the living room. It is not ideal, but it works. Bayaraa and I baptized Molly. That same day, 15 Mongolians were baptized, including five men and a married couple whose little boy was healed last month. For the first time, many of those baptized were over 20 years old. One teacher was around 45. God is answering our prayers for older people to come to faith.

All told, we have now baptized 149. Eleven of them have moved away from Erdenet. Thirty-five are still here, but we never see them. We take this seriously but don't get distraught over it. We have to go on although we constantly evaluate the way we accept people for baptism. To address this we have started a New Believer's Course. For 4 evenings we cover the bare basics of God, Jesus, the Holy Spirit, and the Christian life. Interested people attend these evenings, in any order, before they are invited to give their lives to Christ. Rather than delay baptism or treat it as a graduation exercise, we are delaying conversion until the people have a clear idea of what they are joining. The feedback we received from our "backsliders" was they were merely interested, were baptized, and stopped coming when they learned enough to realize there was a significant cost to following Christ. We hope more communication up front will address this problem. Their ignorance of Christianity and Christ is staggering, and we have to remind ourselves there is no Christian background here at all.

Over 200 came to the last "celebration service" where all the house churches meet for corporate worship, dramas, prayer, and sharing of the Word. The Sunday school has around 150 kids, and the youth meeting around 60 people, many of whom are baptized. Of the baptized believers, almost exactly one-fourth are male and around one-third over 22 years of age. Almost all of these guys and older folks are new since the Holy Spirit was poured out in April.

In response to requests from other Mongolian churches desiring to move away from the standard "big Sunday meeting" format, and into house churches, we are planning a seminar in Ulaanbaatar. Our three elders-to-be will teach and share experiences, and we have invited leaders from six provinces where there are churches or "groups" that are interested.

Saturday, June 18th, 1994

The lapse of time since the last entry gives some idea of how busy things have been here lately. The day before yesterday Louise and I celebrated our 10th wedding anniversary by going out on a date to the restaurant at Erdenet's Selenge Hotel. The only item on the menu actually in stock was mutton stew. We laughed and tried to remember how we'd celebrated each of our previous anniversaries.

Yesterday, Magnus and Maria left for Sweden on the train. We were sad to see them go. We also waved good-bye to one of my Russian church helpers, Ludmilla, who is visiting family for the summer. We had five visitors up from Ulaanbaatar on this crazy day, too; four *Mongolian Enterprises International* coworkers and a *Navigators* guy. Monday is my last English class for the summer and the beginning of all the leadership meetings I will be helping with in the Mongolian church. The Russian church held their first baptism last Sunday, and Anna, Albert, Lydia, Eugenia, Tamara, Luda, and Ludmilla entered the family. These are, to our knowledge, the first Russian believers ever baptized in Mongolia. Our Russian church is small but vital. Erdenet's Russians typically summer in Mother Russia, so in the fall many more will attend. We are concentrating on getting the essentials of obedience to Christ into these 10 sheep so when more come we will have a prepared core.

The Mongolian church is facing a busy summer. Our summer program in July will be our first alone. Last year we shared a program with a church from Ulaanbaatar. We also have baptisms, celebrations, World Prayer Day (for which we've rented the outdoor stadium), all-church prayer meetings, short-term teams from the States, and many leadership trainings and meetings planned.

Looking back on this unexpected and all-important outpouring of grace, we can see so many small, almost unnoticed, things that God carefully orchestrated to prepare the ground for the waterfall of wonders that was on its way. It really wasn't as sudden as it seemed at the time to those of us caught up in the middle of it. Our shift to a more indigenous Biblical terminology had really occurred in many smaller steps: early on, Bayaraa had translated Genesis from an Inner Mongolian source that used *Burkhan* (and though we changed it to the then more acceptable Yurtuntseen Etzin, we put a disclaimer on page one explaining both terms); we adopted the 'Red Bible' as soon it was available; talked, prayed, discussed, met, evaluated and made adjustments in what we were doing and teaching; and finally we decided to "change God's name." The Father was hard at work for many months so the Mongolians would respond to the healings, gifts, and deliverance He caused to burst forth with the April clouds.

SIXTEEN

Alone at the Helm

When summer finally arrived, our team paused from the frantic activity into which "Miracle April" had plunged us. On June 17th, 1994, Magnus and Maria left Erdenet to take their first break home. When almost the entire church turned out on the railway platform to see our team's leaders off for their extended time in Sweden, we were, without realizing it, setting a pattern that would be followed whenever a missionary left Erdenet. We had a worship service right next to the train as all of the other travelers and their families and friends looked on with jaws agape. No one in Mongolia had ever seen anything like this large crowd of crying and smiling Mongolians, singing about God and hugging a blond foreign couple, all accompanied by guitar. It was quite a scene. With Magnus and Maria gone, Louise and I were now alone and in charge until summer's end.

Reality quickly set in. Sitting in our kitchen that evening, Louise and I prayed for my mother who was celebrating her retirement that day on the other side of the world. We felt incredibly far away, isolated and vulnerable. We were eagerly counting the days to my mom and stepdad's visit in August. For the next three months we would be the only church planters for hundreds of kilometers. We had a quickly growing Mongolian church movement on our hands and were barely conversational in the language, and a Russian group I could only lead through a Mongolian translator who spoke all three languages. As I met with the various leaders for training and discipleship, I realized how much I'd leaned on Magnus' linguistic proficiency in the past. With no other English speakers around us, our language skills quickly improved. We prepared house church group lessons, met with the elders-to-be, led the house church leaders meetings, and dealt with problems as they came up.

The Russian congregation held its first baptism service at a sauna for miners up at the edge of the second largest open pit mine in all of Asia. There was a small plunge pool outside the hot room. Alex, the only man being baptized, arranged for the facility and had thoughtfully filled the pool with hot water. I have nothing against comfort, and I'm rarely accused of being traditional, but I felt compelled to insist he drain and refill it with more tepid water. It just wouldn't seem like baptism otherwise. While he was fixing the pool, the ladies were changing. When they came out I was shocked. They were in their underwear. Not one had brought any bathing suit or clothes in which they could get wet. I told them they had to cover up. They seemed puzzled by my prudery, but compliantly trooped back to the dressing room. When they emerged again, Alex, Ganaa, and I were stunned to see an apparition—six Roman matrons in full toga. They'd found bed sheets. The baptism immediately took on what I imagined to be a decidedly New Testament flavor.

On the way to the mine I had tried to memorize the Russian words I would say as I baptized each believer. "Ya chrescho vas vo emeia, Oatsa, ee Seena, ee Swetova Duka." For some reason I developed a mental block and was unable to repeat the whole thing without "cheating" and checking the scrap of paper I'd jotted it down upon. As I baptized the first toga-clad lady, I blanked and looked around for my "crib notes" just as a wavelet washed them right off the edge of the pool. Everyone had a good laugh and helped by whispering the next words whenever I got stuck. It really was a significant time for the Russian church and for me. It was my first missionary baptism, and my first multiple baptism.

Yesuseen Choolgan (Jesus' Gathering or Assembly), the name the church in Erdenet settled on, was having its first "Summer Program" in 1994, and it turned out to be both wildly successful and terribly trying. The year before, a group of our people had joined an Ulaanbaatar church for their retreat and enjoyed it enough to plan one for us. Our leadership contracted a former Russian youth camp about 60 kilometers (40 miles) northeast of Erdenet in the spacious and green Selenge River valley. The leadership of our church had been busy planning a week of teaching, games, recreation, fellowship and fun. We didn't need to worry about food provisions or preparation since that was part of what we were paying the camp to provide. We were assured the dining hall and kitchen was staffed and ready for our group of 80. When the hired trucks dropped us off we were stunned by the natural beauty of the landscape.

Unfortunately, we weren't the only ones who found the setting irresistible. As soon our truck stopped moving, clouds of bloodthirsty mosquitoes filled the air around us. The camp itself was somewhat run-down yet beguilingly whimsical in its construction. There were actual planes and tanks for the children to play on and, even though decay had begun to set in, facilities which were nicer than most. The building where our family stayed was built to look like a ship on land. We had a private room with windows, unlike the rest of our group who made do with cabins. We kept them all closed tight, choosing the considerable heat over the involuntary blood donations to the local insects. Privately we thought the food was terrible, but we put a good face on things and tried to clean our plates. The kitchen had apparently hit the mother lode of a sale on tripe. The main course at every meal was cow stomach. The church folks kept encouraging us to take advantage of the special meals the camp staff were always offering to us. Like good missionaries, though, we insisted on being treated like everyone else. Our girls chose to fast for the week, eating mostly yogurt and bread. The yogurt was served daily as a snack at two o'clock in the afternoon. Our leadership was upset with this camp custom but apparently unable to get the staff to change the time. The problem was Mongolians consider yogurt to be the equivalent of a powerful sleeping pill. They were convinced the camp was trying to ruin the afternoon teaching sessions by putting our group to sleep. It really did seem to have that effect on Mongolians. My family, however, relished the daily yogurt breaks.

So what was so wonderful about this week at "Camp Torture?" Our church family. We grew so close to our Mongolian brothers and sisters. I taught every day, but the best lesson was one Louise and I did together. The older folks and parents asked us to do a Biblical Question and Answer period with them. We ended up talking for three hours, and we all had a marvelous time. It was so satisfying to answer questions from God's Word and have 15 people simultaneously gasp "Aimar goy yuum bay!" (How frighteningly good it is!) as they understood an eternal truth for the first time. This was what I always knew mission was really about. We also had glorious times of worship and some fun new dramas from the drama team. For recreation we had six tournaments: chess, soccer, volleyball, basketball, drama, and balloon tossing. My team won in soccer and basketball. Normally, I have an aversion to sports, but my lofty six feet four inches (183cm) in a nation of vertically-challenged people quickly made basketball my favorite game. Louise's drama team won that competition. Melody won an uncontested toad collecting award.

When the week was over, we were all tired, hungry, and happy. We would miss the close fellowship and closeness of living together as a church, but we were ready to return to the relative comfort of Erdenet. One of our trucks ran out of gas on the way home, and half of the church was stuck in the middle of nowhere until two a.m., when they finally arrived home on foot.

Several days after Family Camp, I overheard the leaders talking about lousy food. I asked what food they were referring to. "The camp's, of course," they responded. It turns out everyone agreed the food was the worst they had ever eaten in their lives, and they couldn't understand why we insisted on eating it when something better was being offered. We all had a great laugh about this mix-up.

In the beginning, the believers in Erdenet had only met in small groups in living rooms. As the numbers of these groups increased, it became both attractive and feasible to gather them together periodically is a larger congregational meeting we termed a "Celebration" but usually just called "Big Meeting." We would rent a hall once a month on a Sunday and announce to the house groups where and when the Celebration would be. We were forced to change the venue fairly often as the government owned all of the buildings and would hound us out of whichever we were using once they realized they were renting to Christians. It was a benign form of persecution, hardly deserving the name when compared to what followers of Christ endure in many countries. Besides, it didn't affect us very much because "church" was happening in apartments all over the city, and the big meeting was not essential. On a number of occasions our "landlord" evicted us as we were setting up for the Celebration service, and we merely posted a leader out front to let everyone know the meeting was cancelled. The life and ministry of the Body of Christ went on with hardly a ripple.

As time went on, the elders-to-be came to Magnus and me and asked for more frequent big meetings. They reasoned that everyone enjoyed getting together for corporate worship, dramas, and testimonies, and they found seeing the growing numbers of believers very encouraging. They also pointed out that the people were giving generously, in accordance with the command of Jesus they'd been taught, and there was enough money coming in to rent a hall more often. We gave our consent and the Celebration was increased to every other Sunday. This worked very well and the excitement level rose proportionately. Eventually, there were enough funds coming in to rent a place every Sunday, and we could tell everyone liked the large gathering even though it took far more energy and resources to pull off than a house group. The house churches continued in the weekdays, and the big meeting became our regular Sunday event.

After a couple months, however, we noticed something was wrong. We were meeting with the house group leaders in the regular training meeting and they were taking turns sharing statistics on their groups to give us all an idea how things were going. A puzzling and disturbing trend began to emerge as we looked at the data. The house churches had stopped growing, and worse still, had stopped multiplying. They weren't shrinking, but all had basically hit a plateau. The big Celebration meeting continued to grow every Sunday, though. The more we questioned the leaders, the more it became clear—believers older in faith continued in the small house groups, but the new people were choosing the Celebration as their connection with the church. No matter how much we consistently stressed participation in the house groups as the only way to be a real part of the Body, we were giving out a stronger, contradictory non-verbal message every Sunday morning. Since 90 percent of our time and energy and money went into just three to four hours on Sunday mornings, the new believers assumed this was our main event, despite our protestations to the contrary. It was certainly easier to come and be a part of an audience than to enter a home and be discipled by those who knew you well as you learned to be an active participant—the "king and priest" of Revelations 1:6.

The Mongolian leaders and I were horrified. As we prayed about what to do, we kept circling around a solution none of us wanted but that eventually proved to be the only way to get our church back on God's track. We came to the painful decision to cancel the Sunday Celebrations.

The next Sunday morning, after the testimony, worship, dramas, and sharing of God's Word, we had all the house church leaders stand around the outside of the movie theatre auditorium we were renting. We announced this was our last big gathering for the foreseeable future, and anyone who considered themselves a part of the Body would need to be involved in a house church, as this was the only expression available from now on. The leaders were arranged by district, and we pointed them out geographically. We asked everyone to walk over to the leader whose group was closest to their home. Almost everyone did. Then the leaders took down their names and told them where and when the next gathering was taking place. And that was it.

The fruit of this drastic action was dramatic. Within a couple weeks all of the groups needed to multiply as they were all too big. The new believers were being taught to obey Jesus at last, and new life flushed through the arteries of the Body. After a couple of months we resumed Celebration meeting just once a month—and it was good.

I wish I could tell you we'd learned our lessons, and everything went well from this point onward. But I can't. We eventually slid from monthly, to bi-monthly Celebrations. These gatherings were so popular and fun we once again tried to have them every Sunday—and the same story played out again with similar results. The house churches were just not sustainable at the center of the church's life when the big meetings were weekly. We never did find a solution that pleased everyone on this issue. It seemed we were always experimenting with Celebration frequency—once a month, twice a month, or every week?

Years later at a house church seminar in England I found my answer to this dilemma. A pastor asked the presenter, Tony Dale, how often the big meetings should be. My attention was riveted. This was our big burning question. The answer completely surprised me. It was one that never had even crossed our minds. Tony answered with a question: "When did the New Testament house churches gather for a larger city-wide or regional gathering?" Tony had to provide the answer because no one else in the crowded room of church planters and leaders could come up with an answer. "When they had a reason to gather the house church together, like when the Apostle Paul would visit." And just like that I had the answer we had sought for so long in Erdenet and since. Whenever there was a real reason (visiting apostle, prophet, teacher, worship group, testimonies about miracles, etc.) we could gather all the churches in a large Celebration. The only excuse to come together which wasn't valid or Biblical was the one we'd always prioritized —the calendar!

SEVENTEEN

Battle with the God of Hell

The West is infatuated with national religion of Mongolia: Tibetan Buddhism. The Dalai Lama is the darling of western media and winner of the Nobel Peace Prize. Benefit concerts and documentary films are honoring the people of Tibet, the pillars of this religion. Major motion pictures promote Tibetan Buddhism, and stars like Richard Gere and Steven Seagal have become its apostles in America. This ancient religion has become the trendy pop-faith of the hour.

There is an element of trend to the Tibetan Buddhist resurgence in Mongolia, too, but there is more to it than that. Seventy years of the twin religions of Scientific Atheism and Soviet Communism were not able to break the hold of the lamas on the soul of Mongolia. Once again, just as before the 1921 Revolution, parents were giving young sons to monasteries to raise as monks, setting up idol shelves in their homes, and visiting temples to prostrate themselves repeatedly before gods of metal and wood. When the urn containing Buddha's ashes was brought to Ulaanbaatar from Bihar, India for a viewing, crowds stood for hours just for a glimpse as they filed by.

I have found a discrepancy between the Tibetan Buddhism peddled in the West as a peaceful and transcendent religion of meditation, and the Buddhism practiced in temples in Nepal, Tibet, and Mongolia. Tibetan Buddhism is one of the world's most openly demonic religions—at least in its homelands. It puts on more innocent clothes when it goes abroad. In Ulaanbaatar there is a sprawling temple complex located on a low hill that survived the Communist Era as a museum, but is again the Tibetan

Buddhist capital of Mongolia. When visiting Gandan Monastery, a visit inside the temples gives one quite a different picture than Richard Gere's interpretation. The room is filled with idols—Buddha seems to be a minor player. Pride of place goes to Yama, the god of death and hell. Images of Yama differ, but certain themes prevail. He is depicted with fangs and a terrifying expression of fierce leering malevolence. He wears a necklace of severed human heads, a cloak of flayed skin, and is often shown consuming a skull-cup of blood. There is often a sexually graphic element in his depictions whether Yama is alone and visibly aroused by lust, or engaged in graphic coupling with his consort Chamundi—a naked she-demon. One element that's always present is the bodies of men, women and animals, even Buddhist lamas, being crushed under the god's feet. Yama is clearly the "star" of Tibetan Buddhist worship, and torture and terror are the main events.

The naive pop version of Tibetan Buddhism in the West keeps a steady stream of "World Travelers" coming to visit the Asian "ends of the earth." The typical "World Traveler" is twenty-something, apparently appreciative of all cultures (except their own), European or American, environmentally and politically correct, and dressed either in retro-hippie or trekking chic. These folks would regularly end up in Erdenet, since it was at the end of the rail line, thinking they had finally reached "the back of beyond." The goal is to go someplace not yet polluted by the people from back home. Erdenet fit the bill nicely until they met an American family of five out doing their shopping. They always resented their illusions being broken this way. However, their illusions about the beauty of Mongolian Buddhism were made of tougher stuff. They were able to rationalize or ignore the ugliness they saw in the temples and continue to follow their path to Nirvana.

Since, in August of '94, Magnus and Maria had returned refreshed from Sweden, our family could take its first trip out of Mongolia in 18 months. We had gone by train to Beijing to meet my parents. Carol and Bud Hadford, my mom and step-dad, had followed the siren song of grandchildren and had been lured into returning with us for a visit to Erdenet. After a year and a half in Mongolia, we were more than ready for change of scenery—anywhere with fresh vegetables and greens. Everyone's favorite experience was the hotel's breakfast buffet. But since we couldn't eat all the time, we took in the major tourist sites, too, including the Great Wall. On a tour bus I ended up sitting next to a young French "World Traveler" who began to share with me his trip through "this utterly fantastic place—Mongolia." Everything about Mongolia was perfect and flawless. He'd been there for a whole three days and would have loved to stay longer. Curious as to what he'd seen, I asked him about a few of the places I enjoyed taking visitors.

"Have you been to Mongolia?" he asked incredulously.

"Well, actually, we live there." I noticed a guarded expression replace the surprise in his face. "In Erdenet," I added.

"What do you do there?"

"Well, I teach English, develop small business seminars, and I work with a church." I had suspected he wouldn't like this last part, and I wasn't disappointed. You'd have thought I'd claimed to club baby harp seals for a living. He launched into a loud diatribe against missionaries, drawing the attention of most of our fellow passengers.

"How can you go in there and destroy that beautiful culture? I can't believe how arrogant you people are! Why do you think you have the right to go and tell them about your religion? They already have a beautiful religion of their own."

When he paused for breath, I was ready. "So, you were in Mongolia for three days? Did you happen to go into any of the temples?"

"Yes, of course . . . beautiful religion . . . best on earth . . . gorgeous art and architecture."

I pressed on, "Did you notice the larger-than-life idols in there?"

"Yes, so what?" his guard went up even higher.

"Then you must've seen Yama right up there, front and center?"

"Yeah?" he admitted, beginning to see the trap but unable to avoid it, "but they are perfectly happy and at peace with their own gods and beautiful religion."

I went on to describe the Tibetan god of Hell in graphic detail, taking care to get his agreement to my depiction at every step. Then I asked him: "Do you think the Mongolians love this god who stomps on them and devours them in every depiction? Or are they just terrified of him? I came to Mongolia to bring Good News, not to destroy culture. I tell Mongolians about a God who loved them so much he allowed himself to be trampled underfoot for them so they would never have to experience Hell or its evil god. Mongolians are responding because they know Good News when they hear it. They're sick of living in spiritual terror."

His face suffused with rage, he spat out at me. "Do you think the Mongols need your Jesus?" The Savior's name came out like a curse.

I was shooting up a prayer for help responding when the Japanese man sitting in the seat behind us jumped to his feet and shouted, "Everybody needs Jesus!"

I was almost as surprised as the French guy by this unexpected "cavalry charge," but I had no time to say anything because this young Japanese brother began excitedly quizzing me: "Are you a real missionary? I have always wanted to meet one. I have been learning so much from God's Word about all of this. I think God may be calling me to be a missionary. Do you think I could do it? Where could I study for this? I am on my way home from Bible School in England. I need to plan my next step. Do you have time to counsel me?

I glanced over at our World Traveler. He was steaming, but what could he say? He had been answered by an Asian from a Buddhist nation who had found something much better: Good News about a God who really loved him. The joy radiating off my new Japanese friend was the best answer possible to the charges he'd made. As I shifted my attentions to him with a sense of relief, I chuckled inwardly. "Father, you set that guy up. It certainly wasn't fair to put this fired-up Asian evangelist right behind me to answer that question. You probably had fun arranging all this. Oh . . . and thanks!" The young Frenchman didn't speak a word for the rest of the bus trip—to the Wall or on our return. Our family enjoyed the whole day at the Great Wall fellowshipping with our new little brother from the Land of the Rising Sun. It was an unlooked for privilege to share with and minister to this ardent and loving Japanese disciple. Days like this made relishing our time away unavoidable, but we longed to be back in Erdenet as well. We were anxious not to miss anything.

Within a year of the church's birth, our decrepit Russian-built apartment block in Erdenet was already a hotbed of Christian activity. Bayaraa, the Mongolian believer who'd moved to Erdenet with Magnus and Maria to help plant the church, also lived in our building. The apartment she shared with her sisters served as the meeting place of one of house groups.

Our family began to attend this house church soon after our move to Erdenet. We enjoyed the worship and singing, and struggling to understand the teaching was good for learning language. It was great to be a part of such a close-knit and loving group.

What none of us knew was that a Buddhist family upstairs was listening to our meetings through the ductwork. A brother and two sisters had been faithfully gathering around the smoke hole in their kitchen every Wednesday night. The acoustics were perfect. The older sister got to know Bayaraa as they studied together at the university where the Alphonces were English teachers. It wasn't long before Bayaraa and her sister paid the family a visit and led them to Christ.

What an encouragement it was to know people were being drawn to Jesus just by listening to our worship. The group eagerly confirmed their salvation and began to disciple this family. The eldest sister, Bolortuya, grew up in Christ quickly. She and her mother evangelized their extended family living in the ger suburbs outside the city. Grandmother, uncles and aunts, nieces and nephews all eagerly responded to the gospel.

Mongolians trapped in Tibetan Buddhism will typically have an idol shelf at the rear of the ger or in the corner of the living room. This is comprised of a small shelf with a picture or statue of a god, some candles, and offerings of food and money. Bolortuya's family was no exception, and their question of what to do with this altar brought on a small crisis. Our young church had never had to think through a policy about getting rid of idolatrous paraphernalia. Up to this point we had never experienced a whole family coming to faith, and we never encouraged the young teenage girls to destroy their family idol shelves. Even though idols were in their homes, these items of worship were not theirs to dispose, but rather belonged to the entire family. But in this situation, with a whole family believing, our advice was they should rid themselves of it. The family decided to invite a few church leaders over and burn the idol shelf.

Almost immediately, one of the new believers in the family fell ill. She happened to be the oldest and most honored member of the family, Grandmother. Mongolian society gives grandmothers pride of place in the hierarchy of their mildly matriarchal family structure. Over the next several days Bolortuya's grandmother's condition worsened, until the family began to despair of her life. Relatives living out in the countryside or in distant towns were called and told that this woman wanted them to visit her. In a culture that has a strong taboo against mentioning death, even impending death, this was commonly understood as code for "Hurry, she's dying." The extended family began to gather and await the inevitable.

Bolortuya's other grandmother and her aunt, both devout Buddhists, noticed the missing idol shelf as soon as they stepped over the threshold. The idol shelf is the determining geographical space in the Mongolian ger, and its absence must have been glaring. The two ladies' disapproval was obvious, though no mention of the sacrilege was made.

As the new believers in the family prayed and discussed the situation, they began to realize that there were a number of other Tibetan worship items in the home. They decided that these too must be consigned to the flames. Later we heard from Bolortuya the entire household had bravely agreed to this plan. The paraphernalia was taken out into the yard and burned. The family prayed the whole time for God's protection from the evil spirits. Following the bonfire, they prayed for Grandmother she made an amazing full recovery.

Bolortuya and her mother showed up at our place with a number of questions. We began by explaining to them that Satan, the prince of darkness, is the power and authority behind the idols. Their family's conversion, followed by the dismantling and burning of the altar, had enraged the powers of darkness. The attack on Grandmother's health that followed was their attempt to reassert their authority over this family. The forgotten idolatrous items had continued to hold open the door for this kind of spiritual attack.

As the good news spread, the entire church was encouraged by this victory over demonic forces they had feared all their lives. Jesus had brought the battle to Yama and his legions, as He rescued Mongolian people from a dungeon of terror.

EIGHTEEN

Gossiping the Gospel

We had been trained to expect that cross-cultural evangelism would be one of the first and most difficult hurdles our team would face. I know that many church planting teams working among unreached groups experience much of their struggle just getting the Good News across the cultural divide in a bold and effective manner. We were ready for this battle, but it never came. The one church planting task our team did not handle "in-house" was evangelism. We outsourced this job to overseas Asians.

Mongolians have a natural gifting when it comes to sharing their faith. They just can't keep good news to themselves. After short-term teams of Mongolian believers won a foothold for God in Erdenet, we had watched in amazement as those first converts, not hindered by cultural differences, quickly began to win their friends and neighbors to Christ. In the first year the teenaged girls who formed the early core won their peers, but through summer and fall of '94, the Gospel spread like a grassfire through all age groups and both genders. Our New Believers classes were crowded, with many older people getting saved, and even some of our shyest and most unassuming members leading their neighbors to Christ. The believers poured out their hearts in prayer for family, neighbors, their countrymen and even other nations in our weekly prayer gatherings and in the house church meetings. And those prayers were answered.

We church planters were so quickly thrust into discipling the growing

band of converts that we never really had to do much evangelism ourselves—at least among Mongolians. But we did look for opportunities
anyway, at work, on the long overnight train journeys between
Ulaanbaatar and Erdenet, and as we lived out our lives in the community. Indeed, with so many Mongolian believers, it made little sense to
cross barriers of language and culture to carry the Good News ourselves
when we were far more effective training Mongolians to win their own
people. We had learned during our training that when locals began
sharing the Gospel with their neighbors, it was a signal to the church
planting team to shift gears and concentrate their energies on discipleship and leadership training. But, what is foolish to men is often the wisdom of God. As I recall from my diary, the first day of November '94
was such a case.

"Last night my bike was stolen. It was really my own fault. I went to
meet two Australians in Erdenet on a temporary business assignment. I
heard they had some videos they might loan us, and I wanted to surprise Louise, somewhat homebound with the baby due yesterday, and
Ann-Marie, the Swedish midwife who had come up from Ulaanbaatar
to attend the birth. I parked my bike outside their hotel and neglected
to lock it, reasoning I would only be a minute, and we'd never had a
theft since leaving the capital city. Upstairs I found the Aussies were
out, but a friendly Croatian man invited me into his room. I really like
meeting folks from new countries, so I went in. After exchanging pleas-
antries, I made a fatal mistake. I admitted my ignorance of the underly-
ing issues in his country's war and asked him to explain. (New Life Rule:
Never ask a native of what was Yugoslavia to explain the Balkan conflict) Two and a half hours later I insisted I had to go, and yes, I would
come again, but my "due-anytime" wife might be worried about my un-
explained disappearance. It was now ten thirty and Louise was expecting me home at eight o'clock. I went over to where I'd parked my bike
and it was gone. I started home on foot and met Magnus and a group of
our church girls. They were a search party helping the police to look for
me. Apparently Louise had been a bit concerned. Chagrined, I walked
home with them and reported by phone to the police: American found,
bike stolen.

This morning I had to get up at five thirty a.m. for the School of Discipleship meeting at six o'clock. After the meeting, Toogee, one of the trainees, asked to borrow my bicycle—a daily occurrence. He and his best friend, Tsogoo, are our church's "hooligans." This word is one of the very few that's the same in English and Mongolian. These two had been the leaders of a fierce gang in Erdenet. At 15 and 16 they already have a feared reputation. About six months ago they came to faith and were baptized, though they still have numerous rough edges. Fighting, smoking, drinking, loitering, and other hooligan pastimes still seem to be going on in a somewhat diminished way. I am glad they have never been anything but respectful and kind toward us. This is nice because they live in our building. God led us to accept their applications for the School of Discipleship even though we were forced to make major changes in prayer partner assignments because they had been in fist-fights with so many of our other male disciples. After three sessions, we are already seeing real changes. When I told Toogee my bike was stolen last night, he asked for the details, listened carefully, then grunted and stalked away. I saw him talking to Tsogtbaatar (whom we call "the Hooligan King"), and when I turned back, they were gone. I assumed they'd gone home to bed.

Forty-five minutes later I opened the door to find our hooligan-disciples (grinning), my bicycle (in pieces), and two small boys (very frightened; their shirt collars firmly in hooligan hands). They explained they'd asked around (apparently their contacts with the underworld are intact) and caught these small thieves taking my bike apart. A few pieces were still missing, as was the ringleader, so they sent one boy (named October) off to fetch his boss and the missing parts. The other boy, Altansook, was kept in our living room as a hostage for their return. Since he was sitting there all alone while Toogee and Tsogoo reassembled my bike in the hall, I began to talk with him. He was 13, small for his age and quite pathetic. I told him that he, like all the rest of us, was "gemtei" (with sin). I explained that B Burkhan, the living God could not abide sin and he and all of us were lost and dying. Using the Bible I showed him God's solution to his problem. "For Burkhan so loved the world..." It is wonderful how being caught red-handed strips us of our excuses. He certainly couldn't deny his need for a Savior. When I came to the end of my

Mongolian and still wanted to tell him more, God provided one of our church's elders-to-be, Odgerel (Star-light), to come over and share more with him. I told him I forgave him and invited him to receive Jesus—which he gladly did. He spent the rest of his captivity reading the Bible. He was enthralled. He promised to come to the middle school Bible Study I will teach tomorrow. We embraced as new brothers as I sent him off with Toogee and Tsogoo to find his escaped friends. I told him if they returned with the parts, I would keep their names from the authorities. Otherwise, first thing tomorrow the names and addresses of those two would be turned in to the police.

A few hours later, right in the middle of our team meeting with Magnus, Maria, and Anne-Marie (our Swedish midwife), the two hooligans showed up. They had the missing parts and felons: October and the ringleader, Amarbat, both aged 14. Magnus and I shared Good News with them. When I expressed my forgiveness and love, those tough angry eyes suddenly got very moist. When I said the good feeling my forgiveness gave them could be magnified a thousand times with God's total forgiveness, they were really touched. Amarbat asked, "Could someone like me come to your meeting to hear about Jesus?" It was wonderful to hear Magnus say, "Of course! Jesus came for gemtei huumus (sinners) just like you." They will join their friend at the meeting tomorrow. I can't wait to have my bike stolen again.".

NINETEEN

Erdenet's First Foreign Birth

Our fourth child—and very first son—was born the very next day, November 2nd, 1994. I really feel the telling of birth stories should belong to those who do the hard work, so here's what happened in Louise's own words (from a letter she wrote to a friend in Nevada):

> I have been thinking of you a lot lately. I guess because there are few people I know that have four children and lived to tell about it. How I wish I could call you. I'll have to make do with the antique art of letter writing.

> I woke up at two a.m. on the 2nd of November with mild contractions. I ignored them and went back to sleep. At about five o'clock I got up to see if this was really it. I cleaned the living room and swept the floor while timing the contractions. At six, I went back to bed to see if I could get some sleep, because I knew I was in for a long day. Brian became coherent enough for me to tell him what was happening and he showed as much excitement as a slug. We slept until the natives got too restless to ignore anymore. I got up and made breakfast for the starving masses. We had home-made granola and Tang. Who would have guessed I'd ever consider orange flavoring a treat?

> After breakfast I walked over to Magnus and Maria's to tell my Swedish midwife—yes, God loves me enough to send the very best! — we were in for a busy day. Ann-Marie (my midwife) was much more excited than Brian had been at six a.m. Magnus was astounded I could be so calm about the whole thing. I had a cup of tea with the

Swedes and then went home to homeschool. I figured home school might be more sporadic after the baby was born, so I wanted to get in one last day. The girls were disappointed — they figured a new sibling was a sure excuse for a holiday.

Maria came over later in the morning to ask what she could do, and I sent her out to do the shopping. She came back a little later with the needed foodstuffs and then took Alice to her house. Alice needed some special attention, and Maria was perfect for the job. Alice, being a fine connoisseur of bathtubs, asked Maria if she could take a bath in their tub. She was as happy as a clam. Molly and I finished school around noon, just after Brian and Melody finished her studies, and I got some lunch together. My contractions had slowed way down. Ann-Marie had come over prepared for a long stay. She checked the baby's heart and head — the heart was right on and the head was still a little high. She could still move it a little. She suggested we go out for a walk. This was exactly what I needed. We took a nice long stroll in the hills behind the city. The baby picked a great day to come into the world; the sky was deep blue with no clouds, and the temperature was in the mid-forties (7°C), really beautiful. The walk helped the contractions along. When we got back to our apartment, Ann-Marie checked me and things were really progressing. I had a bite to eat.

About this time Magnus showed up in a rush with all his camera stuff (he was supposed to film the events of the day) in tow. He had gotten a frantic call from the mother of our good friend Ganaa, who translates for the Russian house church. Ganaa's mom had told Magnus the baby was born and he thought he had missed it. We were all baffled. Then Melody came in from playing. Apparently, she had gone to see Ganaa to tell her what was happening, but Ganaa was at work. So Melody told her mother in fractured Mongolian. Minutes after Magnus appeared, Ganaa showed up, having excused herself from a teachers' meeting. Maria and Alice came back a few minutes later. The house was full now and my contractions were coming harder and closer. There were already 15 people in our small apartment when four more Mongolian friends came by to see the show. Ann-Marie had brought the video *Anne of Green Gables,* so everyone was watching the movie, and glancing over at me whenever I looked uncomfortable. The whole concept of privacy doesn't translate very well across cultures. I finally asked Ann-Marie to shoo everyone not actually related to me out except for Magnus and Maria. Brian remembered that he was supposed to be teaching a Bible study to the junior high youth. He offered to find someone else to lead the meeting, but I was happy to get him out from under foot.

By three forty-five my contractions were two to three minutes apart and I was singing through them. My sister had told me this helped in her labors with her two boys. It sure is more fun than boring old breathing. Brian came home around five; and Maria and Ann-Marie started making dinner for everyone. I had roasted a leg of pig the day before, so we had plenty of leftover meat. The aroma was tantalizing and it would have been bliss, but the labor pains were killing my appetite. I tried lying down, but my contractions and daughters kept me awake. The girls kept popping in and out of the bedroom to see if the baby was here yet.

The next time Ann-Marie examined me, at five thirty, things had begun to move along. I was eight centimeters dilated. We began to get a bit worried that Carleen might miss the birth. Several days before, we had asked Carleen Curley, the Peace Corps worker in town, to be present at the birth so she could testify the baby is an American citizen for the U.S. Embassy. The Consulate had told us they could not issue a passport without a "Certificate of Live Birth Abroad," and this required the statement of a non-related American citizen to verify that the baby really came from these American parents. Brian asked Magnus to go out and find her and bring her back to save us a red-tape nightmare.

Just minutes after Magnus rushed across town to check for Carleen at her apartment, Carleen came by to see how we were doing. We asked her where Magnus was and she looked puzzled. She had no idea I was even in labor. She'd wondered why Ganaa had left their teachers' meeting at the Foreign Language Institute so abruptly. We had a good laugh over the mix-up and had to send Maria out to look for Magnus who was now panicking at his inability to find Carleen. Eventually everyone was back where they were supposed to be.

Carleen had also happened to bring pancake batter for the next day's breakfast. She was divinely inspired in this. Carleen has been a real blessing to us. She comes from a large Catholic family and does not hold to the silly cosmic beliefs many Peace Corps personnel seem to hold. She also has good morals and an incredible work ethic.

At 6:03 p.m. according to Ann-Marie's records, I was fully dilated and she broke the water membrane. I immediately felt like pushing. That part is sort of fuzzy for me, I think I pushed three times and Jedidiah was born. His head came out and then a hand and then he started crying. Then I pushed the rest of him out and Brian yelled "It's a BOY!" This brought everyone in the house crowding into our bedroom to see the excitement. Ann-Marie checked and declared him very healthy. That was 6:11 p.m.; it seemed so much longer to me at the time.

The girls were so excited about their new brother. The sound of Melody sobbing, "it's a boy, it's a boy," drowned out the congratulations of the adults. Ann-Marie measured and examined the baby: all his parts were where they are supposed to be and the correct number. He was 52.6 cm (20.7") and weighed 4 kg (8.9 lbs.) Getting his weight was difficult, like so many simple things here. We borrowed a huge scale from the church's bakery, but they did not have all the weights for the scale, so Magnus and Brian used canned goods on the one side as counter-weights to Jedidiah on the other. It made for a funny memory.

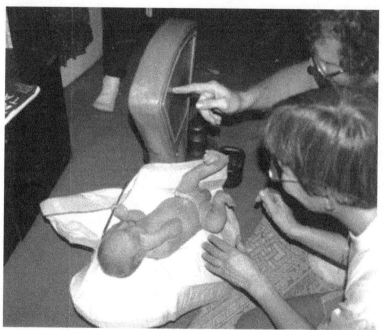

An hour after the birth I'd showered (breaking a Mongolian birth taboo) and was up eating the succulent and tasty pork dinner Maria had prepared. I feel like I've really accomplished something. Jed is the first non-Mongolian baby born in the twenty-year history of Erdenet City. The local newspaper ran a story about the birth, and it is the talk of the town.

Brian went right away to get the Mongolian birth certificate. It was really hilarious to have this official explaining that if they were to give Jed a birth certificate, then he might claim Mongolian citizenship. The fear is this could open the door to floods of foreigners moving to Mongolia to have their babies and get in on the wonderful benefits of being a citizen of this country. Brian tried to explain he would probably prefer not to surrender his American citizenship, so he could stay the same nationality as the rest of his family, but the guy would not budge. It is a good thing we did everything right to get the American birth certificate.

I hate the first three months of babyhood; I wish I could just sleep through it all. Ha-ha, not even close. Sleep deprivation does funny things to your mind. It is only worse here in this strange land. The Mongolians have such odd beliefs about new motherhood and all. The mother is not allowed to leave the house for a month and a half and she must keep her ears covered or plugged at all times. The thinking behind this seems to be the baby left a large hole behind in your body and "evil" things can get in through your ears. You would also think they could get in through your nose and mouth, but this is not a concern. The mother should not bathe for at least a month. The baby needs to be wrapped up tight, with only the tiniest part of his face showing. Even in summer they wrap their babies so tightly they all have heat rash. Moreover, Mongolians have no cultural taboos against giving unsolicited advice. I could scream because of all the advice I have received. I have taken to hiding in the bedroom when there is a knock at the door, and if it is someone who will be free with his or her advice, I stay there. Sometimes this works, but often they just walk right into the bedroom to see the baby. Please write. I need to know there is one sane person left on the earth.

Ugh! There went the electricity. I am sick of this. Thank God for battery power, even so, I'll take the hint and say goodbye.

Love, Louise

TWENTY

Shock and Awe

Amid our joy over Jedidiah Patrick's birth, no one on our team or in the church marked the fact we had just entered the gates of Hell. Satan chose this moment to unleash an intense and violent counterattack against us that would threaten to completely consume everything God had done in Erdenet.

During the summer we had hosted a short-term team from a church in Minneapolis that had some strange beliefs and practices, especially concerning spiritual gifts and leadership. Their visit had not gone well for the Erdenet church, and we had been relieved to see them off at the train station. We had never heard anything further from them, so we were shocked to run into four of them a day after Jed's birth. They had come to stay, with instructions from their pastor to start a "more spiritual" church in Erdenet and to keep their activities a secret from our team if possible. As the only other Americans in the city, the secret was out within hours of their arrival. We tried to talk with them, but they had their orders to work apart from us, and the meeting ended on a sour note. This first real opposition shook us, but we had no idea what was already in motion.

A week after the birth, I was strolling across the city plaza, and I was stunned to see four young smiling American guys taking in the sights. Even with heavy coats on over the distinctive white shirts and ties, it was obvious they were Mormon missionaries. Non-Mongols of any kind were an unusual sight, and our team had been the only resident *gadaad humuus* (foreigners) in town. Sending up a prayer-arrow that they were only tourists, I went over and introduced myself. My heart sank as they told me that they already knew who I was, and they had just moved into an apartment on the other side of town. They'd secured teaching contracts at the Foreign Language Institute, where the Alphonces taught English.

Magnus found out from the principal of his school she had hired five new English teachers from America. We knew there were four Mormon boys, but we hadn't yet met the fifth teacher, a girl from San Diego, CA. It turned out she had come to start a Baha'i congregation in Erdenet. That same week, we heard some Mongolians who had been converted to a Korean cult, commonly called the "Witness Lee," Church (a.k.a. Living Stream Ministry or the Local Church) had moved up from Ulaanbaatar and had already started a small church on the east side of Erdenet. Part of their practice was to trudge up the hill before dawn and greet the day with screaming praise. This did not endear them to the neighbors who, unfortunately, thought they were part of our church.

It seemed inconceivable that in less than a week we had gone from working completely unopposed as the only church in the city to contending with four groups, three of them cults! All four sects immediately targeted the believers of Jesus' Assembly. I sent a teaching on Mormonism versus the Bible through all our home groups and into the daughter churches outside of Erdenet, just in the nick of time. The day after our whole church had been exposed to the clear differences between Biblical Christianity and the Latter Day Saints; the Mormons began their door-to-door witnessing campaign. It didn't go as well as they had hoped—they failed to convert even one of the believers. The Mormon church of about 40 that eventually developed was comprised almost exclusively of English students motivated by promised trips to the United States and scholarships to Brigham Young University in Utah.

The "American Ladies," as we called the team from Minneapolis, went right to work setting up their church. It was easy to see what they had found wanting in our approach to church planting. Their method was more a duplicate of the Sunday big meeting approach that characterizes most churches in the West. Our meeting in simple small churches, primarily in homes all over town, must have struck them as weak and odd. They imported a large sound system, electric instruments (not only breaking sound missionary contextualization practice, but also requiring nonexistent 110 voltage), and materials for starting a Bible School, and right away gathered a group and began services. They brought a Bulgarian woman who spoke Russian to the Mongolians to help things get rolling because no one spoke Mongolian. They connected with two young women who were deacons in Jesus' Assembly, the church we were planting. A real spirit of rebellion and independence erupted in these deacons and began to spread. Within a few days it seemed as if Jesus' Assembly would split. We tried talking with these deacons and their followers, but the offer of instant leadership without any discipleship was too attractive.

Odgerel (whose name means: Starlight), an elder-in-training, spent quite a bit of time reasoning with the rebels. The spirits that were working on them caused him to be filled with doubt and completely demoralized. He made plans to abandon the church and move down to Ulaanbaatar to become a babysitter for his sister's family. This was such a shock because he'd been so passionate for Christ. We spent several hours pleading with him to change his mind, and it was like talking to a brick wall. There was a strong sense we were dealing with an entirely different person who merely looked like our friend. Magnus, Maria, and I were at a complete loss. We were almost resigned to losing Odgerel, when Bayaraa spoke up. She said, "I don't think talking to Odgerel will do anything. We need to pray and command this spirit to leave." Talk about being humbled! Instantly we realized we were experiencing a spiritual attack, not a human crisis. We surrounded Odgerel, and

Bayaraa led out in prayer, rebuking the demon and commanding it to quit oppressing our brother. After about 15 minutes of praying, it left and Odgerel began to sob. He repented and shared how he had felt compelled to leave even though he didn't want to go. Despair had covered him like a blanket. He felt cleansed and wanted to go immediately on a two-day retreat for fasting and prayer in the countryside. We blessed him and sent him off. (A year and a half later Odgerel would be appointed elder and pastor of the church in Erdenet, so, in hindsight, we should have expected a battle like this over him.) Our team gathered with the rest of our church leaders and prayed hard, asking God to open the eyes of those in rebellion and limit the spread of damage through the rest of the body. About three days later all those that had left with the two rebellious deacons returned, repenting in tears. God healed the split, but we were all shaken by how close we had come.

At this same time, both our family, and the Alphonces, came under the threat of eviction from our apartments. Our old 'friend' Sukhbat, now in charge of the Housing Authority, was infamous for being quite wicked and taking bribes. She could be paid to snatch a family's home and award it to the one who bribed her. Apparently, she had "buyers" for both of our team's apartments. Sukhbat sent word we should hand in our "house books" and move out. We refused and later received notice she was having us evicted. We discovered a Mongolian law making it illegal to evict anyone between September and May due to the harshness of Mongolia's winters. Our hope soared but then fell again when we found out the cops were in on the dirty deal. Sukhbat had bribed the police to do the eviction job. We had friends go and fight this eviction at City Hall, but no one was motivated to cross this woman. She went on a break out of town and we were told the evictions would take place upon her return. Living under the strain of impending eviction would be stressful anywhere. But in Asia's deep-freeze, with four children, and one a newborn, stressful doesn't even begin to describe it. Daily battles with red tape to try to foil this woman's plans were also wearing us down. All the other attacks against the church made the overall situation seem impossible.

Around the middle of December, the "Housing Tsarina" returned and put the wheels in motion. It really seemed as if we would all be in the hotel for Christmas with our belongings on the street, when Magnus had a scathingly brilliant idea. We sent word to the police they were welcome to come and evict us at any time. We were going to videotape the proceedings and cooperate in every way. They demanded to know why we were going to film them. We informed them CNN would probably find the tape interesting and do a story on how Mongolians were breaking their own laws in the mistreatment of their foreign guests. The police immediately decided the fallout from this was a higher price than the bribes they'd received, and pulled out of the deal. Sukhbat had paperwork but no muscle, and so, no apartments for her "buyers." After a month of tension and red tape, it was over.

I felt as if our team was playing that "Whack-A-Mole" arcade game where you have to keep hitting the moles that pop endlessly out of holes. As soon as we resolved one crisis, another popped up. Right after we saved our apartments, Oyuun (not her real name), a girl who had been serving as leader of the worship team, had to be confronted about sexual sin with one of the young hooligans who had been part of the church. This young guy had never made any effort to enter in to the life of the church but had been a fixture on the outskirts for some time. Like a wolf around a flock of sheep. Oyuun was resistant at first, but finally softened and confessed. Bayaraa and Maria prayed through her repentance with her and extended her grace, but it was clear we were going to have to think through what should happen when leaders fall in sin. As we sought God and His Word and shared with each other and the elders-to-be, we came up with a restoration plan for these situations. The leader who fell and repented would be removed from public ministry for a period of several months. This was a time for getting closer to God and being discipled by church leadership. There was also a requirement for those in leadership to publicly confess at whatever level was appropriate. For example: a regular believer would confess to their house group, a deacon would share their repentance at a deacons' meeting, and an elder would repent before the entire congregation. Oyuun was happy to do anything to make things right, both with God and with her brothers and sisters. We all saw immediately how individual sin could hurt the whole church as her fellow deacons wept while she shared with them and then later as we limped through worship at our celebration meetings without Oyuun's musical skills. We hoped she would be restored enough by Easter to lead worship at the Easter celebration.

The attacks had just begun. Too many horrid things happened to our team and Jesus' Assembly during November and December to be recounted here. One of the most disheartening was finding that two of our top leaders had gone to a party and allowed old friends to cajole them into drinking too much. Several in the church had witnessed their drunkenness, and we were left with more tearful and repentant Mongolians under church discipline and restoration.

At home was the added stress of a new baby. Jed, a fussy and difficult baby, had not once allowed us a night's sleep. He was an incredibly light sleeper and woke up screaming on occasions too numerous to recall.

On top of the mental distress of sleep deprivation, we were all suffering from the cold. Outside, the mercury never poked above -20°F, while inside, our ground floor apartment was an icebox. Frost gathered on the inside of our door in December and was not to go away until March. On one occasion Louise knelt to wipe up water splashed onto the kitchen floor while she was doing dishes. Instead, she had to pick it up and put it back into the sink, already frozen solid! One day I noticed the outside door to the basement under our flat had been left open. I went to close it to increase the insulating properties of this room of dead air right under our apartment. What I saw would have made me cry, if I hadn't laughed. A pipe had been dripping and the resultant ice flow had filled the room from floor to ceiling with an enormous stalagmite. It was so huge that at its base ice filled the room. No wonder we were freezing up above. We were camped on a glacier.

As a result, we had to wear sweaters and coats inside the house and keep several borrowed heaters going round the clock. When I went to pay my electric meter bill, the man refused to believe a single apartment could consume so much power. "As much as a school," he groused to me. Only Alice seemed immune to the effects of the cold. She danced around the apartment in a bathing suit and wiggled out of any other clothes we put on her. Mongolian visitors were horrified and would chase her with blankets. The constant numbing cold and spiritual attacks wore us down.

Just after the middle of December, Louise and 6.5-week-old Jedidiah got out of town for a bit of a break from all this. They went down on the train to Ulaanbaatar with Magnus and Maria. Louise took the opportunity to take the baby to a missionary doctor there. Dr. David Meece cheered us with the news that Jed was perfectly healthy and in the top percentiles in all measurements.

Another ray of bright light appeared to cheer us. The Bible School in Abakan, Siberia, had sent a young Russian couple to work with our team. Ruslan and Svetlana were full of faith and fire, and we loved them from the first. Svetlana had been the leader of the team who'd kicked off the Holy Spirit outpouring in "Miracle April" and now she was back with a husband, a baby in the womb, and a long term calling to Mongolia.

As wonderful as these reinforcements were, they couldn't hide the hard facts we were facing. We had been taking a beating for two months that had shaken both our team and the church. The attacks on Odgerel, Oyuun, and the church split had only been the opening volley. Many others had begun to fall away, fall into sin, come under oppression, or give way to bitterness and anger. There were so many things going wrong we were not at all sure the church would survive. Towards the end of December, our team met in tears and seriously considered whether withdrawal wasn't the best option. It really seemed as if there was no recovery from the deep hurts the Body had sustained. We were unable to come to a decision about staying or leaving, so we were stuck with struggling on until we knew better, but we were all bone-weary and running out of hope. Things didn't seem as if they could get much worse, but they were about to do just that.

TWENTY-ONE

The Worst Christmas Ever

"History has shown that throughout the ages, whenever the Kingdom advanced, someone first had to pay a terrible price."
Phil Butler

The Foreign Language Institute, where Magnus, Maria and I taught English classes, had had its Christmas party on the evening of December 23rd. We'd all walked over to the party to enjoy the festivities with our students. The mood had been happy and festive and conversations provided many opportunities to share the true reason for celebrating this holiday. Our friend Carleen, whose Peace Corps job was teaching English at this school, had worked very hard at training the entertainment for the party. The language students spirited song-and-dance rendition in English of "Rocking around the Christmas Tree" had had us almost falling out of our chairs with laughter.

Jedidiah had been the real show-stealer though. Mongolians love babies and he'd been passed from person to person all over the crowded room. We kept a watch on him from where we were seated, not wanting him to be overwhelmed. It was easy to spot his bright blue Mongolian dehl. A lady in my architecture firm had made it for Jed as a birth present and it fit perfectly. His tasteful choice of elegant native dress had been wildly popular with Erdenet high society, at least among the English student and teacher set. With all the attention and passing around, Jed had stayed amazingly peaceful. He hadn't cried once, and many remarked on what a good baby he was. Of course, they did it in the acceptable Mongolian way to complement an infant or child. "Mohai hoohid" which translates as "ugly child," is actually praise designed to avoid demonic attention.

When the party ended, our team had walked home together through the frigid December night. Louise had Jed sleeping, tucked away in the baby sling hanging across her chest and inside her warm coat. The city had been very quiet. Christmas was not widely celebrated in Mongolia; the Institute had wanted the party merely for a cultural experience. The only ones in the entire city who planned to celebrate the Savior's coming to Earth were the members of our church. As we walked home down the deserted main avenue we talked of the church's Christmas party, which was to be the very next night. Louise had written a song called "Lullaby for the Baby King," which our family had been planning to sing at the party—excited at the added meaning of holding a new baby while singing these lyrics. While we were discussing party plans, Louise slipped on the icy sidewalk and fell smack on her bottom. Amazingly, Jed hadn't woken, and Louise, beyond her sense of coolness, was uninjured.

Our apartment was the first one our little group had come to and we hugged goodnight and let ourselves in while Magnus and Maria walked on to their building, another five minute walk. I'd put our sleepy daughters to bed in their room while Louise nursed Jed in the living room near his bed—warm with thick wool carpet, sheepskin fleece, blankets, comforter, and warm footy pajamas. We were trying to get him used to sleeping through the night. It would be the second night we'd let him cry himself to sleep. We were hoping his protests about not being in bed with us, and about wanting to be held and fed each time he woke, would be less this time than the first night we'd tried it. But, after Jed had finished feeding, he was really happy, and as we lay him down on his bed, he beamed the biggest smile at us—his first ever. He even kept smiling while I got the camera out and snapped a photo. We wanted to take more pictures, but not wanting to lose that good mood, kissed him goodnight, turned off the lights, and crept softly to our room. Louise told me to leave the camera out to remind us to take more pictures in the morning. "Now that he can smile, it should be easy to get some great photos," she'd said.

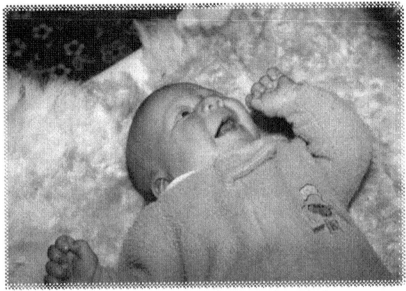

For the first night in two months, Louise and I slept like logs.

Around six in the morning, Louise had suddenly awoken. She immediately knew something had gone dreadfully wrong.

Rushing out to the living room, Louise flips on the lights. There is no movement from the covers on the floor. Louise pulls off the blankets and sees Jed lying face-down, as we'd left him, but something about his head looks wrong. She reaches out and touches him. She feels absolutely no warmth. She pulls his stiff form up against her chest and just knows. Time stops. Louise hears herself scream but can't feel herself do anything at all.

I jolt bolt upright in bed at the sound. I am running for the living room and meet Louise in the hallway. I hear, "Jed is dead," and my world caves in. I can't breathe at first, but I hear the girls calling out from their room and make myself tell them to stay put. I go to the body of my son and pick him up, as Louise crawls back into our bed and slowly coils into a fetal position, moaning. She chants one thought over and over in her head, "God is good, God is good, God is good."

I hold my son's body and know he's gone. I begin to ask God to bring Jedidiah back from death. My daughters are crying and scared, but they obediently stay in their room. Their sobs tear me away from the edge of the pit where I am teetering. I go to the room which my three living children share and sit down on the lower bunk. I hold all three of them as I tell them that Jed had left us during the night and has gone to live with Jesus. "You mean he's dead?" asks Melody. Her face already drenched with tears. My heart is breaking for the second time in less than ten minutes. I nod. Wailing breaks out from Melody and Molly, and I join them. Alice, too young to understand, is crying from fear and sympathy. This is, I decide, the worst moment in my life. Louise appears in the door and announces she is going to get Magnus and Maria. The girls and I just huddle and cry and pray and wait for her return. I feel like maybe I should be doing something, anything, with Jed's body, but I can't think of anything more useful than holding my daughters and grieving with them.

Louise has gone into shock. She can't feel the -30°C (-22°F) cold of the Mongolian winter morning. She's numb inside herself, and stumbles through the snow and ice. When she reaches the door of the Alphonce's fifth floor flat, she has to lean on the doorbell for what seems like ages to get a response. Magnus and Maria think it's a drunk mistaking his floor and are understandably reluctant to get out of their warm bed. When they finally answer the door, they too enter our nightmare.

Louise returns with our deeply shocked and grief-stricken partners. Looking at their faces I have a perverse thought. 'Good! I'm not the only one who thinks this is unspeakably hideous. Someone else feels it too.' I feel guilty for thinking this, but I understand later that this is precisely why we're told to "grieve with those who grieve."

I move Jed's body to our bedroom and Magnus and I begin to really pray agonized prayers over it. We are calling on Jesus with all we have to raise my son from the dead. While we pray I have my eyes open. Unable to keep looking at my son's lifeless body and continue to pray with faith, I look out our bedroom window onto Erdenet's main avenue. The sun is coming up, and I am shocked to see people starting to move around outside, going about their business, as if nothing has happened. The stinking world has come to an end and these people don't even realize it! It is impossible for me to conceive of life just going on as before. I close the curtains and keep howling out pleas to God.

While Magnus and I are praying, Molly comes quietly into the room. I stared at her in disbelief at how much grief has changed her. Her eyes are red and puffy, her blond locks tangled and bedraggled, and the tears still flow down her cheeks. She is grieving for her brother as deeply as any six-year-old has ever grieved. She hasn't stopped sobbing since I told her the news. I worry that looking at his body, as she is doing, might unhinge her. I can't imagine what this has already to her young faith and impression of God as her heavenly Father. I ask her, "Molly, can you still believe that God is good?" And she answers immediately, "Oh yes, daddy! And He's here in this room with us right now." As she says this, Magnus and I sense the presence of Christ in such a powerful way. Jesus is in the bedroom! Jesus is grieving with us. I have never felt the Lord's presence in that potent a form before or since. Even though the miracle we sought doesn't come, we begin to feel a hope well up that makes no human sense in our circumstances.

Maria is comforting Louise in the kitchen. She's reading to her from the eighth chapter of Romans and urging her to hold onto the fact God is somehow working things together for good. It seems written for us, since we love Him and are called by Him according to His purposes. Magnus, the children and I all join Louise and Maria in the kitchen for some food and to talk about what needs to happen next. We decide that Magnus should tell the elders-to-be and the rest of our team. We are worried about the church. Two solid months of spiritual attacks have weakened the fellowship to the breaking point. How will they cope with seeing their apostles struck down as well? Since this evening was to be the first-ever Christmas celebration for most in the church, we feel that, no matter what, we need to delay a general announcement until after the party is over.

Magnus goes out to round up the leaders and Ruslan and Svetlana, our new Russian teammates. After he leaves, I decide to run over to our friend Ganaa's. Her fluent command of Mongolian, Russian and English is going be needed as we deal with officials later in the day. When Ganaa comes to the door and I tell her the sad news, she reacts with violent anger. She screams and kicks a chair down the hallway. I don't know whether she is enraged at this latest of Satan's assaults or if this is just a Mongolian reaction to death. When she recovers her composure, she wants to help in any way she can. I send her to City Hall to find out what legal procedures we need to follow.

When I get home, the Mongolian elders-to-be are beginning to arrive. Ruslan and Svetlana are already there. All have been crying and exchanging hugs with the family. We crowd into our bedroom, praying. I sit on the bed with Jed's body in my lap, and the others all lay their hands on me or the body. They pray intensely. It feels wonderful to hear voices calling out in Swedish, Russian, Mongolian, and English, imploring God to return life into Jed's still body. I am thinking that if any prayer would result in a resurrection miracle, these are the ones. Ruslan is particularly impassioned. I can't understand very much of the Russian, but I know from the tone that God is going to require a really good reason not to grant Ruslan's prayer. The praying goes on and on. After some time I hear something very distinctly in my spirit. "He is not coming back. It's time to say 'goodbye.'" I look over at Louise and in a non-verbal way, as only married couples can, she communicates with me that she's heard the same thing. As I begin to try to accept the loss as God has instructed, I continue to feel His presence, heavy and real. I want the praying to stop so that I can stand up and begin to move on to whatever is next, but I can't think of a way to get everyone to take their hands off and stop praying. I feel suffocated, but I don't want to be rude. So I wait.

When they finally stop praying, I share what God has told me, and Louise confirms that she's heard the same thing. Magnus shares a vision of Jed and Jesus playing with a ball on a lawn beside a waterfall in heaven. We are tremendously encouraged. And then we all start crying again.

Bayaraa calls for an ambulance, but is told that a doctor has just died and they can't come for some time. "Is there only one ambulance in Erdenet?" I ask. The Mongol leaders wrap up Jed's body for burial in a long piece of cloth. Then Louise and I wrap him in a final blanket that has special meaning—a hand-knit one from a friend back in the States. We settle in to wait. We talk and pray and share and sip tea with our brothers and sisters. Waves of tears periodically overtake us. It becomes the longest day ever.

Magnus goes back to his apartment and phones David Andrianoff, the director of JCS International, his umbrella mission agency. David has better access to international phone calls in Ulaanbaatar, and he takes on the task of informing our families back in the States. He is so kind and thoughtful. To avoid our parents hearing the news of their grandson's death over the phone, he calls the pastor of one of our supporting churches. The pastor doesn't answer, so David leaves a message on his answering machine: "Please call me in Mongolia as soon as possible at this number. It is urgent." Miraculously, this pastor calls David—a complete stranger—in Ulaanbaatar. David tells him what has happened and asks him to drive over to my mother's house and break the news in person. He is able to provide support when my folks need it. My mom calls Louise's parents and breaks the news to them and to our other supporting churches. Later, in the evening, we receive calls at Magnus' apartment from two of our pastors and from our parents.

David further blesses and comforts us by sending his car and driver all the way up to Erdenet to deliver two dear friends. Joy McConnell, a nurse from New Zealand, and Helen Richardson, the Leatherwood children' school teacher. They brave the icy road to Erdenet at a time when few would (we had never been on it!) and make it in record time—arriving that evening to be with us. We feel wonderfully mothered in lieu of our own parents' presence. David continues to serve us by setting things in motion with the US Embassy and Jedidiah's American doctor in Ulaanbaatar for the issuing of a death certificate.

On that longest of afternoons we have a surprise visit that is both difficult and strangely helpful. One of the Peace Corps workers is a large young lawyer named Roger. We had gotten to know him a bit and quite liked him, though his teaching schedule meant we saw little of him. Roger had conceived a plan to brighten up Christmas for the only American children within 200 kilometers: ours. Our doorbell buzzes and when we answer it we find Santa has arrived. "Ho! Ho! Ho!" he booms. Roger has arrived with gifts for the girls. When he sees the tears and hears the reason for them, he is horrified at his timing. We spend a lot of time reassuring him and telling him that there is no way he could have known. The thought is very sweet, and it lifts the girls' spirits as nothing else has done all day. Bells jingle as Roger respectfully removes his red and white St. Nick cap. Santa's now in the house, crying with us.

While we are comforting "Santa Claus," Bolortuya and Bayaraa quietly and lovingly go about preparing Jed's body to be taken to the morgue. I don't know what they're doing, exactly, but when we go into the bedroom again we find his body is bound and swaddled as any Mongolian baby would be, and the whole bundle wrapped in a Sesame Street blanket. We are so grateful for these quiet and loving gifts of service.

We had been told to await the ambulance and not to leave the house. Frequent calls to the hospital let us know that it would be a long wait as the doctor's death had thrown their systems into disarray. Finally, as dusk is falling, the ambulance arrives in front of our stairwell. Mongolian law stipulates that a parent must accompany the body of a child until it is signed over to the morgue. I carry Jed's body and get into the ambulance with our friends, Ganaa, Bolortuya and Bayaraa. The ride across town to the hospital is eerily quiet. What do you talk about driving to a morgue? We pull up in front of a small stand-alone, single-story brick building behind the hospital. This is the morgue.

The driver unlocks the metal door and explains that I need to take my son's body in and place it somewhere inside. I think these are very strange and unspecific instructions until I go inside. There are dozens of dead bodies lying on every available platform. It is a charnel house. I am surrounded by death. My heart sinks to a new low as I contemplate having to leave my precious son in such a place. I feel like I'm abandoning him. I search for a place, and find a small rolling metal table with nothing on it and, sobbing now, lay down my small bundle. His Sesame Street blanket is the only color in the room. The contrast is stark, and I feel like I might not survive this room of death. I emerge from that place with a look on my face that causes all three friends to hold me and cry again with me. As we ride in a cab back across Erdenet, I ask why all those bodies are piled in there. My three friends are surprised that I didn't know that winter burial in Mongolia is next to impossible because the ground is frozen. You simply can't get a spade into the ground to turn it over. I had never thought of this. How would the authorities dig a grave for my son, I wonder. Or would I have to do it? This thought overwhelms me. I silently tell God that He has to figure all this out for me. I can't do it.

The cab stops in front of the large elementary school in our district. All three girls get out, and I remember that the church's Christmas party is starting and that they have to dry their tears and go in there as if all is well. I pray for courage for each of them as the cab delivers me at the base of the stairs to the Alphonce apartment where our family is spending the night. None of us has any desire to stay in our own place. Louise, the girls, Maria, Joy and Helen are all there when I arrive. Magnus has just left for the Christmas party. The plan is to tell the church the bad news after the party finishes.

As we sit, share, talk and nibble away at Swedish Christmas goodies, I keep feeling I am in the wrong place. I try to push the thought away but it stays there, intruding on my grief and my time with family and friends. As I think about where I 'should be,' I tell everyone where I wished that I could be. "This would be so much easier if only we could be with our parents in California!" It really seems as if the hardest part is bearing this awful experience at the ends of the earth, so far from home and family. I think of how my mother always knows just what to do for the girls and how wonderful her presence would be for them and

Grieve with those who grieve. Joy and Helen.

for Louise and for me. Louise is having many of the same longings for her family. We are overwhelmed with homesickness. In the midst of these thoughts, it comes again . . . an impression that I am needed elsewhere. Suddenly I am unable to crowd out the thought anymore. I know God wants me to leave the warm apartment and trudge over to the Christmas party.

"No way!" I say to God. "Father, that's really asking too much. I can't go to a party tonight. I'm not sure when I will ever feel like a party again. I don't even want it to be Christmas! I can't believe you want me to do this, considering what I have just lost—this was my only son!"

I've no sooner formed this thought than I realize with horror the answer that God could give me, but gracefully doesn't. "I know something about losing an only son, Brian. And for Me it all started at Christmas as well." He doesn't need to say a thing. I tell everyone, "There is someplace I need to be. Please pray for me." I go out into the entry hall and put on my winter survival gear: sweater, jacket, heavy coat, gloves, scarf, extra socks, boots, and stocking cap. I reluctantly step out into the bitter cold.

When I arrive in the multipurpose room at the school, I see that everyone is gathered at the far end. Just then a collective sobbing breaks out. Everyone is crying and when someone spots me I am suddenly surrounded by weeping Mongolian brothers and sisters. Magnus had just made his announcement as I was coming in the doors. As we huddle together grieving and holding each other, I realize that God has answered my complaint. I had longed to be with my family. He had created family for me here, in this room, right at the very ends of the earth!

TWENTY-TWO

The Letter

The sun defied all my expectations and came up that Christmas morning. Just 24 hours earlier we had awakened to a horror that Christmas Eve and Christmas Day never broke. I got out of bed and went straight to the desk, knowing somehow I had to communicate what was happening to friends and family back home.

Christmas Day, 1994, Erdenet, Mongolia

Dear Family,

Today is Christmas Day. Yesterday our son died. This letter will be tough to write. I usually enjoy writing to you and the words flow easily. There are no words for this. Yesterday morning Louise woke to find a perfect baby boy lying dead in his bed. Jedidiah was 52 days old.

I wish you could have known my son. I wish you could have held him and seen how beautiful his hands, eyelashes, lips, everything was. He learned to smile in his last week. He had a smile more gorgeous than a sunrise. Jed used to stare so intently at our faces—just as if he was memorizing every detail.

I don't understand this "Sudden Infant Death Syndrome." I know whoever named it never lost a baby to it. The name should reflect that something in the parent suddenly dies. I have heard a few facts which provide a sort of cold comfort.

Our living in Mongolia had nothing to do with this. The highest prevalence of S.I.D.S. is in New Zealand, a Western country. It usually strikes healthy boys, under six months, during the winter. Jed had a full checkup by an American doctor just a week before he died. He was perfectly healthy.

Yesterday was the longest day of our lives. Louise woke and noticed it was six a.m. and Jed hadn't awakened her all night. She knew. Her scream woke me to a nightmare I have yet to awaken from. I ran to where he was sleeping and picked up my only son. Jed was not there. I prayed for God to raise him from the dead. He didn't. Louise and I wept in shock and disbelief. The girls woke when Louise had screamed, but had obeyed my command to stay in bed. They were calling to find out what was wrong. I had to go in and hold them and tell them their little brother was dead. I won't even try to describe this.

Louise went to get Magnus and Maria. They got up and came immediately. Praise God for our team. There is no way we could have walked through this without them. Magnus and I labored over Jed's body again in anguished prayer. I knew (and know) God could return life to Jed, but I began to realize the answer this time was this body was no longer a vessel for Jedidiah's life. Later a few Mongolian Christians and a Russian man, Ruslan, who'd just arrived to join our team and help me with the Russian church, came to pray over the body again. While they were praying, God told me to say good-bye to my son. At the same time He gave Magnus a vision:

> "There was a river with a waterfall next to a wide green lawn. Jedidiah, looking about five years old, was kicking a big colored ball around. Magnus looked to see where he was kicking it and saw Jesus. Jesus was playing with Jed. Jed turned around and flashed his beautiful smile and waved. Then he ran to Jesus."

We waited almost all day for the ambulance. The hospital insisted one parent accompany the body at all times, so when it came, I rode to the morgue holding what had been my son. Even knowing beyond a shadow of a doubt Jed was with Jesus, leaving him on that gurney in that horrible place was perhaps the most difficult thing I've ever done. No doctor was on hand, so we are still waiting for a death certificate before we can bury him. We don't know where they will let us bury him. We have been told not to ask. Just go privately into the hills with a few friends. It is sometimes easier to apologize than to ask permission.

Later that day was the Mongolian church Christmas Eve dinner party. We decided to only let a few of our closest friends and leaders know what had happened. At the end of the party Magnus made the announcement and began to explain. We were all spending the night at Magnus and Maria's, and the Spirit prompted me to walk over to the party. I walked in just as Magnus finished telling the church Jed had gone home. Everyone was weeping as I went up and shared our pain and our hope and faith. We have family here in Mongolia!

We called Magnus' boss in Ulaanbaatar and he informed all our friends there. He and Rick Leatherwood immediately dispatched two close women friends of ours to Erdenet by jeep to be with us. Helen and Joy have been a huge blessing, as has Carleen, our Erdenet Peace Corps friend.

We deeply love you and appreciate you,

Brian, Louise, Melody, Molly, and Alice Hogan

TWENTY-THREE

Hope Can't Freeze

Christmas Day came and went in a blur. Other than getting up early, going back to my apartment and writing that letter, I can't remember much that happened that day. I know the kids opened presents but I can't picture it at all. Missionary friends were my only memorable gifts that Christmas. Rick and Laura Leatherwood and their four kids came up on the train. Lance Reinhart and Dawne Caldwell arrived on the same train. Dawne's was a face from home. In fact we were sent by the Los Osos Christian Fellowship. We'd mobilized her through Perspectives back in '89, and she was working with street kids in Ulaanbaatar. Dawne had been up to visit before and was a favorite of the Erdenet believers as she trained and encouraged the drama team. In younger days Dawne had been an actress on stage and in film. She'd had a speaking role (as Dawne Damon) in the 1970s sitcom M.A.S.H. "Auntie Dawne" was adopted family and her presence took some of the sting away from going through this so far from home. These brothers and sisters put their lives on hold to surround us with love, comfort and practical help beyond the burial.

Practical details kept demanding attention. The question of what to do about burial proved particularly vexing. None of the options seemed very comforting or even acceptable. We began to realize that, as much as we were committed to adapting to our adopted culture and doing things the Mongolian way as much as possible, sometimes we had to "draw the line." In three areas we were unable (or unwilling) to give up our own culture's ways: birth, death and breakfast. Every culture prescribes its own very distinct ways of how people should come into the world: suggesting new and intriguing practices to a woman who is in labor is not recommended; every culture prescribes it own distinct ways of how people should leave the world—as we were soon to discover; and no culture, other than the Mongolian one, offers you sheep's head to eat before noon.

We knew we wanted to bury Jedidiah in Mongolia. He had lived his entire life there. The farthest he had ever been from Erdenet was the brief trip into Ulaanbaatar for a medical checkup with a missionary doctor. Whatever significance and connection his brief life had was with Mongolia. Though our embassy offered to help with the details, the ordeal of transporting his body to the United States seemed both unnecessary and inappropriate. Jed's body belonged in the soil of Mongolia, his country.

There was a city cemetery just west of Erdenet's city limits, and we were assured a plot would be made available to us. As we talked with the believers, it became apparent we would not be in control of the funeral or anything that followed. Buddhist priests had taken over the caretaking there, and they conducted the rituals for all those interred in that cemetery. Louise and I didn't really want those rituals performed at his grave that might set an example for others.

An older believing couple came by to share in our grief. They had lost a child as well to what was probably undiagnosed SIDS. We were blessed by their visit and we were all comforted in sharing our grief, old and new. Then, trying to be helpful, they offered a suggestion for the burial dilemma. They began by describing the traditional Mongolian "open-air burial" practice to us. Before the 1921 Revolution, the unclad corpse was usually placed on a cart pulled by horse or cow and driven out to an uninhabited area even nomads didn't use. These places are sacred and only visited for funeral-related events. In other areas, especially in South Mongolia, the corpse was placed on a horse's back and upon reaching a lonely spot on the steppe; the horse was urged to gallop until the corpse was thrown off. This way the ghost is rendered incapable of following the bereaved home. In both practices, the body is then returned to nature by being devoured by hungry birds and animals.

Not seeing our growing looks of horror, they then excitedly described the modern synthesis of these ancient customs. "You are lucky the law just changed," they said. These days, the body is driven out to the remote and lonely spot in a car. Upon arrival, the body is placed upon the top of the car and the funeral party gets back inside. Then everyone covers their eyes (including the driver) while the driver "floors it" and the vehicle lurches off across the steppes. The body falls off and no one knows exactly where it is. The dogs, vultures, and wolves then tear it to shreds and eat it.

We managed to thank our friends for sharing this "option" with us, but tried to tactfully explain we would be unable to utilize this "new freedom" due to our own taboos. There is no way I could let my son be bounced off a car roof and left out on the steppe to be devoured by wolves. I was fairly sure that even having heard about it was going to give me nightmares.

I went to bed Tuesday night and couldn't sleep. All I could think about was that my son's body was still in that morgue, and we had no decent options for burial. I began to seriously consider whether I could break in that night, take Jed's body, and hike off over the hills to bury him myself. I kept thinking, "It is easier to apologize than to ask permission." After spending much of the night in sleeplessness, I eventually talked myself out of the idea. I realized the extreme cold would probably kill me long before I could hack a hole deep enough in frozen rocky soil. I was so frustrated by my inability to accomplish even this: as his father, I owed it to Jedidiah to give him a proper burial. I finally gave it to God, my Father, and sleep came at last.

The next day dawned and after breakfast, Magnus and Maria had worked everything out. They had spent several hours at the hospital securing a death certificate, without which the body could not be released. The doctor had initially refused to complete the paperwork because SIDS is not a recognized cause of death in Mongolia, and he flat out refused to check the box for "Cause of death: unknown." He had been insisting on attributing the death to "Double Pneumonia" rather than admitting he knew of no cause. Fortunately, our friend Zagdaa had gone with Magnus and Maria. Her children had actually survived double pneumonia and she knew what it looked like. We had gone to her home with Jed for a Christmas party on his last day of life. She got right into the doctor's face and told him this child was perfectly healthy and there was no way he was going to say Jed had pneumonia. After arguing with him for a while, Zagdaa noticed the death certificate was completed except for "Cause of Death." She grabbed it off the desk and told the astonished doctor they were finished with him and stalked out, Magnus and Maria trailing in her wake. When they gave it to us, the box for "Unknown" was marked. (Later the American embassy arranged for a "Certificate of Death Abroad" that used information provided by the missionary doctor who had examined Jed a week before his death. The official cause of death was registered as: Sudden Infant Death Syndrome.)

The Alphonces and church leaders had already arranged for the morgue to release the body to us. And, best of all, they had come up with a plan for how and where to bury Jed. An elder-to-be, an older man named Lhagva, worked in an elected position as a city official in one of the ger suburbs. He was able, through his position, to secure us a permit to travel with human remains in a vehicle. The ordinary purpose of this permit was transport to the city cemetery, but the destination was not indicated in writing. Lhagva suggested that we drive out to a lonely hillside where not even nomads would ever camp. We were so relieved. All of the worries of the night were swept away. I placed a call to the bank where I'd taught English and the bank president immediately made their van and her husband, a driver, available for our use.

In the middle of the day, December 28, Louise, Molly, Magnus, Maria, Lance Reinhart, Rick Leatherwood, Lhagva, Tuvshin (Zagdaa's husband), and I all piled into a gray Russian van and drove out of Erdenet with the body of my son. Jed was still wrapped in a crocheted blanket and Sesame Street quilt, stabbing reminders of our own culture, family, and friends back home. We drove out east of the city, several kilometers past the train station. We turned off the road and went a few more kilometers overland up into some hills to the north. When Lhagva had found a spot that didn't violate any taboos and would not offend any locals, we stopped and began digging a grave. It was a place that would be really lovely after winter released its grip. There were a few trees and in four months the hillside would be covered in grass and wildflowers.

I started in with a shovel but discovered at once that without serious pick work that soil was not moving. It was completely frozen. I was digging rock! I had imagined I would do the bulk of the digging. It seemed like a father's duty. But the reality was I quickly tired and gratefully handed off to the many willing hands of friends. The job was just as impossible as I'd feverishly imagined the night before. The wind was blowing at least 24 kilometers per hour (15mph) and the temperature was a minimum of -26°C (-15°F). That made wind-chill factor a bone freezing -39° in Fahrenheit or Celsius. Lance was filming for us so we would be able to include loved ones far away. The wind made a roaring sound that almost drowned our voices on the video. It was so bitterly cold Molly, who had insisted on coming with us to say goodbye to the brother she loved so dearly, had to return to the van with her mother and Maria—she would not have survived long outside. The men struggled to hack deep enough into the ground for a decent grave before any extremities were lost to frostbite.

It seemed like forever, but eventually we were ready for what would have to be a quick graveside service. I went down to the van and fetched

Louise, Molly and Maria, and I carried my son's body for the last time. As we stood huddled around that bare hole in the Mongolian earth, I knelt and laid Jed's shell into his grave. The finality of this action overwhelmed me and I began to sob as I knelt over the grave. I could hear the others crying around me. Our tears froze on our faces and fell to the earth in Jed's grave, frozen like gems. After I stood up, Tuvshin and Lhagva quickly filled in the grave, shoveling back in the dirt we'd just wrenched from the ground at such cost.

Our dear friend and mission director, Rick, shared from the words of Jesus: "My Father wants everyone who sees the Son to have faith in him and to have eternal life. Then I will raise them to life on the last day." John 6:40 (CEV). We sang a song we'd chosen, "There is a Redeemer" by Melody Green. I could remember when, years before, I had heard how she'd lost her little ones and husband, Keith, in a plane crash, thinking, "How could anyone make it through losing their child?" It seemed appropriate that we were worshiping with a song penned by one "acquainted with grief."

A Precious Seed Planted

After singing, we prayed this seed we planted and watered with tears would result in much fruit for the kingdom of God in Mongolia. After we finished our service, I started to wander around gathering rocks to outline the pile of earth. It looked too bare and unloved. The others understood without words and joined me. Before long the grave was surrounded by rocks and had a rock cross on top. We found a large stone covered with orange lichen and several of us managed to roll it over so there would be a headstone. At this point, driven away by the onset of frost-bite, we hurried back into the van and returned toward Erdenet. Looking back as we drove away, I could see the grave until it was swallowed from my view by the vast hillside. I thought, "That is probably the first Christian grave in Mongolia since the Nestorians were here in the 13th Century." It also struck me Jedidiah was the first American ever born in Erdenet, and, as far as we know, the first American to die in Mongolia. Whatever the historical significance, a piece of our heart was now forever buried in the soil of Mongolia.

When we made it back and were dropped off at our apartment, we entered to the bustle and smells of a feast in preparation. The church leaders had come over earlier in the day and told us a shared meal at the home of the grieving family was customarily served to all of the extended family and friends. We told them there was no way we could possibly put on a feast in our present state; even preparing meals for our own small family was beyond us right now. They quickly assured us they were not expecting anything of us. Mongolian families would count on the help of relatives, who came around them after a death, and the church was our family in Mongolia. They would take care of the feast. Relieved, we agreed. During the burial, we had forgotten this was happening and were strangely cheered and comforted by a warm flat full of friends and the smells of good food.

Before long a steady stream of guests began to arrive. As they entered, each person handed me a cash gift. I was horrified at first. We had lived with the knowledge that, as poor as we were, we were far wealthier than almost everyone in Erdenet. Being handed money by people with nothing to spare was hard to take. Bayaraa saw my dismay and quickly whispered that I had to accept. It was custom and there was no polite way to refuse the gifts. I stood there in our entry hall feeling humbled and astounded by the generosity of these Mongolian people.

The apartment was overflowing, but somehow everyone was served. Friends from work and town passed through and left after greeting us and eating something, but many from the church stayed on. As the stream of guests diminished at last, those not cleaning up in the kitchen gathered in the living room with Louise and me. We shared our hope with them as we told of words and scriptures that had been encouraging us over the past few days. Louise and I sang a worship duet in English and someone led us all in Mongolian worship on the guitar. The time flew by and before long, everyone was leaving to go over and set up the "Women's Palace" for the evening's meeting. It was the church's regularly scheduled Old Testament storytelling time, but tonight it was doubling as Jed's Memorial service.

The day before, Magnus had mentioned that though it was my turn to take the story up at the next day's meeting, he would be willing to carry on alone until I felt up to it. We had been trading off every week, storying our way through the Old Testament. Every Wednesday, we'd check how far the other had gotten in "God's Story" and pick up the thread there. I asked Magnus how far he'd made it last week, and he paused. I asked again and he said in a lowered voice, "Abraham is just about to offer up his only son." I was speechless. It hit me how God was in charge of details like this even on our bleakest days. I told Magnus, "Thanks, but I think I'm supposed to tell this story."

As the last guests left, we went with them over to the rented hall, which doubled on many nights as Erdenet's disco. We walked into a packed room. I walked up to the front and told the story of what God had asked of Abraham. We were not very far into the story before I was getting choked up and many in the crowd were crying. We wept our way through the story somehow, and it felt as if we had all experienced the real story of that ancient grief and loss and redemption for the first time. I tied it all into Christmas and we understood that the Father had sent that sweet, holy baby into this world knowing he would die here. That was the real and hidden meaning of the holiday we had celebrated so joyfully in the past. Loss and sacrifice are the price paid for joy and salvation. We'd never experience Christmas the same again.

I took my seat with Louise and our girls. We were sitting in front next to "Auntie Dawne" and our Peace Corps friend, Carleen. Rick Leatherwood brought his four kids and our three girls up to lead several kids' songs. Mongolians love action songs, and this was a big hit. The mood changed and lifted. It seemed strangely appropriate Jed's home going should be celebrated with children's worship he soon would have loved. After Rick finished, Magnus and Maria surprised us all with a song they had been practicing as a gift to us—a beautiful duet of Graverobber, from the Christian rock band Petra. The lyrics captured perfectly where we had been finding our hope since Jed left.

Jed's Memorial service with Dawne Caldwell

Afterward, we worshipped in Mongolian and with The House of the Lord, the Vineyard worship song Louise sang throughout her labor just two months before. I went to the front and shared my heart with the church. It was clear we were not going through this alone. The church had been under attack for almost two months, and our team had been having serious doubts as to whether the infant church was going to make it.

Jed's had not been the only death. We were all still reeling from a second death that followed Jed's by two days. The day before, a deaf young teen from our house church died of no apparent cause. The doctors claimed it was kidney failure, but she had seemed perfectly healthy. This was a special child who'd always seemed to overcome her mental challenges with an uncluttered spirituality that made others want to experience the Father like she did. The shock and grief this caused seemed overwhelming on top of all we had already absorbed. Death seemed to be all around us. I felt I had to say something to encourage the battered believers. I told them we had been going through a lot, and I wasn't sure how it all would end, but I wanted them to know Satan had gone too far. He had crossed a line with these deaths.

"I don't know what any of you are going to do, but as for me and my house, we are going to serve the Lord! We are going to tear away at the enemy's kingdom for the rest of our lives, and if Satan doesn't like it then he had better kill all of us!"

The mood changed noticeably from then on; the church began to return to the fight. I sat down again, Magnus shared from the Bible, and afterward everyone gathered around us and prayed for our family. It was both beautiful and hard. The fact that almost all of our son's memorial service was in a language we were still struggling with seemed to increase our painful feelings of separation from parents and home. Both Louise and I were inwardly praying we would be back in the States very soon.

It was not to be.

TWENTY-FOUR

Something Breaks

The church leaders were encouraged by what I shared at the memorial service and called for 24 hours of fasting and prayer against the attack we had been enduring since the beginning of November. All of the leadership met for worship and prayer at an all-night gathering in the Alphonce apartment. As we called out to the Lord in unity, something happened. At three in the morning, simultaneously, we heard a thunderous crack. Everyone in the room looked up at the same instant. It wasn't audible, I don't think, but we all "heard" it. It was like a small branch breaking in a silent forest. We were all looking around, not sure what to do, and a new believer who had tagged along to this leaders' gathering, asked, "Does this mean we can go home now?" We all nervously laughed a little at his blunt question. Magnus suggested we sing a song first and then go on home, so that's what we did. The attack was over. We sensed it then, but we saw it in the weeks to come. Spiritual battles still lay ahead, but the withering onslaught of November and December had ended. All of the serious hits we had taken were healed and restored in the weeks to come. The deaf girl and my firstborn son were the only permanent casualties.

Both Louise and I shared a strong desire to take a trip back to California to grieve with our parents and families and allow the girls to reconnect with their grandparents. It seemed a foregone conclusion this was the best time to take our oft-delayed first furlough from Mongolia.

Our family had broken a record among the Mongolian missionary community, and no one envied us. Without trying to we had become the family who had served longest on the field without a visit home. Other than a brief visit to Beijing, we hadn't left Mongolia since we'd arrived over two years before. Most mission agencies classified Mongolia as a "hardship field" and mandated regular trips out for their workers. Neither of our organizations, YWAM and Mongolian Enterprises International (MEI), had any settled policies or guidelines on this, so we'd made our own plans. Back in early '94 we had planned a vacation before our move to Erdenet. We had reasoned that if we couldn't get all the way home to California, we could at least get to someplace warm and comfortable. We'd heard about an inexpensive paradise in Thailand many missionary friends had frequented. We had put our request in at an MEI staff meeting and, although there was no policy on vacations, a brand-new policy was made up on the spot. We were told that to help us bond with the culture; no out-of-country trips were allowed during the first two years. Louise had fled the meeting in tears, and I had started butting heads with the leadership. In a few days I had almost managed to get us drummed out of the mission. God had intervened at the last moment by giving Louise a revelation about what was really going on—a "spirit of opposition" had been dogging our steps for years and was manifesting itself again. As soon as the Holy Spirit revealed this entity, we had countered it easily. We had prayed and I'd gone to the meeting where I was to be fired. I had requested to speak first and had shared what the Lord had showed us. God had confirmed my words to the leaders and we all forgave each other. In fact, Rick Leatherwood had been so adamant the enemy would not win, he'd immediately launched into high gear in helping us move to Erdenet. God had triumphed, but in all the excitement the original cause had been completely forgotten and we moved without getting a break. In an amusing endnote to this story, we later received word in Erdenet that the entire staff of MEI (except the Hogan family) had taken a break out of country. Rick had changed the policy and discovered all were overdue for a vacation and had mandated a trip out.

We hadn't had another chance to go anywhere after we got to Erdenet. Magnus and Maria had badly needed a visit home to Sweden, so we had been left in charge for most of the summer of '94. We hadn't wanted to travel while Louise was in advanced pregnancy so an autumn trip had been out, and then we'd been busy with a newborn when winter arrived.

Now, with losing Jedidiah, taking a break seemed the most sane and logical course of action. We and everyone else assumed we would be heading home to grieve and recoup as soon as it could be arranged. Throughout the whole period following that hideous Christmas both Louise and I were conscious of an almost overwhelming desire to be with our parents and families. From a ministry angle it made a lot of sense as well. To break out weeping when folks come over to be discipled just isn't very uplifting.

We had the funds. Our supporters had given generously and the Southern Baptist workers in Ulaanbaatar had taken up a collection. We were honored, humbled and blessed by their large gift. As we began to make plans and to talk about how to buy tickets, an unexpected word came from God. I began to pay attention to a nagging and growing impression that we were not supposed to leave Erdenet at this time. It didn't seem possible the Father would ask us to stay on after losing Jed, yet that was just the thing I began to sense Him asking us to do. I remember actually reminding God that we were in deep grief and incapable of being joyful witnesses. If we could just go "home" I promised we would "heal up" and return as much stronger workers for His kingdom in Mongolia. I was so intent on continuing to plan our break I almost "won" the internal debate I was waging. I had no idea the secret weapon God held in reserve. As we were drinking precious real coffee one morning, Louise casually mentioned she'd been feeling we were supposed to stay on in Erdenet and walk through our grief in front of the Mongolian believers. I was floored. Louise had been dying for a respite from the harsh life we led in Mongolia since before we had moved to Erdenet. As soon as she voiced what she had been hearing, I knew it was from God. There was no way for this to come from Louise's flesh or human desires. As we talked about it, we cried, knowing it would be several more incredibly hard months before we would see "home." We shared what we were feeling with Magnus and Maria, and they confirmed they had also been hearing this, but they couldn't very well ask us to stay. We had needed to hear it from God for ourselves.

So we did our early and heaviest grieving in Erdenet. We wept in front of guests and visitors, at church gatherings, and at home alone. It was embarrassing and awkward, as Mongolian culture does not encourage display of emotion. I often wondered why God wanted us to go through this there. It didn't seem to be helping His cause. I would not get any insight into this for some time.

The day after Christmas I sent a fax out as a response to the faxes and calls we were receiving from all over:

> So, how are we doing? It's like the guy said in *Sleepless in Seattle* . . . 'you get up, remind yourself to breathe in and out' . . . We are all going through grief, in different ways and different stages. Alice doesn't fully understand death, but misses Jed. Melody has sobbed, denied, and been flippant, wild, and stable, depending on the moment. Molly is hardest hit. It breaks your heart to hear her wracking sobs. She is experiencing empty arms in a terrible way. She and Jed shared a special bond since the day he was born. She could often hold and calm him when even Louise couldn't. She is dealing with her grief though, not stuffing it down. Louise has managed to stave off guilt and accusation, and deeply mourn the loss. We are binding her breasts, which, heavy and full of milk, are a constant reminder. The tears come in waves. Sometimes you almost forget for a bit, and then you feel guilty for not crying. I find myself mourning the baby we had that I want to hold, and the boy that I will never play with, and the man I'll never have for my friend. We all went to the Christmas service last night. Over 700 Mongols packed the largest hall in town. The Christmas Play caused us both to weep. My mother had just asked in her letter if Jed would be the Baby Jesus in this play. Instead Jesus is holding our son.

A few weeks later I wrote to our friends and support team:

> "We are doing very well. Our faith is unshaken, and we are testifying to God's tender care. He always does the most loving

and right things for us, and to us. 'Yea, though He slays me, yet will I praise Him!'

We are passing through the stages of grief, and God in His mercy seems to time the hardest times of one for the strong times of another. We have been drawn very close as a family through this loss. Two visions have encouraged us greatly: Magnus' vision of Jed at around five years old, playing with Jesus; and Rick Leatherwood's vision of Jed as a fine strong man in the prime of life and health, exceedingly beautiful.

'Where is your victory, O Death? Where is your sting?'"

TWENTY-FIVE

Faces of Grief

The year 1995 began in much the same manner as the previous year, and yet everything seemed so different from just a year before. Once again we saw the New Year in around our kitchen table with Lance Reinhart. We forged a tradition that would become a yearly ritual during our stay in Mongolia. New Year's Eve was always with Lance, and we'd dent the chalked ceiling in our kitchen with a cork from a bottle of Russian champagne at the stroke of midnight. Thus there is a slowly growing array of scattered indentations on our ceiling with the year penciled beside each. It was both sad and odd to reflect that just a year before we had been happily chattering about plans to move to Erdenet and were not even pregnant, and now, a year later, the three of us were back together both sadder and wiser. We had a much clearer view of the cost that comes with our calling. That Brian of a year before seemed like a complete stranger to the grieving Dad I now was.

As we moved through January and February, we began to discover grief as a force we knew nothing about, nor did anyone around us seem to have anything useful to add. Bizarre and unexpected side effects appeared. Louise had been noticing her sense of taste had diminished to the point where all her food tasted like sawdust. Emotionally, the well seemed to run dry at the same time. She was deeply sad but couldn't seem to really cry. She felt like something was stuck in her and she lost the ability to be passionate about anything. I noticed she'd quit voicing any opinions about plans I made. This shocked me. Louise had never been a "yes woman" or shy about her opinion. This new Louise worried me, even if it did make my life easier.

I continued to grieve, too. I would burst out in tears at random moments. It wasn't that others would rub my wound. It was an internal thing. I would think of Jed and something I'd never be able to do with him and just start weeping over what I'd lost. Each girl handled the loss in her own way. Friends sent us a couple of books on grief and we knew everyone goes though grief differently, so we just tried to support each child as best we could. Molly grieved most like me. She would cry as it hit her, and then recover and move forward. Alice seemed not to get the death thing at all. She made comments from time to time, but mostly just slid back into being the youngest child. In some ways we wondered if she was relieved that the weird and unwelcome displacement from her position as our baby had ended so quickly.

Melody was all over the map. There was no order to her grief. One minute she'd do denial, flip a switch into wild sobbing, and then just as quickly she'd be running around the house as if nothing had happened. We worried she didn't seem to be dealing with her feelings, but shoving them away as soon as she could. Louise and I just tried to parent each through this as best as we knew how, sharing our trust that their brother was with the One we all wanted to be with and we would be together again someday. We also made sure that we spoke as a family about all of the wonderful ways God was meeting our needs and caring for us. We were feeling His presence and help in ways we never had before.

With very limited phone and fax service and no email availability in Erdenet, we had to rely on the Mongolian Post Office for communication with our home support network. This proved both a blessing and a curse. Throughout the winter and spring every trip to check our mail at the Post Office was like negotiating an emotional mine field. We were encouraged and comforted by the deluge of letters and cards we received from people reacting to the letter I had written on Christmas Day. The impact it had on people around the globe was phenomenal. As people shared their grief and reactions with us, we were strangely encouraged. One family read the letter while driving and had to pull their car over to scream and weep as a family. As terrible as this was, Louise and I were blessed by their response. To know others felt it so deeply filled a need in us. It was horrible. It deserved some screaming, some reaction.

Mongolian culture does not allow for speech about the dead after the funeral, and all our Mongolian friends had gone silent on us just as we were really feeling a need to talk about what we were going through. Hearing reactions and shared emotions from friends abroad helped us process the things we were feeling. We began to understand the power of "grieving with those who grieve."

At the same time, many of the packages and cards we opened just ripped open our wounds. We discovered an unforeseen trial of living in one of the earth's most remote places. Because the mail was so slow and unreliable, along with sympathy cards we were still receiving "new baby" congratulations, and even Christmas gifts for Jed. Many of my birthday gifts and cards come bearing wishes for the "father of a new son." Our emotions were dragged all over the map by every day's batch of mail. If we'd been going through this at home, we'd never have had to open and read Christmas and "Congrats, You finally got a baby boy!" and sympathy cards all at one sitting. We actually would wait some days until Maria could come by before wading into it, unable to face it by ourselves. We took to sorting it out by postmark to try and get some clue as to the contents and cut down on surprises for which we were unprepared.

We found some comfort in stepping quickly back into most of our church and team responsibilities. I handed over the Russian congregation to Ruslan and Svetlana. I had been leading it with the help of Ganaa, our friend and Russian-English translator, since April the year before. I was unable to meet this small fellowship's needs. The Russians were so different from Mongolians. Where the Mongolian believers were so open and eager to embrace anything you taught them, the Russians tended to process everything intellectually. It took a group argument before a simple Biblical truth could be accepted. I spoke almost no Russian, so I was left out of these debating sessions. Ganaa would be so offended that they seemed to be disagreeing with me she would jump in and rebuke them in fluent Russian. I would sit there listening to a babble of raised voices for maybe five or ten minutes. When it finally resolved, Ganaa and the church would all look to me to continue again. I'd ask Ganaa, "Did we win?" "Oh, yes," she'd reply smiling, and we'd go on with the teaching. Even though this seemed to work, in an odd way, I believed a cultural insider could lead the small church better. I couldn't tell whether things they did, religious things, were merely cultural form or whether they carried non-Biblical meanings. I was trying to be sensitive to a culture I hadn't learned through a language I didn't speak, and I knew I was in over my head.

Rather than add neglect to this already troubled mix, I turned the group over to Ruslan without any transition. The timing of their arrival a couple weeks before Jed's death was pure Jesus! And the handover worked like a dream. Ruslan immediately corrected a few small things I had been reluctant to address, and because he spoke as a Russian, he had the knowledge and authority to pull it off. He and Svetlana also brought an experience of faith and triumph in financial provision that encouraged the believers. As a worship leader, Ruslan offered far more than I.

Ruslan came to our apartment regularly for English lessons with Louise. Svetlana was already semi-fluent. She was seven months pregnant with their first son. They'd just marked their seventh month of wedded life. The Russian church tripled in size under Svetlana and Ruslan's direction, and they opened a Sunday school for 20 Russian boys that Melody enjoyed attending. Ruslan reported, "I love childrens!"

I'd spent eight months concentrating on training the Russian believers to simply obey Jesus' basic commands, and that formed the foundation for their life together in Him. I had also baptized them and that, in the minds of these disciples, gave me an enduring father's role in the life of their church.

TWENTY-SIX

Flexible is Too Rigid

Another kind of unwelcome surprise arrived with our mail. An international Christian news magazine carried a blurb about the church in Erdenet and our team in their January issue. The report paired the name "Brian Hogan" with the word "missionary." Even with religious liberty guaranteed by the constitution, the situation in Mongolia still warranted more discretion than this. This well-meant publicity jeopardized the papers of all our team in Erdenet. All we could do was ask our home team to pray God would protect the work and make certain eyes blind to this publication.

Our yearly contract with 'MONAR' Architectural Company was coming due and Mr. Orgil, the boss, was eager to renew for a third year. The English classes I had been teaching in Erdenet had proved very lucrative for the firm. We had been discussing several other small business start-ups as well. All our plans hit a major snag when the Ministry of Labor unexpectedly denied our application for a renewal of our visa. They said 'MONAR' had no business placing foreigners in Erdenet since they had no Mongolian employees there to supervise me. The Labor Ministry canceled our new contract when 'MONAR' submitted it, leaving us only a month to secure a new visa. We suspected the magazine publicity had brought this upon us. In any case, we suddenly found ourselves with no source of a visa and therefore no clear way to stay on in Mongolia.

We weren't the only ones on the team experiencing visa problems. Svetlana and Ruslan were to secure a work permit, and they were dealing with a firstborn son who was determinedly coming into the world, ready or not. Baby Rueben ended up appearing on March sixth, before a visa ever did. Magnus and Maria had received a miracle the year before when the Foreign Language Institute pulled an "impossible" visa for Swedes to teach English out of a hat. They had been informed then this next year's visa would be "completely impossible, there is no way you will stay another year." And yet, as we all labored over this in prayer at our team meetings, God did the impossible and the Labor Ministry granted their visa to the utter mystification of the school and the local police.

After exhausting all the possibilities of continuing on with the company I'd been working for since our arrival in Mongolia, I figured it was time to hunt up a new employer. If I couldn't manage to land a new contract, then our upcoming furlough would be quite a bit longer than we wanted. We had folks all over the globe praying. With less than a week left in Mongolia, I landed an interview with a top manager in the all-powerful "Erdenet Concern," the largest copper mine in Asia and Erdenet's reason for existence. He began my interview by explaining to me that the company was a Russian-Mongolian joint venture, and they had no other nationalities working there. "This would make me your first American," I countered. He asked what I was capable of doing, and I said, "Anything you need." I rattled off some ideas like proofreading their contracts in English, fixing computers and training their users, teaching English, etc. We had quite a tussle over whether I had to work full-time (like all their other employees) or half-time, as I insisted. I convinced him there was no way I could home-school my children, shop for food all over the city, and work full-time. It just wasn't practical as an expatriate without extended family support. He ended up hiring me as a manager in the mine's Commercial Department. I had no idea what the job entailed, but the contract came with a letter of invitation. We would be able to get our visas and re-enter Mongolia! We'd seen again and again there was no way to hang on in this land without being as flexible in our plans as a jellyfish.

All through the excitement of securing future secular employment, I continued to teach and lead in the Erdenet School of Discipleship. Our first group of students was enthusiastically plowing through the lessons and materials we had prepared. I taught the weeks on Biblical Basis of Missions and the History of the World Christian Movement early in the school, then sat in on several weeks taught by guest missionaries from Ulaanbaatar and Sweden, and finally taught on Culture during our last week in Erdenet. The students were excited about finishing the classroom phase and spending the summer months in outreach trips across Mongolia—the first Mongolian short-term missionaries!

Before we'd moved up to Erdenet, Louise and I had become quite close to Lance Reinhart. Lance had done his YWAM missionary training with us

Lance Reinhart

in Oregon, but it wasn't until we were all struggling to adapt to a new country that we really deepened our relationships. Lance boarded with a motherly Mongolian woman who worked for the director of the school where he taught English. Her son was also living at home, and he and Lance were both in their early twenties. In this total immersion environment, Lance's language proficiency soon surpassed most foreigners. Even so, he would frequently get hungry for familiar faces and food and show up at our apartment in search of chocolate chip cookies and peanut butter.

These visits were fun for all of us. We'd play games, have discussions about everything from the sublime to the ridiculous, and, after we acquired a toaster, we'd eat toast—a luxury in a land that lacked the concept of toasting bread. Lance would usually just "pop in for a few minutes," then, several hours later, accept our invitation to dinner, and finally miss the last bus of the night at eleven p.m. and be "forced" to stay for breakfast. We all enjoyed these impromptu camp outs and always made sure Lance would ring his "Mongolian Mom" to keep her from worrying.

When we had moved to Erdenet, we were able to lure him up from Ulaanbaatar fairly often. Magnus and Maria saw in him what we had already recognized; quiet determination that really got things done, wonderful ability to train and equip others from behind the scenes, and dry wit that made life in Mongolia so much more bearable. The four of us agreed that Lance was meant to be on our church planting team. Lance, however, was not sure. We had already noticed that the more one of us tried to get him to do something the more he resisted. I, on the other hand, tend toward artful persuasion as my first and foremost tool. It made for an interesting standoff, and after a year of cajoling, tempting, and begging Lance to move up to Erdenet, I finally gave up.

A couple months later Lance announced he was joining our team.

The timing was perfect. Lance moved into our apartment as we left on our first vacation home. He finished teaching my English classes and other projects, was hired on by the Foreign Language Institute, and had found a posh furnished apartment with incredibly cheap rent to move into when we returned. A mining executive leaving Erdenet to study in Colorado had wanted a Westerner to housesit his fancy apartment for a year, and had met Lance on his way out of town. God worked out every detail as soon as Lance made his move.

As the first "single" to join the team, Lance was to experience a different side of missionary life in Erdenet than the rest of us. One evening, not long after moving into his own place, he answered a typically Mongolian constant knocking at the door. At the door were three very lovely young women from his English class, all smiles and nervous giggles. His Mongolian "mother" had trained him well, and Lance hospitably invited them in, led to seats in the living room, and set about making tea in the kitchen, wondering what they had come for. After tea was served, and all the conversational niceties about health, herds, and relatives covered, the leader of the delegation, at the prodding of the other two, sat up on the edge of her chair, cleared her throat, and pulled out a piece of paper. In slow and halting English she read Lance the reason for their visit as the other two beamed at him.

Lance choked and nearly sprayed his mouthful of tea across the room, "What?!"

And the beautiful girl repeated with more assurance, "From ancient times we have longed to come and be intimate with you."

After a shocked silence, Lance recovered enough to tell them he was sure they didn't mean what they were saying. No, she protested in Mongolian, they had looked up each word so carefully in the Mongolian-English dictionary. Lance asked her to tell him in Mongolian what she was failing to get across in English.

"We have been wanting to get acquainted with you for weeks now, Teacher."

The Teacher was relieved, but much too embarrassed to explain to the puzzled girls what they had actually said in English. Having all experienced how wrong translation efforts can be—especially those referenced solely from the dictionary, with its bewildering array of word choices—we all laughed until we cried when Lance shared this story at our team meeting.

Lance's great contribution, beyond the refreshment and laughter he brought, was his skill in preparing and training the believers to take over things Magnus and I had been doing. The Discipleship School was one of these.

The idea for a discipleship training program had come to me during October of '94. I had felt our church's biggest liability was a shallowness that rapid numerical growth and newness of everyone's faith had made difficult to address. As I thought about what had created the high levels of intensity and commitment that Louise and I had always known as normal Christianity, I realized that the Vineyard School of Discipleship where we had first met was a perfect incubator for these qualities. Surely it would be possible to translate what worked from that program into something that would fit the culture here in Erdenet. During our team meeting, I began to think out loud to Magnus. We needed some structure to give training in depth to those who wanted more, training that was practical and based on doing rather than mere hearing. We also needed a higher level of commitment from students than church attendance required. We hoped a high degree of interaction with our disciples would help them to catch intensity and commitment directly from us as we modeled what the Word taught. Relationship between the students would also be a priority so they could be trained to use their gifts together in love.

We knew God was behind this from the beginning. That very evening, Magnus and I feverishly planned and organized far into the night, and less than two weeks later we were sorting through 50 applications for the first school. We had personal interviews with all 50, and on the last day of October we started with our first 20 students. Not all that happens on Halloween is "of the devil." We had contacted missionaries from Ulaanbaatar to come up and teach a week each in the six-month long school. Most responded positively and excitedly, as what we were doing was needed in all the churches in Mongolia.

There was one Bible School in the capital. However, students were removed from their church involvement, filled with information by visiting professors and pastors who knew little or nothing about the local context, and given little opportunity to exercise what they learned in practical ministry. Students were paid a stipend to attend, and this practice attracted many with questionable motives. The "fruit" we'd seen from this particular "tree" had been rotten.

We wanted good fruit, so we deliberately designed our "Disciples' School" to discourage the "professional student" mentality. No student was paid—we charged tuition. It wasn't much by Western standards, but to the people in our church, it was sacrificial. Our goal was to build income into the school from the beginning, so it could continue without reliance on outside funds (and without the strings such funds often entailed). I also wanted to make sure we were training heads of households. In our training we had learned that this is the best pool from which to draw church leadership in most societies. Our problem was these folks typically were already employed. We certainly didn't want anyone to quit their job to attend our school. There were too many unemployed people in the church to begin with. We decided to have class at the ungodly hour of six a.m. so students could go to work afterwards. For most this meant a long trudge to class before dawn—under stars strewn like diamonds across black velvet—in winter temperatures that averaged -20°C (-13°F) during the day. This would keep away all but the extremely committed.

We hadn't known that it was completely unheard of in Mongolia to meet for anything before eight a.m. We found out the first day of class. We all showed up at the "Women's Palace" (just a Communist meeting hall— it sounds much fancier than it is) we had rented—only to find it dark and locked up tight. The students pounded, shouted, and eventually tossed pebbles at upstairs windows to awaken the *jijuur* (watchperson). After 45 minutes in the bitter pre-dawn cold, a very angry woman opened the door and proceeded to give the entire class a tongue-lashing. We meekly slipped in past her as she yelled at us. We held our first class. I found out later, that Odgerel, went back that afternoon to meet with this jijuur. She had calmed down and was even a bit sheepish, but Odgerel was seething. He asked what she thought she was doing that morning. Why hadn't she been up to let us in as he had arranged the day before? She replied that of course she had thought he was kidding when he'd told her we needed the hall at six a.m. No Mongolian people would get out of bed so early for any kind of meeting. Odgerel reminded her there had been 20 Mongolians waiting outside the door that morning. She asked with frank amazement "What kind of Mongolians rise so early." He replied, "Mongolians who believe Jesus rose from the dead."

Disciples in the Erdenet Disciples' School

The first Erdenet Disciples' School exceeded our dreams. Most students were ministering in leadership positions before the school was half over. It had been hard work for our team. All the preparation was from scratch. Magnus and I did quite a bit of the teaching, and Louise or Maria sat in on class with every guest speaker and hosted them all in our homes. Six months of bone-numbing early mornings had taken their toll, and it was an occasion of both joy and relief when we hit the final outreach and presented graduation certificates before a cheering church. We thought we might be ready to do it again after another six months.

The elders-to-be had other plans. They came to us and asked when the next Disciples' School was starting. When we told them we had no immediate plans for another school, they were shocked. It turned out they had students already lined up. The church had been so blessed and excited by the initial school they wanted to do another right away. I almost passed out just considering it. They refused to take no for an answer and we ended up negotiating a second school. We thought we could make it bearable by having this one meet in the afternoons. When we mentioned the new time slot, though, the elders-to-be balked. "Everyone thinks it must be so early to separate the true disciples from those whose faith is weak," they insisted.

We managed to stave off our eager Mongolian leadership until September when we promised to train the batch of disciples they had lined up. We could already see this course would become a permanent discipling structure within the church, and there was no way the church planters could keep running it. We needed to pass on leadership, and quickly.

Lance saved the day. He stepped in to lead the second Disciples' School with the understanding this school would have Mongolian staff-in-training. Lance's spiritual gifts were a perfect match for this task. He carefully modeled every step for his helpers and after the conclusion of a school equal in impact to the first, he handed the administration of the Erdenet Disciples' School over to the leaders he'd trained. They immediately started a third school, and these have continued to produce committed believers and leaders having "grown up" into a full YWAM DTS in Erdenet.

Even as Lance was settling in to the rhythms of life on our church planting team in Erdenet, we were preparing to grow even larger. A Swedish baker, Mats Berbres was working his way through the visa maze to join our team. His arrival, along with that of Svetlana's baby, Reuben, would bring our team roster to 12: three Swedes, six Americans, and three Russians. Our four Mongolian "elders-to-be" could probably be counted, too, although we had separate leadership meetings. One of our principles of church planting was to keep the local leaders off the apostolic

team because this team is only temporary—like scaffolding—disman-
tled as the local, indigenous Church takes shape. The Mongolian leadership would stay while we were going to leave. Our team wanted
church members to identify with leaders from their own culture, not
ours. It was equally important that the "elders-to-be" continue to find
membership and identification with their own people, and not with our
church planting team.

During our training we had been warned that multi-cultural teams are
far more stressful than the homogenous variety. We were amazed to
discover we experienced no tension or conflict on our team. I have never
experienced this before or since, even with same-culture Americans.
God is bigger even than the mission strategy books.

*Clockwise from left: Lance, Brian, Louise, Ruslan holding Reuben,
Sveta, Mats, Magnus, Molly, Maria, Melody, Alice*

TWENTY-SEVEN

You Deserve a Break

Leaving Erdenet, even for three and a half months, proved bittersweet. The evening of Easter Sunday, we were escorted to the train station by the deacons, elders-to-be, our team and other church friends. We stood in a huge circle on the platform and worshipped, prayed, hugged, cried, received gifts, and confirmed our love for one another. Mongolians on the train just gaped. Those traveling that day had never before seen anything like the fellowship the Spirit brings. Melody and Molly sobbed, "I don't want to leave here!"

We barely managed to board the train after hugging our way through the crowd who had come to see us off. Lance was filming the event on our video camera which we were leaving behind in Erdenet. We planned, however, to take the tape home with us. Suddenly as the train jolted forward and started to roll along the platform, Lance realized he had absent-mindedly gotten caught up in the emotion of the moment as he watched the viewfinder. He also discovered the pressing crowd of those seeing us off had pushed him off the platform and into an enclosed grassy area nearby. A three-foot high metal fence and several meters stood between him and my outstretched arm as I leaned out of our open compartment window. In a harrowing scene, I watched him hurdle the fence, sprint alongside the train, all the while trying to eject the tape from the camcorder. Unfortunately, the scene ended up resembling Michelangelo's Creation of Man on the Sistine ceiling; my arm stretching from the window toward the cassette in Lance's outstretched fingers. As the train hurried me away, empty-handed, everyone on the platform, church member and heathen alike, breathed a corporate sigh of disappointment.

**Airport Goodbyes: Helen Richardson, Laura & Rick Leatherwood
and their children: Jessica, David, Daniel, and Jonathon**

In Ulaanbaatar the next day, we had a smaller but equally loving send-off at the airport. The Leatherwood family and Helen Richardson sang us off in style. All too soon we were bound for Beijing. We had one night at a luxury hotel where we had great fellowship with a friend who worked at the hotel and got us the room at her rate.

Our flight from Beijing to Tokyo had more in common with an amusement park rollercoaster than any flight we'd ever taken. Melody and Alice were both positively green. Molly had her headphones on while she shoveled airline food into her mouth. She exclaimed, "I love to fly!" to loud groans of protest from both sisters. After an hour of watching sumo wrestling on the overhead TV monitors in Tokyo-Narita airport (and buying tablets for motion sickness at prices usually reserved for illegal narcotics), we got in line to board our flight to Los Angeles. Alice, who had just turned four, asked if we could take a bus instead. "How about a boat?" asked Melody, displaying a greater grasp of geography. This leg of the trip was much smoother, but poor Melody never did fully get her "air legs."

My parents and Louise's sister's family met us at our gate in Los Angeles International Airport. We had a joyous reunion in the terminal (the lost pleasures of pre-9/11 air travel) before having to tear away to finish our journey to Seattle where Louise's mom and dad met us.

We had a wonderful and relaxing road trip down the west coast. A short stay in Salem, Oregon, at the YWAM base where we'd been trained, provided another exhilarating reunion and a chance to share what God had been doing. The audience at Community Night responded in a way that drove home how remarkable the events in Erdenet really were. Back on the road we enjoyed majestic redwoods, snacks, exploring the prison on Alcatraz Island, great restaurant meals. America, what a wonderful place!

People always ask if we've ever experienced reverse culture-shock. Louise always responds, "Hey, no problem. I grew up here." Alice, of course, didn't remember the United States at all. The sights and sounds overwhelmed her. Even Melody had some surprises. Upon seeing a garden hose in a pastor's yard, she called to her sisters: "Hey you guys. Look at this thing. It's neat." I noticed a complete lack of desire for things when wandering around Wal-Mart. None of us knew what to do with all that stuff at the supermarket. But, all in all, we fit right back in just fine.

We had a great visit home to California's Central Coast, but it was exceedingly full and often exhausting. We spoke in a different church every Sunday, and ate dinner and lunch (and sometimes breakfast) with different families almost every meal. Somehow, we also managed to cram in trips to Arizona and Los Angeles, a YWAM Conference on Frontier Mission in Seoul, Korea for me, dental and eye appointments for everyone, and corrective eye surgery so I could shed my glasses. In the cold Mongolian winters, they were perpetually frosted or steamed over. We had to bite our tongues when people would comment on how nice it was we were taking a break—Erdenet was far more restful.

When we had passed through the Northern California redwood forests, I had made a special point to meet and connect with a YWAM leader I had been corresponding with about church planting. Kevin and Laura Sutter were leading a ministry in Arcata, California called YWAM's Church Planting Coaches. Their mission was to "train and sustain YWAM's church planting teams among the unreached." While in Mongolia, I'd come across an article Kevin wrote that was a perfect mirror for the principles our team had adopted. I wrote him, and it turned out we'd been trained by the same guy, George Patterson. Anyway, when we drove through his area, Kevin met us for a meal. We forged a bond and vowed to find ways to collaborate in the future. Kevin also invited us to attend an upcoming conference the YWAM was holding in Korea. We had been feeling somewhat separated from YWAM because of our experiences with J.C.S. International during our first few months on the field. The J.C.S. director had equated leaving that umbrella organization with quitting YWAM (which had agreed be under the J.C.S. umbrella). Kevin assured us we were welcome, and indeed needed, at the Conference on Frontier Mission near Seoul.

Louise couldn't go, but I was able to join YWAM church planters and international leaders for a week of fellowship, relationship building, reports and strategy, in a large woodland conference center outside Korea's capital city. It turned out Magnus and Maria and other friends from Mongolia were also there, having come a week earlier for the global mission conference GCOWE. In fact, our Erdenet team was the star attraction of the entire conference.

My spirit was especially encouraged as I shared with YWAM's top leaders, including the new international president - Jim Stier. Jim took extra time to listen to me and assured me over and over we were still YWAMers, regardless of our status with J.C.S. I made new friends, caught up with old ones, talked about our post-Mongolia future, and cemented our relationships with our YWAM family. We were encouraged to consider ourselves to be working with YWAM on an international level and Mongolian Enterprises International within Mongolia. Everything was perfect after my mouth recovered from that first bite of kimchee (extremely hot pickled cabbage, served with every meal there).

Louise also received healing through a side trip she took on her own. One of our sending churches, the Twin-Cities Vineyard, was taking a group to speak and minister at the Airport Vineyard Christian Fellowship in Toronto, Canada. A move of God had been taking place there for a year or so that we had been hearing about in far off Mongolia. Louise was invited to join this group. She tried to tell them she felt like she had nothing to give. Her grief over Jed had turned into a numbness that was robbing life of all its flavors. "Everything still tastes like sawdust" she told me one night. She didn't feel like she could pray for others when she was so needy of a breakthrough for herself. The ministry team dismissed her objections. Here is her account:

"The second night we were there I prayed for many people, then one of my fellow teammates prayed for me. The presence of the Holy Spirit was so heavy I found it hard to stand. The Lord spoke to me and told me he had been saving all the tears I had cried in the last two years and he was going to pour them out on me in laughter. I laughed from the gut. Then I thought of specific times I had cried in Mongolia and I laughed. I remembered the frozen tears on the day we buried Jed and I laughed and laughed. I said to myself, "This is not funny," and I laughed again. The next day another team member prayed for me again and this time the Lord showed me He is raising up an army that will laugh in the face of the enemy. I remembered all the battles we fought last year and I laughed again. God had indeed turned my mourning into dancing, and his joy into my strength. The last night I was there I had the opportunity to share what the Lord had done for me in front of the whole assembly, numbering a few thousand people. They heard how God is moving in Mongolia. I am looking forward to getting back to Mongolia with the blessing stored in my earthen vessel."

During our time in the USA, we really missed our team back in Erdenet. The relationships had become so tight. They had become our family in such a real way. Knowing we were headed back made the absence easier, but we began to anticipate the pain of a future good-bye when we would leave Mongolia for good. When I saw them in Korea, Maria filled me in on how the church was doing in our absence. The mother congregation in Erdenet now had over 350 attending the big "celebration service." Our church had, the previous year, planted its first daughter church in the county seat 60 km. (37 mi.) from Erdenet. Now that daughter congregation in Bulgan had planted a daughter church in another, even more remote, town (a granddaughter church.).

This furlough was even more than we had hoped for. The Father had come through for us and fulfilled desires and needs we weren't even aware of ourselves. Of course, you can never see everyone you want to see, or do everything you'd like to do, but we tried. Somehow after extending our time in the States by an extra month, we felt refreshed and ready to return to Erdenet, even filled with a sense of anticipation. Louise and I wondered, "What will God do this year?" Our team had already begun to discuss the timetable for handing things over to Mongolians and leaving. Our tentative planned withdrawal was a year away. The goal was to hand the church over to fully trained Mongolian elders and disengage the team from the church at that time.

We arrived back in Mongolia on July 15th, 1995 after a three-day journey via Tokyo and Beijing. We were all looking forward to getting up to Erdenet and seeing our team and church again. I was also intrigued about beginning my new work at the copper mine soon after we settled back in.

Home is wherever you are. Bayaraa's family with my parents.

TWENTY-EIGHT

Back to our Little House on the Steppes

I woke up knowing the buses wouldn't come. Friday morning, on the last day of our church's summer program, the departure back to Erdenet was scheduled for noon, and I knew it wouldn't happen.

Other than this disturbing awareness, it was the perfect final day to our week-long stay at the holiday camp on the Selenge River, about two hours north of Erdenet. "Family Camp," as the believers called it, had been an ideal way for us to jump back into life in Mongolia, and we'd left Erdenet for camp soon after our return to town. The weather was perfect Mongolian high summer: middle to high eighties, light breezes, few bugs, distant clouds. Our morning meeting was the most powerful of the week. People were standing on the benches and dancing in worship. Ruslan gave an impassioned message about sharing the Good News, and people were healed. One older woman had walked in on crutches. When we prayed for her, she collapsed under the power of God. God told me: "I am going to use this woman as a vessel for my glory." When we helped her up there were no signs of any healing, except on her face. I doubted the word God had given me, so He repeated it. I whispered it to Magnus and let the service continue. Later, during testimonies, this woman came down, walking and dancing. God had healed her legs. The church went nuts. Then Magnus shared my word from God and she began to weep with joy. It turns out she had been one of the top national dancers under Communism. She had been part of a cultural exchange program with North Korea, chosen to bring Korean dance back to Mongolia. The mine in Erdenet had hired her and brought her family here to perform in the city's Culture Palace. Then an injury had ended her career, income, dancing, walking, everything. Her former patrons had subsequently abandoned her and she'd sunk into poverty and despair. She had met Jesus only weeks before and now she had new legs. She will now glorify the Khan of Khans as a vessel for His glory.

When this meeting finally ended (and no one wanted it to end), we found the buses hadn't arrived. When we sent someone out to call about this we discovered the man who had our money had never given it to the bus company, so they weren't sending any until they were paid. Maybe tomorrow, the leaders assured us.

I decided to walk to the nearest town to get a car for the three families with children: mine, Svetlana, Ruslan and their new baby Reuben, and a single mom with two kids. Lance came along to keep me company on this five-kilometer (3 mi.) march. It was a warm summer day and we took nothing with us. We stopped at gers along the way to ask directions, perhaps borrow horses, and eat. Feeding guests is mandatory at gers and we were fed tarag (yoghurt), currants, aaruul and urum (dried milk curds and clotted cream), and water with complete ecosystems included.

The silliest episode occurred as we were trudging down a track in a particularly deserted stretch of countryside. A Mongolian man in a dehl (the national dress) rode up on a horse. I asked him (in Mongolian) how far away the town of Hyalganat was, and the conversation went something like this:

Brian: Are you well? How far is Hyalganat?

Rider: (greets us and replies to my question in Russian)

Brian: We are not Russians.

Rider: (more unintelligible Russian)

Lance: We don't understand Russian.

Brian: We speak Mongolian.

Rider (finally switching to Mongolian): What's your name?

Brian: My name is Brian.

Lance: My name is Lance. How far is Hyalganat from here?

Rider: Five kilometers. I am looking for paint. Do you have any paint?

Brian: (in English) Did he say he is a painter?

Lance: (English) I think so. (Mongolian) What?

Rider: Do you have paint?

Brian: No, none.

Lance and I exchange puzzled looks—where would we have paint hidden?

Rider: Do you want any fish?

Lance: No, not right now.

Brian: We need a car or horses.

Rider: I don't have any.

Brian: Okay, bye.

Rider (riding off down the dirt track): Bye.

Brian: (in English) What was that all about?

Lance: I don't know. I guess this is a trade road.

Anyway, we finally arrived in the tiny lumber mill town and found that an acquaintance of mine with a car had just driven in for Hyalganat's twentieth anniversary celebration (festivities conveniently beginning that evening). The driver had been night watchman at the bank where I'd taught my English class the year before. I once arrived for class to find him with a torn shirt and the bank floor splattered with blood. Without a weapon, he had just violently put two bank robbers to flight. This guy was huge.

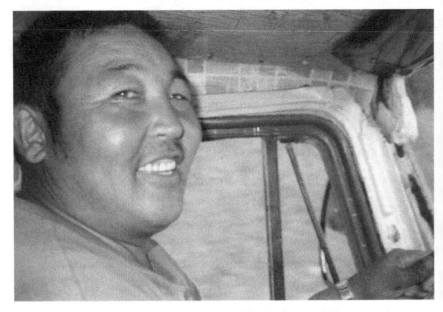

The Bank's Night Watchman

Thankfully he was one of the good guys. He agreed to drive us back to the camp and pick up the families needing to get back to the city. As we made our way down to Erdenet in this overcrowded "taxi" we saw the buses lumbering slowly along in the opposite direction to pick up the 150 people still stranded. By God's grace just after midnight everyone was home from camp.

Back in town, Magnus shared a conversation he had heard at camp through the thin cabin wall. Molly (six years) and Alice (almost four) had been quarreling in the next room. Magnus was trying to prepare a Bible lesson, but his ears tuned in to the following exchange:

Molly: "So what are you going to do about it?"
Alice: "I'm going to pray."
A long silence followed. Magnus pasted his ear to the wall.
Molly (breaking in): "Well, what did God say?"
Alice: "God told me to tell you to 'Shut up!'"
Magnus spent several minutes stifling laughter and gasping for breath.

We had barely returned to Erdenet City when the "Jesus Festival" was upon us. The impetus for this event had come from the outside. A team of Germans was coming to town for a month of mercy ministry among the poor and asked our church to help them culminate their outreach with a large evangelistic meeting. Their HELP International director was flying in from Germany to speak. We had been impressed with this group through shared ministry experiences and we happily agreed.

Meanwhile, the Lord was working a wonderful reconciliation between our team and the "American Ladies" who had been sent from Minnesota to Erdenet almost a year before to start up a church and Bible school. Relations between us and the "American Ladies" had not begun on a very good note. From the time they arrived and immediately tried to deceive us about their intentions, the two teams had viewed one another with distrust. But God was at work. Ruslan and Svetlana quietly worked on developing relationship with the other team. Eventually, they reported to our team that the "American Ladies" wanted to have us over for dinner and make things right. They were very lonely and had undergone huge amounts of culture shock. Mongolia was working its magic—no . . . the Holy Spirit was working at bringing unity to God's people, using Mongolia as His tool. I am not sure whether Ruslan was confused or brilliant, but it was clear when our entire team showed up at the ladies' apartment that they hadn't been aware of the invitation they'd issued us! They scrambled to find food while we glared at Ruslan. Yet, somehow a meal was served, hearts were bared, and repentance and forgiveness flowed from both sides. As real relationship grew between the two teams of missionaries, we all agreed it was imperative the two churches work together and without competition in reaching our city. As we talked, we learned their pastor from Minneapolis was leading an outreach team of Americans in the same week of the German meetings. This town wasn't big enough for the both of them. Or was it...?

God impressed all of us that His Name would be most glorified by a joint effort. A huge two-day outdoor festival was planned; featuring the German leader teaching one day, and the American woman pastor teaching the next. Before and after would be three days of teaching in indoor venues. We let the Germans and Americans know, and they agreed to cooperate. The Mongolian church leaders went to work on the permit process.

This part was hideous. To use any outdoor venue meant getting permission from just about every official in town, and 90% of them were openly hostile to Christians. A lot of prayer and daily visits finally secured us the Naadam Stadium—a venue nearly sacred due to the cultural importance attached to the summer Naadam festival. We rejoiced until the stadium boss told us we couldn't touch the grass. The stadium was completely covered in grass. So we started over...

At last we got a green light to use the soccer stadium, which had more seating and was located right behind the Sports Palace in the center of the city. A day before the Festival we found out the copper mining company (my employer) owned this field. We had neglected to secure their permission. They were furious. Neither the police nor city hall had mentioned this as they gave their permits. With great difficulty we resolved this new roadblock. The morning of the festival, the American team arrived in town.... without police permission to be there. Magnus told them that without this permit they couldn't lead in any outdoor meetings, as this would endanger the believers with the already fuming police, who thought our church invited "all these foreigners" to town.

Their pastor assured Magnus she could get the police to permit them to minister because she'd forged a relationship with them last summer. She went to the police and they informed her that her team had to leave town on the evening train. They were welcome to return once they had been issued travel permits. This woman had a problem with her temper and exploded: "You can arrest me, but the Holy Spirit has sent me to Erdenet, and I'm not going anywhere!" The police responded by promptly canceling the Festival, scheduled to begin in three hours.

Our leaders went again to the police and finally convinced them these Americans were not from our church, had not been invited by us, would not be in the festival, and were on their own. The police finally grudgingly allowed the festival, but with no foreign involvement whatsoever.

So, an hour before the Festival began, the whole thing fell onto our church, including all the speaking. The Germans were out and so were the Americans. Police, citing safety concerns, were swarming the stadium to make sure no foreigner even left the stands. The Mongolian believers were scared but determined to pull it off. The German evangelist, Walter Heidenreich, was fantastic. He laid hands on Zorigoo, our most gifted evangelist and leader of our daughter church in Bulgan, and asked God to pass on his anointing to Zorigoo. Walter then declared, "This is what I came here to see—Mongolians being raised up into ministry."

Mongolian Evangelists

The worship band arrived, all dressed in dehls for the first time. We were so excited to see this decision the Spirit had helped them to make. Early on we had urged traditional dress on the leaders and they had reacted strongly against the suggestion. "The dehl is for bumpkins. I'd look like my grandmother!" Now they had "heard from God" to have their moms and grandmothers make dehls for them. There was a palpable sense of honoring their elders and their culture that no one had seen before in these city kids. Worship was wonderful and the stands quickly filled with 1700 Mongolians. This was the largest Christian meeting in the history of our church and maybe of the church in Mongolia. The drama team performed. And when Zorigoo preached the Gospel over half the crowd responded and received prayer.

The second day went much the same, with about 1500 attending. This was exactly what God had been planning all along. We wouldn't have thought to plan such a huge event if these foreign short-term teams and speakers hadn't prompted us. Then God, in His sovereignty, gave the whole meeting to the Mongolian believers and the results were spectacular. He "tricked" us into organizing this whole thing so He could give it to His church.

The Mongolian believers experienced a terrific surge of faith, confidence, and release through this event. Even the teams from the West were excited by the results of the police department's prohibition. The church made a huge leap forward, ready now to stand without foreign support. The police themselves were impressed by how culturally correct this event was. The Chief of Police called our elders-to-be in and told them he was impressed with the Christians and could see why many Mongolians were now "turning to this way." He also marveled there had been no drunken brawls during the events—something he declared to be impossible in Mongolia. He told them our church could do anything it desired in Erdenet from then on.

Meanwhile, our family was still getting settled back in again after our furlough. There was plenty to do in the church. Seventeen of our more committed leaders had left for Bible School in Siberia the same day we had arrived back from America. I was shocked the decision had been to send them away for training when our Disciples' School was well equipped to train leaders right in the context of the church. "Train leaders locally" was one of our team's New Testament church planting

Off to study in Siberia!

principles. Not only does it keep the leaders grounded in what God is doing among their people, but it facilitates modeling from the church planters to the emerging leaders. Disciples learn ministry skills best by watching and imitating a discipler. It was going to be hard to model things for these disciples in Siberia. Magnus told me those going felt like they had heard clearly from God about the Bible School opportunity, so there really was no point in second guessing things as their train headed north. There was much to do in seeing new folks raised up to replace these folks in the ministries left leaderless. At home, we were restarting our Home School. I was teaching Melody fourth grade, and Louise taught Molly second. Alice even had a few preschool books this year. We were beginning production on our new cottage food industry—making our own cheese and jerky with supplies brought back from the States. Keeping a varied, healthy and appetizing diet in Erdenet kept us hopping.

We had returned to find our flat under a cloud of bureaucratic doubt, again. Sukhbat, our nemesis at the government housing office, always on the prowl for bribes, grabbed our house book (or deed), and refused to give it back to anyone but the original leaseholder, a nomadic shepherd who was not to be found. These constant struggles were wearing us out—spiritually and physically. Our new visas were also being contested in Ulaanbaatar, and we were, for a time, "illegal aliens." My new employer, the "Erdenet Concern" copper mine, assured us this would shortly be resolved, but this situation weighed on us. We did get encouraged when Magnus, Maria, and Lance were granted "miracle visas" that had seemed impossible just a month before.

TWENTY-NINE

Mongols Follow the Khan of Khans

As summer drew to a close, I found my time being filled with curriculum development for our second "Disciples' School" class starting September 25th. Twenty-two had graduated from the first class, and the conferring of diplomas at Sunday's celebration service had excitement at a fever pitch. This time around we had 40 applications for the 30 slots. We were still praying over the applications at our weekly team meeting on September 21, the day after we'd all celebrated Melody's tenth birthday. We finished the meeting to discover snow had covered the city in a thick white blanket while we feasted and discussed the School of Discipleship applications. What a shock. It seemed way too early in the year for winter to start. The radiators hooked to centrally supplied city heating were still not working properly, but we had purchased two electric heaters to supplement them. Even if our power bills went sky high, as Mongolian friends grimly warned us, we were not going to spend another six months shivering inside our home.

We had to meet again to discuss other Disciples' School issues. Student feedback had prompted changes. This class was to be shorter in duration (three months instead of six) and more intensive (an extra early morning session every week). At the students' urging we kept classes in the very early morning, and resolved to be even tougher about the rules and fees and attendance. So, a leaner, meaner, Disciples' School was ready to turn out more solid disciples of Jesus. The leadership was in Lance's capable hands this time, much to the relief of Magnus and me.

He directed while training two alumni from the first class to take over for the next one.

Magnus and I designed a curriculum around these subjects: Quiet time and Hearing God; New and Old Testament Surveys; Witnessing & Discipling Others; Intercession & Spiritual Warfare; Spiritual Gifts Inventory*; Relationships & Forgiveness; Signs and Wonders; Ministry to the Poor & Oppressed; Inductive Bible Study*; Biblical Basis of Missions*; Church History*; and House Church Methods & Leadership. Our team and Erdenet church leaders taught every week. Guest instructors from Ulaanbaatar filled in the few gaps. I thoroughly enjoyed teaching four of the weeks. (*subjects I taught)

At the same time, we discovered Erdenet was going to be treated to two completely different paradigms for training up leaders. The three lady missionaries from Minneapolis informed us that their Bible school would open soon. This was fine with us and we encouraged them in their efforts. Both teams had continued to cooperate with the Spirit in His work of reconciliation. They began to solicit our counsel about their plans and strategy for the Bible School. We were diligently trying to give honest advice without giving offense.

In this, the Lord chose to use Louise and me. Magnus had advised the American ladies that their curriculum looked great, except for the format which was too academic for the young Mongolian Church. He also warned them their plan to pay their students financial incentives to attend classes had already been tried in Ulaanbaatar. It had failed miserably to produce sound disciples and succeeded in causing trouble and divisions.

There are about a million sound historical, cultural, missiological, psychological, and spiritual reasons to avoid paying national believers to obey Jesus Christ, but to enumerate them goes beyond the scope of my story. For now, let me just say many missionaries have learned this through much blood, sweat, tears, and failure. In any case, the ladies didn't really hear Magnus' warnings due to a curious cultural difference between Americans and Swedes. My countrymen (and I include myself in this generalization) are used to a fairly direct communication style (some would even say blunt and obnoxious), whereas most Swedish folk tend to understate and hint in an effort to be diplomatic. Americans, as a result, sometimes miss the fact that they have just been corrected by Swedes. This phenomenon is even more pronounced when the ultra-blunt Mongolians are on the receiving end of rebukes.

Several days after Magnus had spoken with them, the ladies were excitedly sharing how they had received the funds from their home church to pay all their Bible students. I felt the Spirit of God prompting me to share my concerns with them, American to American. I took their team leader to a restaurant and told her clearly the pitfalls in their path. I was stunned by her positive reaction. She was genuinely grateful. She asked me for books that backed up my assertions so she could effectively communicate the change in plans to her home pastor. By the next day, all three were voraciously reading the missions books I'd supplied. Our two teams met, and the ladies announced their unanimous decision not to pay students. They still needed to convince the "powers-that-be" at home, whose strategy this was in the first place, but they said they were prepared to obey God rather than man if it came to that. God's incredible goodness continued to amaze and confound us all.

This wasn't the first time I'd had to provide on-the-job training for under-trained American missionaries. I began to understand that this was one reason why the Lord sent a mission educator all the way to Mongolia. All the mistakes that can be made already have been made in the last two centuries, and I was glad to use my knowledge of mission history to help prevent the same mistakes being repeated on the Mongolians.

Bayaraa, the original believer who moved to Erdenet with the Alphonces to plant the church, and an elder-to-be, had been studying English at the Foreign Language Institute. I had been teaching classes there along with Magnus and Maria until we had gone on furlough. Lance had taken my post there in our absence. Since my return, I had been idle as far as secular work, since our visas had been contested. After I signed a new contract with the mine, the ministry of Labor approved the visas. However, there remained the issue of an outstanding fine for the month and a half we were "illegal aliens." It took another couple of weeks for the mine to decide they were responsible for this fine. Until they paid the fine, we could not receive the police residence permits and, therefore, could not work. It was trying, and yet, God redeemed the time. Bayaraa came to our apartment with several of her classmates, all former students of mine, and presented a plan. All of these young women had come to faith through Bayaraa's witnessing and wanted to grow in their walk with the Lord. In fact she had led 25 students to faith in Christ. No wonder her full name, Erdenbayar, translates to "Joyful Treasure." However, their class load made regular involvement in Jesus' Assembly's house churches difficult. Bayaraa had suggested they form an English students' house church and conduct it entirely in English. This way they could be discipled and work on improving their English at the same time. All the students were already comfortable with me since I had been their teacher in the spring semester. I thought it sounded like a terrific idea and I readily agreed to lead the "club." We dubbed our gathering: FACES for 'Fellowship and Christian English Study.' We began meeting at our house to study together a discipleship book in English: How Christians Grow. It was thrilling to see these young women grow up in their new-found faith. A decade later I had several Christian leaders approach me and remind me they had been members of our FACES club.

FACES—our English language house church
Bolortuya (Chap. 18) on left and Bayaraa, front middle in black coat

During this time, we were struggling to get our residence permits and visa issues settled, our apartment situation had gone critical, and then miraculously it was resolved. It had to be the prayers of our supporters! The problem was we had never been the true owners of the flat we had attempted to purchase in Erdenet. The best we could do was to buy the "right to rent." The building and all the apartments within were owned by the State. Now we were being told even what we had bought was only as good as the word of the seller, an old herdsman who had been awarded use of the flat by the government. He had sold it to us because with 12 children and flocks an apartment in the city was of no earthly use to his family. Cash, however, was desirable. The old herdsman was honorable, but he'd moved far off with his flocks, and therein laid our peril. His "prodigal" son tried to use his father's absence to seize our home and evict us. He bribed Sukhbat, the corrupt head of the Housing Department, and was given an official eviction notice to serve us. This same woman had a week earlier demanded to see our "deed" and had failed to return it. We suspected that our old enemy was up to something nefarious.

The herdsman's son came to the door waving this official paper and yelling at Louise when I was out. When I returned, she told me; we asked advice of our Mongolian friends who'd helped with the original purchase. They said the best thing to do was to physically snatch the document away from him. The power to evict was not in the decision — it was actually in the stamped document itself. Since he'd obtained it through an expensive bribe, they reasoned that he wouldn't be able to replace it easily. When he came back, I was ready for him. I did not let on I could understand his speech and acted puzzled by what the paper was all about. I took it to read it, and before he stepped in through our door, I pushed it shut and slammed the bolt home. He continued to bang on our metal door for some time, but I just shouted he should bring the police if he had legitimate business with me. I had been assured the last thing he wanted was more hands greedy for bribes involved in this.

This was a very discouraging and low time for us. In our imaginations the corrupt housing ministry lady had grown to become an evil Housing Tsarina. Our documents were still on her desk! It was only a matter of time before Sukhbat made a move to evict us for another "buyer" willing to grease her palms. After talking and praying with our team, we decided standing firm couldn't really hurt us. Miraculously, our documents were returned without comment a few days later. We never saw or heard from Sukhbat again.

The herdsman's son continued to come by and harass us periodically. Once he even brought his wife and pointed out our furnishings saying, in our hearing, "This will all be ours soon." Eventually, he made the mistake of coming by when a extremely tall male Mongolian friend was visiting us. Our friend tore into him verbally with proof of his double-dealing and threatened him with exposure to the authorities. The young man crumpled like a punctured sub at the bottom of the Pacific trench. By the end of September, the whole plot had completely disappeared, our residence permits were granted, and we felt secure. I started work at the copper mine the first week of October.

The tallest Mongol in the world lived right upstairs from us. A believer, Shavraa attended Jesus' Assembly when he wasn't off playing basketball. He later played for the Harlem Globetrotters.

THIRTY

Heading into the Home Stretch

October had flown by and it was November second, Jedidiah's birthday. Our team gathered around and helped us commemorate that day of joy just a year before and the pain that inevitably followed. It was a year since the attack had hit us like a tsunami. The robust growth and health of the church was in marked contrast to its struggles of the previous November and December when even survival looked unlikely. When Christmas came Louise sent the following letter to our friends and supporters:

Christmas is upon us already. I had hoped it would never come again, but there is no stopping time, and that's as it should be. This Christmas will be filled with bittersweet memories for us. As most of you know, a year ago our baby son Jedidiah went home to live with Jesus. I think of him now and I wonder what he would have been like now. He would have been 13 months old. Would he be walking, as all his sisters were at this age? How many words would he know? What color hair would he have? Melody and Molly were almost completely bald at this age. What color eyes does he have? Do I finally have a child with brown eyes like mine? I will not know these questions until I reach the Promised Land.

I am not going to tell you this has been an easy year and I have always felt the Lord's loving hands and trusted His goodness. This would be a lie. Grief is a strange thing. There have been days when I have been angry at God, angry at Jed, angry at the world. There have been days when I have wished it had been me and not him—days when the anguish and sorrow seem so deep I was sure I would drown. There have also been days where I have known the Lord's presence stronger than ever before in my life—days where I have felt comforted by the Lord himself; others where He used you to comfort me.

There are still so many unanswered questions—questions I will not get answers to in my lifetime. But the one thing I can say without reservation is that I know when I get to heaven Jed will be there to greet me with Jesus. This is, after all, the goal we have as parents, that our children will make it to heaven. Well, I have one down—three to go.

Christmas does not seem a time to look at hard realities and yet, isn't that why Jesus came to earth in the first place? His death means life to me. I understand this giving of an only son far better than ever before. I fear Christmas will always be a difficult time for me because of the memories it will stir up. Please pray for us now, even though we know with absolute certainty Jed is safe with Jesus, we still hurt, and the wound his death caused still needs to heal. Our continuing need to talk about something that makes others so uncomfortable helps us to relate with the lepers in the Bible. I know it has been a year, and so I should be over this, but I will carry a tiny bit of this sorrow with me for the rest of my life until I hold my son in heaven.

The good news we have for you is that the birth of our Savior is being celebrated all over Mongolia this Christmas. That is something that, up until a few years ago, had never happened here since the time of Creation. This is what our desire was in obeying our call to come here three years ago. In the small view, this knowledge doesn't ease our pain of loss at all, but, in the big picture, it makes all the difference.

Christmas festivities for the Hogan family were a pale shadow of Christmases past. Louise and I could barely summon the inner resources to prepare for the joyful traditions and practices our daughters expected. We, ourselves, certainly didn't feel like celebrating. This holiday would never be the same for us. Still, the sheer busyness kept us going somehow. We took part in the huge Christmas Dinner the church put on in a rented hall a few days before Christmas. So many people showed up that the tight conditions would have been a trial for anyone with even slight claustrophobia. The collective exhalations of the revelers condensed on the cold concrete walls and windows and ran in growing rivulets down onto the floor. The Mongolians loved the dinner party, and we enjoyed the walk home in the bitter cold, but fresh night air.

Our team really came through for us and picked up the slack in our holiday cheer. Once the big day arrived, they all came over, and we spent the day together, opening gifts and eating. The church's Christmas Service was hard for us. The year before, we'd talked of having Jed play a live baby Jesus in the Nativity drama, and seeing a doll in the manger brought fresh tears to Louise. Afterwards, we all returned to our apartment. Lance and the Swedes put together the most fantastic international feast with goose and pies and some Swedish delicacies that were new to us. One potato dish was called Jansson's Temptation and involved anchovies. It was healing to laugh, exchange gifts and customs, and just play with these folks who'd become such dear and close friends to us.

A traditional Swedish Santa Lucia in Mongolia (Alphonces & Mats)

Lance Reinhart, Louise, and I brought in the new year, 1996, in the same way we had welcomed the previous two—we aimed the large green bottle of Russian champagne at the powdery whitewashed ceiling of our Soviet-era kitchen—and let 'er rip. We'd discovered by accident in an identical kitchen in Ulaanbaatar in the first moments of '94 that the cork made a nice mark in the paint. It had become a tradition for the three of us to celebrate together and "mark the ceiling." In our kitchen in Erdenet, a small dated piece of masking tape marked the new blemish and joined a partner that proudly marked the place the 1995 New Year's cork had hit. We remembered how that celebration had been a brief spark of joy in the dark days following Jed's death—an act of defiance against Housing Tsarinas and the spiritual forces arrayed against us and our own grief-stricken hearts and minds. This year was different.

We spoke of the changes and growth we'd witnessed over the past year. Lance had joined our team in March, and his gifts in discipling the believers to rapidly take up any ministry he started, had made him an incredible asset. Due to Lance's efforts, our School of Discipleship was running along great—completely in Mongolian hands. Our excitement grew as we shared together all of the pieces each had added. It had been becoming more and more obvious for several months that the end was in sight.

As a team we'd taken stock earlier that week, and had realized with pleasure that our days in Mongolia were numbered. Throughout our time together as a team, we had placed a real priority on evaluation. We knew if we didn't regularly evaluate our activities in light of our end goal, we would never reach that goal. We needed constantly to track our progress. Often this forced us to drop activities which, as good as they were, didn't bring us closer to our goal. During a team meeting in the last week of December we were excited to hear several accounts of how Erdenet's civic leadership was pleased with the church and its impact on the city. They particularly commented on the Mongolian character of the church. One leader declared he had opposed the church when he thought it was a foreign import, but "now that I see it is completely Mongolian I am very happy to have Jesus' Assembly here in Erdenet." We also noted how older people continued to respond to the Good

News, and how the church movement had just about matched the age and gender demographics of the city. This was a huge change from the first year and a half when we had been essentially an all-girl youth group. Most exciting was the realization that the Mongolian leaders were doing virtually everything for themselves. The only activities still in foreign hands were a couple of Bible Studies, the literature production, and the training of the elders-to-be.

Our direct apostolic role was drawing to a close at an ever accelerating pace. We began to dream that maybe by summer it would be time to dismantle the scaffolding and allow God's glorious construction to stand on its own. It was almost electric in that small kitchen as we realized our prayers, dreams and hopes were actually coming to pass. We had no idea how far those hopes, dreams, and prayers would be surpassed.

Louise and I admitted to Lance we had begun sending out feelers to YWAM operating locations around the world to see if they had a place for us to pursue what we sensed God wanted to do next with our family. He had been giving us a desire to train others in what we had learned and experienced in the task of starting movements of multiplying churches among unreached peoples. It was thrilling to think of the impact of dozens and even hundreds of teams out doing this on the frontiers.

Lance began to open up as well. He had discovered a desire to return to Oregon and complete his college education. He'd seen how a business or economics degree could open doors in Mongolia and elsewhere, at the same time equipping him to reach out through micro-enterprise and other "business as mission" ventures. We all chuckled as we remembered how during our training in Salem, Oregon, we'd taken a test that identified Lance's main motivational gifting as money and finance. That test had proved uncannily accurate for each of us. Louise had come out with "Bring to Completion" as her top motivation, and I had gotten "Be Key, Be Central." Both of these described our roles on the team to a tee. We even joked, with some seriousness, that Louise's prayers for God to allow us to leave Mongolia, the hardest place we'd ever been, had probably caused God to advance the timetable for our team's finishing. He certainly knew He had created in Louise a servant who would never leave a task unfinished.

Magnus and Maria had been thinking ahead. Even after the churches didn't need our oversight and leadership, they still wouldn't have the ability to train Mongolian believers as cross-cultural missionaries. This task would still need to be done by outsiders, at least until some Mongolians got the experience and training to lead the missionary training by themselves. The Alphonces had begun to pray about offering that ministry to the Mongolian leadership who, we felt certain, would eagerly accept. The church had been a hotbed of mission fervor for a long time.

Since Mats Berbres, our rather tall and round Swedish baker, had basically "gone native" from the day he arrived, we all assumed he would go on living in Erdenet and probably end up marrying one of the incredibly lovely and amazingly competent local believers. Mats had arrived the previous summer and immediately commissioned a full traditional Mongolian outfit, complete with historic accessories. He had out-Mongoled Mongolians, and the local lads had been stung into emulating his style. He actually started a revival craze for the hurem, a colorful brocaded jacket that had slipped into fashion history and museum cases until Mats had one tailor-made. Suddenly, it seemed every guy in Erdenet from 18 to 25 was wearing a brand-new hurem.

Svetlana and Ruslan had a baby boy to contend with and another on the way. With all the turmoil back home in Russia, life in Erdenet and their leadership in the Russian congregation had more to offer their young family than a return to Siberia. We all figured they would stay on for several years and continue to work with the Russian population of Erdenet. Magnus and I had both been trying to train Ruslan and Sveta in missions, a subject their Bible School had covered too lightly, but neither of us had been able to devote the time we felt we should have to this task.

MATS: Mongol-Acting Toast Salesman

We ended up talking till far on into the wee hours with our friend and partner, Lance, and for the first year since we'd begun doing New Year's together, when we were finished, Lance left and walked home. Always before he'd had to spend the night, either because he had missed the last bus, or because his apartment was on the other end of Ulaanbaatar, and we laughed about this new innovation—breakfast on January first without Lance—and tried to lure him with toast, his favorite. It was so good finally having him on the team, and even though it had taken a couple years, God's timing was perfect.

Three weeks later we were caught up in the celebration of a third birthday. The third is a very special birthday observance in Mongolia. The male child receives his first haircut on that day, and the shearing is performed by all the guests at his party. Typically, the little boy goes around the room with a bag and a pair of scissors. Each person cuts off a lock of beautiful soft virgin jet-black baby hair and drops the lock and some paper money into the bag. These little guys make money like nobody's business.

The birthday we were celebrating was not for a little Mongolian boy, however. We were gathered to honor a precious and beautiful three-year-old Mongolian girl. And this little lady was already betrothed at her tender age. Jesus' Assembly in Erdenet, Jesus' bride, was three years old. Her growth and development had outstripped everyone's expectations and she was almost ready for an independent journey following her Bridegroom.

The church leadership had arranged to hire the local movie theater for the birthday bash. That wasn't unusual. Our large celebration gatherings were pretty much forced into being in the cinema or the Women's Palace discothèque. On rare occasions the copper mine would allow us to rent "Gornyeck," the Culture Palace, which at 750 seats had the largest capacity in the city. When the day arrived, 350 Mongolians filled the theater to capacity. It was actually a shock to see the vivid evidence of growth right before our eyes. In a church that gathered in homes all over the city and beyond, we easily lost track of the actual numbers of those coming to Christ. What was even more exciting to me was the obvious fact that the makeup of the crowd was indistinguishable from the population on the streets outside the theater. We had been a "youth church," even a "teen girls club," for so long it sent a thrill up my spine to note there was no particular subset of society dominating our gatherings anymore. There were old men and women (some ancient), children and babies, and everything in between. We had guys and girls, sportsmen and handicapped people, country folk wearing dehls and city dwellers in suits, rich mine workers and poor shepherds, Russians from our Russian church, even a deaf congregation with sign language interpreters. Jesus had infiltrated every part of Erdenet society. This was a real and visible answer to many prayers and pleadings.

Since we had finally arrived at a point where the church's need for our involvement was shrinking, it was easier to focus on the more mundane (and normal) aspects of life in Mongolia. My job at the "Erdenet Concern" copper mine was, in turns, challenging, dull, and frustrating. I had to figure out how to manage huge and complex purchases of copper ore and its transport by train as far as the Chinese border. I had to deal with my sole customer (Caterpillar Inc.), the assay firm providing ore analysis, the train freight company, the smelters in China, and the Chinese customs and border folks. Between purchases, things would get slow, making the hours crawl by. I would try to make myself useful in other ways, like fixing computers and teaching English to mine executives, but I was often bored. I had repeatedly asked for additional clients, thinking it odd I was entrusted with only a single customer. Eventually the word trickled back down to me that one of the top bosses was refusing to let me have any more contracts because I was a security risk. He thought I worked for the C.I.A. When I collapsed in gales of laughter at this, my Mongolian associate hastened to add that the bigwig was not sure I was spying for the Americans: "You might be an agent of the Vatican." Well, at least this cleared up the mystery. I was glad I had insisted on only working half-time. I could use the free hours to put together some Mongolian tracts on the differences between Mormonism and a Biblical faith. The Mormons had recently posted four additional young missionaries to our city, bringing their total to six. Since they tended to seek out believers over regular pagans, we needed to teach God's people about the falsehoods the young Mormon "Elders" were concealing from them. Their classic lead-in was "We believe the same as Brian and Magnus, but God has shown us just a little bit more." The teaching we had done when they first arrived in November 1994 and these tracts to help new folks coming in seemed to do the trick. We didn't lose anyone to this cult group. The members they were able to gather were mostly from the Foreign Language Institute and were all hoping for trips to Utah.

Louise began teaching English to a group of Russian ladies who were members of the Russian daughter church we had planted. These women had so much fun in these classes, I was envious. They loved Louise and gave her many precious gifts to show their appreciation. Louise was also doing private lessons in the home of a brilliant wheelchair bound Mongolian girl. Bayanaa had become a part of the church, and Louise enjoyed her time with this sharp girl whose English was already beyond that of most our Mongolian friends. Bayanaa's home life was very difficult and abusive, and there was a lot of hurt she and Louise prayed their way through. The three Peace Corps volunteers who were assigned to

Erdenet, and another two that were 60 kilometers west of us, out in Bulgan, were others who received Louise's love and friendship. We made lasting friendships with Carleen in Erdenet and Jerel in Bulgan. Jerel would stay with us and hang out whenever he came through our city, and Carleen's long walks in the hills with Louise were a lifeline for Louise as she grieved for Jed, and moved Carleen toward a lifelong relationship with Jesus. These activities and relationships, along with the fun with our girls, were the high points in Louise's week, because the running of a household in Mongolia is filled with things that can only be described as drudgery. She wrote to a friend: "Convenience here means the yak is already dead before you buy it for food."

Louise and I continued to home school using a literature-based Sonlight Curriculum that was developed by missionaries for missionaries. We loved it, and the material was so engaging that Louise and I looked forward to most of the classes as much as the girls did. Alice could sit in and soak up much of what was going on since there was a good deal of read-aloud involved. With the temperatures so bitterly cold outside, the girls did a lot of indoor imaginative play. However, Melody often went over to the houses of Mongolian friends as well as having them over to play. Even Alice (almost five) started to get groups of little girls coming to the door and asking to play with her. All three girls were happy and healthy, and each of them brought us joy in such completely different ways. The unique personality God puts into each child is another reason it makes sense to speak of "daughter churches."

Melody, Alice and Molly at Jed's gravesite

THIRTY-ONE

A Brand-New Thing

Indigenous: original to the country, not introduced; native, not foreign.

Indigenous Church: "A congregation of believers who live out their lives, including their Christian activity, in the patterns of the local society, and for whom any transformation of that society comes through the guidance of the Holy Spirit and the principles of Scripture."   —William Smalley in "Cultural Implications of an Indigenous Church"

Jesus' Assembly drama team in open-air evangelism.

Our efforts to leave behind all the non-essential elements and cultural "barnacles" that have affixed themselves to our ideas of "church" over the past 17 centuries bore fruit in Erdenet. We had consciously "lightened the package" and simplified church as we carried it into this new culture. We were convinced God wanted to do a new thing here not simply clone the American or European church that sent us. As we observed Jesus' Assembly we saw evidence of a truly indigenous movement emerging.

The basic gathering for every believer was the home church—a small group of 15 or fewer disciples that met every week in an apartment living room, a ger (the felt tents), army barracks, a one-room frame house outside the city limits, or anywhere that served the purpose. These groups would interact with God's Word, pray for each other, reach out in practical ways to the lost, share food and the Lord's Supper together, and share their lives with one another. Communion was done with whatever elements were readily available, often undaa (generic carbonated beverage) or tsai (tea, usually a salty milky broth) and boortsog (hard fried dough). As the groups grew, and they did grow, they would multiply to keep the numbers in each group small and fellowship intimate. House group leaders mentored others to take on the new groups as they were birthed. Groups visited other areas and birthed new house churches in other communities, whether a single house church or a whole cluster of them. Much depended on the population density. One daughter church was started with only three families living isolated in a wide spot on the road north of Erdenet. These families were in charge of maintaining a pump station that supplied water from the Selenge River to the city and mine. When a group of believers on an outing broke down there, a church was born. They called the church "Pump Station Number Four."

The house churches in Erdenet and those in our daughter church of Bulgan would gather periodically for large, city-wide "Celebration Meetings." Often groups from outlying areas would manage to join us. The format of these big gatherings, which took place on Sundays, was decidedly different from any of the missionary team's sending churches. These gatherings met in a rented hall or theater, sang indigenous Mongolian music led by the worship team, offered testimonies from those recently come to Christ or recently healed, dramas created and performed by the church's drama team, performed praise dances in the traditional style, shared items of interest to newcomers and the whole church, learned new songs, shared from the Word, and prayed for those needing healing or a touch from God. Those who shared often dressed in the traditional Mongolian dehl and the worship and dance teams had matching costumes in the traditional style. This was all their idea, and we gave no input. The dramas in particular were a powerful element of the Celebration meeting, and the curious would almost always respond to Jesus through the dramas more than any other single part of the meeting. The forms of worship and greeting newcomers were distinctively Mongolian. Not only were the songs and music written by church members, but they began using Mongolian instruments like the Morin huur (horse-head fiddle) and yatga (harp) on occasion. These big meetings would last from two and a half to three hours, sometimes more. The time was determined by how much the leaders had planned on including, rather than on how long we had rented the building. This caused the foreigners no end of discomfort, as sometimes the next group would be waiting outside for us to vacate, but all the Mongolians, those worshipping and those waiting, seemed to take it in stride. When we would urge the leaders to tie things up, they would reply by listing things still coming: "Ganaa has a new song to teach, and old Batsook has a great testimony of a vision he had last week while herding his sheep." When we would give up and go out front to apologize to the group waiting to use the building, they would respond, "They are not finished yet, are they? No, well, no problem. We can wait." In Mongolia, an event isn't over until it is over. They are what sociologists call an "event-oriented culture" while all of us on the church planting team were from strongly "time-oriented cultures."

When I train new church planters headed for unreached people groups, I tell them that if they are successful, the churches that result will make the church planters uncomfortable. If a church takes on an indigenous character, then it will be outside the comfort zone of the apostolic messengers. It will seem weird to the missionaries. Jesus' Assembly and our daughter churches certainly passed this test. In the midst of our discomfort, we were wild with joy that our "children" had an indigenous Mongolian character that was unique and different from anything any of us had known before. In fact, it was new to the world as well. Jesus had birthed a whole new expression of His eternally living Body.

Morin khuur - traditional horse-head fiddle

Celebration Meeting

THIRTY-TWO

Working Ourselves Out

Evidence that the church in Erdenet was ready to stand on its own in Christ was piling up. It had become routine for our team to ask the Mongolian leaders what they felt should be done about a situation and marvel at the answers they came back with after seeking God's guidance. We had been actively working ourselves out of a job, identifying, one by one, the ministries still relying on one of us. Our goal was to hand over each to a Mongolian disciple, and this began to happen with lightning speed.

One glorious spring day when the temperature, while still south of freezing, had managed to allow ice-melt puddles to form on the black surface of the street, I was finally able to shed my parka and move around in a tee-shirt. Later, our spirits were high as we gathered for our team meeting and realized something else had changed. I was doing my usual task of asking everybody what they had done with the church over the previous week. I would then follow up with a question as to what Mongolian leader they thought was ready to inherit that ministry. Well, one week late in February or early in March of 1996, I came up empty. Beyond the storytelling Magnus and I were doing from the Old Testament, no one on our church planting team had done anything that week. Everything had been handed over. Without any of us realizing, we had worked ourselves into obsolescence. The Mongolian believers were doing everything; we were doing nothing. And no one had even noticed! It felt like the moment that comes when you are teaching a child to ride a bike and they start pedaling along a little faster than you can run and you let go. You see them riding unassisted, and they don't even

know it yet. You just stop, panting, and enjoy the sight of glorious un-
selfconscious freedom. You have stopped being a participant and become, in an instant, a joyous spectator.

We met with the five elders-to-be and shared our discovery with them.
Predictably they protested that they needed us very much. We recounted to them all the evidence to the contrary. They insisted we were
still necessary for so many things. We gently challenged them to name
something. They couldn't come up with anything we were doing. We
helped them understand loving us was not the same as needing us, and
there was nothing disloyal about moving into spiritual adulthood as a
church. We would remain partners with them and would continue to
help, but only at the request of the Mongolian leadership. As we discussed these matters, the tears gave way to a growing excitement, tentative at first, and they began to help us in planning the handover
process we'd follow in the weeks and months to come.

We decided that, at our Celebration meeting on Sunday, March 24 in the
city theater, we would give notice our foreign team was moving into an
advisory capacity to the Mongolian elders-to-be, at their request. This
was designed to ease the church into a new understanding that they, the
Mongolians, were in charge—under Christ the Head, and we were on
our way out. We would formally transfer our authority to the Mongolian leaders at a special ceremony in the near future. We wanted a period
where they exercised effective authority while we continued to be there
if they needed us. We could thus monitor how well the modeling of
servant-leadership had taken. We began functioning as silent observers.

When the time came, we must have explained it right. The church responded in a very excited and positive way, and though many came up
and told us how special and needed we were, no one told us they didn't
think the church was up to following Jesus without us. Maybe some of
the joy was due to the other announcement we made that Sunday morning. Louise and I told the church the wonderful news that God had
given us another baby—we were expecting, due in September. Everyone seemed to understand that while there was no replacing Jedidiah,

there was a restoration God was bestowing on us all. The huge significance of two coming births—a baby Mongolian church movement and a new Hogan baby —increased our sense of excited expectation.

Planning our exit was fun. I could enjoy life in Erdenet without any responsibilities beyond my four hours a day at the copper mine headquarters. We spent a lot of time entertaining our friends, Mongolian and foreign. The long winter was over—in so many ways. And yet, Mongolia still had some drama in store for us.

We were overjoyed. When you feel that good you've just got to share it with those who will understand, or you feel like you'll burst. So we sent out word of our preparations for handing over the churches to the mission community in Ulaanbaatar. As the news spread around the capital city, the reactions began to filter back to us.

"Are you nuts? What are you thinking? You have only been there three years—no way is that long enough to plant a church!"

"I knew all along you wet-behind-the-ears YWAMers would make a mess like this. It is just irresponsible sending out young untrained volunteers to plant churches. Six months of training? Ha!"

"If you'd had Bible School or seminary you'd know there is no way these Mongolians are ready for leadership. It is all going to fall to pieces within weeks of when you leave. You'd better call this off."

"Your 'leaders' out there in Erdenet will not be able to cope with the cult groups already in town and the others that will be drawn to your vulnerable groups like a pack of hungry wolves. They will be easy prey for false teachers. Who is going to defend them?"

"Anyway, the elders just can't be ready. They are going to squabble and fall apart and we will have to go out there and pick up the pieces. This is so irresponsible and inconsiderate of you. We have our own ministries and we are going to have to drop them to take over yours."

"You know there's still sin in this church."

We'd blundered into a firestorm of protests and objections we had no idea even existed. Many of our fellow missionaries, friends and colleagues, seemed to agree we had missed God's will and were abandoning our responsibilities in Erdenet. We were stunned. As we met and swapped the feedback we were getting, we had no idea how to respond. It seemed clear we needed to take what we were receiving seriously. These brothers and sisters had shown fellowship and great kindness to us in the past, especially while we were suffering. They cared for us, and their harsh words were motivated by real concern that we were making a fatal choice by handing over the reins and leaving. And yet to us the evidence we'd reached our goals was still so clear. We didn't know what to do with such contradictory guidance. I commented that rolling back what we had just announced would be like trying to put whipped cream back into the can. How do you take back a ministry someone is already doing better than you had done when it was yours? We were distraught as we considered these things. The veiled threat had not gone unnoticed, either. Some would feel it their responsibility before God to come up after we flew home and wrest away control for the Mongolian churches' own good. We felt we suddenly faced an impossible decision.

As we met and talked, and cried, and prayed under the dark storm clouds of these perplexing issues, some beams of light broke through. The first came from something the Lord reminded Magnus and Maria. Magnus shared he had been thinking about the accusation that there was still sin in the Church in Erdenet.

"That's true," I responded, "We know it better than they do."

"Yeah, it is true, but the Holy Spirit reminded Maria and me that there is still sin in the churches in Sweden that sent us here to Mongolia as well."

A light went on. "Oh, there's sin in the Vineyard Fellowship in California that sent us out too!" Louise replied.

"Well, our Foursquare church in southern Oregon certainly isn't sin-free." interjected Lance.

Ruslan and Sveta added their Siberian home church to this list, and we all realized something. None of us on the church planting team had ever experienced body life in a church that wasn't still struggling with sin. You can't plant something you have never experienced—something no one has ever modeled for you. Even if we stayed on another 20 years, or 120, we were never going to plant a sin-free church. This revelation took a huge load off our shoulders. The sin was ultimately Jesus' problem. He was the Head of His Body. He was used to this work. We could safely leave the work of perfecting His Bride in his scarred hands.

However, there were still a number of issues the missionaries had raised we couldn't answer. I found the answer we were looking for in the 20th chapter of the Book of Acts. When Paul was in this same stage with his churches, he said goodbye to his disciples. I read what he said to these elders of the Ephesus Church:

> You know everything I did during the time I was with you when I first came to Asia. Some . . . plotted against me and caused me a lot of sorrow and trouble. But I served the Lord and was humble. When I preached in public or taught in your homes, I didn't hold back from telling anything that would help you. I told Jews and Gentiles to turn to God and have faith in our Lord Jesus. . . . I have gone from place to place, preaching to you about God's kingdom, but now I know that none of you will ever see me again.

> I tell you today that I am no longer responsible for any of you! I have told you everything God wants you to know. Look after yourselves and everyone the Holy Spirit has placed in your care. Be like shepherds to God's church. It is the flock that he bought with the blood of his own Son.

> I know that after I am gone, others will come like fierce wolves to attack you. Some of your own people will tell lies to win over the Lord's followers. Be on your guard! Remember how day and night for three years I kept warning you with tears in my eyes.

I now place you in God's care. Remember the message about his great kindness! This message can help you and give you what belongs to you as God's people. . . . After Paul had finished speaking, he knelt down with all of them and prayed. Everyone cried and hugged and kissed him.   Acts 20:18-37 (CEV)

This story from our instructional manual for church planting, the New Testament, completed the revelation that Magnus and Maria had begun. The Word of God set us free from the shackles human judgments had laid on our hearts. Suddenly it was so clear—we had heard from God about leaving. Paul had shipped in the same boat we were in now. He knew storms were coming against the young church and its leaders, both from without and from within. But Paul knew something that allowed him to let go. He knew what they had received—forgiveness, faith, the Kingdom, and the love of God, in fact, "everything God wants you to know" was enough to bring them through what was to come. And he knew the church, "the flock," belonged to God who bought it with Jesus' blood. God was able to keep what He had in His hand.

Paul also acknowledged that the elders of the church were not placed there by him, but were called and placed in that function by the Holy Spirit himself. These realizations made us breathe a whole lot easier. We were greatly encouraged and felt strangely close to Paul as we read his words, but we laughed aloud when we realized he had planted the church in Ephesus in just three years. It may not have happened much in recent history, but we now had biblical proof that three years was an adequate time span for the apostolic task.

We picked ourselves up and began to move forward with confidence again toward the destiny we and the Mongolian churches had chosen. We knew our work was almost finished. The church was not perfect, but it was so ready to stand on its own.

THIRTY-THREE

Passing the Baton

Easter Sunday, 1996 made history, both in Mongolia and in the Church of Jesus Christ.

Early that morning the whole team had gathered one last time at Magnus and Maria's fifth floor apartment and shared a breakfast. The Swedes made Swedish pancakes—an act of love for the Americans, since this is normally a dinner entrée in Sweden. We chattered about the exciting events ahead—the Easter service where we would hand over the church to Mongolian leadership, our family's move home to the USA, and the rest of the team's plans for finishing their language teaching contracts and moving away as well. I brought up the fact we needed to make the transfer of authority very clear and even visual for the believers who would be at the Easter Celebration Gathering. We decided the relay race would be an excellent way to portray what was happening. The Mongolian people knew about this Olympic race, and since this was an Olympic year, the games were on everyone's mind. We fashioned a baton from a cardboard paper towel roll and some foil and ribbon to use for the visual pass. After the breakfast dishes were cleared, our whole team walked over to the auditorium rented for the celebration.

The Easter service for Jesus' Assembly of Erdenet was standing room only. Nearly 800 packed out the largest hall in the city. We later discovered that many more had been turned away by the building superintendent, who closed the doors when he saw the crowd. Those who made it in gathered to worship Jesus and to witness the ceremony marking the

About to make the pass, Magnus explains the baton analogy.

passing of authority from our apostolic church planting team to the local elders. We explained and acted out the analogy of a relay race to graphically portray what was taking place. The baton was passed from our family and Magnus, representing the church planters, to a group of Mongolian leaders in full national regalia. It symbolized our time to "run" with this Body was past, and theirs was just beginning. They were so ready! The baton was passed. For the first time in history, a fully indigenous Mongolian church was fully in Mongolian hands—and they were firmly in the nail-scarred hands of Jesus. The entire service was a celebration of joy, even in the midst of good-byes. We had only 450 baptized believers in the congregation, so many of those crowding the room were newcomers and seekers.

As the Mongolian service came to a reluctant close, I raced across town with Ruslan to our Russian daughter church. They were having their second baptism and, as I had done the first one, they wanted me to be there. When I arrived, I discovered the Russian believers expected me to actually enter the pool and baptize. I tried to protest I was unprepared and not dressed for it, but they refused to accept my refusal. I ended up exchanging my slacks for a big towel tied around my waist, and I got in and baptized 13 new believers, including two entire families. I then apologized for having to run, but I was in danger of missing the van taking my family and our bags to the train station. I quickly dried off and redressed—without my soaking wet underwear—and started to run for our apartment. By the time I got home, the underwear, which I was holding as I ran, had frozen into a solid ball around my fist. Dealing with that was an ironic task considering the loftier spiritual pursuits I had been involved with all day. God has ways of bringing one down to earth.

The van was already being loaded and I just made it. Louise, the kids and I squeezed in with all our bags, and many friends and headed off to the train station. When we arrived, there were many hands to get our things over to the train and into our compartment. A great number of

Goodbyes on the train station platform

the Mongolian believers had beaten us to the platform, and we worshipped, prayed, wept, and hugged until the train left. It was heart wrenching for all of us leaving dear friends and teammates with no clear plan for when we would see one another again. Our girls were leaving the home they had lived in longer than any other and the only one Alice could even remember. Trains don't pause for emotions or goodbyes, though, and ours pulled out of the Erdenet station with Mongolian friends running alongside, waving. Louise and I had barely dried our tears when we looked out the window and saw the hill Jedidiah was buried on. A fresh batch of tears sprouted as we remembered what else we were leaving behind.

. . . and we're leaving on a slow train . . .

The next morning our train arrived at the main terminal in Ulaanbaatar, and the Leatherwood family was there to pick us up for our good-bye breakfast with our Mongolian Enterprises coworkers. After breakfast, Helen Richardson, Rick, Laura, and their kids drove us to the airport one last time, and then, after almost three and a half years, we flew away from our adopted country.

THIRTY-FOUR

'The Road Goes Ever on and on'

"Surely you don't disbelieve the prophecies, because you had a hand in bringing them about yourself? You don't really suppose, do you, that all your adventures and escapes were managed by mere luck, just for your sole benefit? You are a very fine person, Mr. Baggins, and I am very fond of you; but you are only quite a little fellow in a wide world after all."

The Hobbit by J.R.R. Tolkien

After leaving Mongolia, we flew to Copenhagen and traveled by rail around Europe for a couple months. Louise and I shared about what God had done in Erdenet with a number of groups at YWAM bases and at the churches of friends in the 11 nations we were able to visit. The girls were good travelers, but some of the finer points of culture were lost on them. Asked at the end of a very full Louvre museum day in Paris what impressed them the most, their answer was not Mona Lisa, Winged Victory, or Venus de Milo. "The donuts in the basement!" was their sole enthusiastic memory. Five months into her pregnancy, Louise voted for The Wedding at Cana, by Renaissance painter Paolo Veronese, but admitted when pressed that her favorite thing about this painting was the comfy bench under it. Things improved when I backed off on the museums, and "The Sound of Music" tour of Salzburg had a much better reception. Europe was a good way to decompress from the life we were leaving behind. The return to California held many shocks that would have been all the harder to face had we attempted the re-entry just hours after leaving Mongolia.

We arrived at my mother's home in Atascadero, California, re-involved ourselves in church life at our two local sending churches, and began to prepare for a home birth at Nana's house. We were planning a move to the Caribbean to work with YWAM in training up and sending church planting missionaries from that region, but we needed to have the baby first. My parents were gracious in providing our large and noisy family a safe haven for the summer.

On the tenth of August, Peter Magnus joined the Hogan family. Our joy at welcoming another son was overwhelming. Jedidiah was not to be replaced, but the Father was faithful in sending us consolation and new beginnings. I plunged into full-time study for a Master's Degree in Ministry, focused on Intercultural Studies, from Hope International University. The school was in Southern California, but I used mentored distance learning and completed my degree from home. I ended up being one of the very first to study through the World Christian Foundations Program developed by Dr. Ralph Winter. It was the most rigorous and rewarding study I've undertaken—a Perspectives course on steroids!

In 1998 we moved again—north this time—to foggy and cool Humboldt County, California. Up among the redwoods on the North Coast we joined a ministry called Church Planting Coaches we'd been exploring since our furlough three years earlier. Kevin and Laura Sutter had been single-handedly running this international service ministry of Youth With A Mission for years and were overjoyed to have reinforcements at last. In 2013 Louise and I bought a house in Fayetteville, Arkansas, changing domicile but not our ministry. From our home in the Ozarks, we continue to train and sustain more than 300 YWAM church planting teams around the globe. I travel and teach extensively in YWAM's training schools and in many Perspectives classes, and we develop resources to equip those desiring to see churches multiply among the unreached.

I've managed to return to Mongolia several times over the years since we left. I savor the hospitality of our old teammate Mats, his lovely wife Chimgee and their beautiful Swedish-Mongolian daughter, Lisa. Chimgee was one of the earliest believers in Erdenet and her sister was the girl who had died the same Christmas as Jed.

The first two times I returned I taught church planting in the SOFM that YWAM Erdenet runs yearly. What an incredible experience to sit in a ger and teach Mongolian missionaries the same New Testament principles God used to bring them into the Kingdom such a short time ago.

On one of these trips I was finally able to place a headstone on the grave.

Visiting Jed's grave

GPS coordinates:
N49°07.471′ E104°09.808′

Our whole family returned together in 2000. The visit was satisfying for all of us and provided some needed catharsis. I made this my last time of teaching in the SOFM by training my replacement. Bayaraa is now an accomplished church planting trainer in her own right. At the very end of the visit, during what was to be our final night in Erdenet, I came down with appendicitis. Unable to be flown out, I ended up under the knife at a small Russian clinic in Erdenet. That harrowing story is recounted in An A to Z of Near-Death Adventures (Asteroidea Books) [to see the author's appendix, turn ahead to page 261]. It would be another five years before I walked on Mongolian soil again.

In November 2005, I was back in Erdenet for the Annual Mongolian Mission Conference. I had been asked to be the keynote speaker. I was stunned to see the very hall where we had passed the baton of leadership in 1996 crammed full to way beyond capacity for a week. There were 1000 people crammed into a room designed for 700. It was standing room only, and they had gone to an invitation-only format several years before because attendance continually outstrips the available space.

A well-dressed middle-aged Mongolian man stepped up to great me during one of the breaks. He introduced himself and quickly added he knew me but I didn't know him. He was one of Jesus' Assembly's current elders. He wanted to share about the day he had "met" me.

"On a Sunday morning in spring 1996, I came with my friend to a large meeting here. There was a lot of happiness and excitement, but it didn't draw me in. Then, towards the end, I saw something I had never seen, never even heard about before. You and some others got up on the stage and did something that stunned me. You handed away real power. You were the leaders of this huge group, and you gave it to these Mongolians and walked away. No one ever does that! I didn't understand what I was seeing but I knew I had to return. Within a month I was a disciple and now, almost 10 years later, I am leading in this church. Your disciples followed your example and passed on their leadership as God led them to new works. I wanted to meet you again and thank you."

At the same conference I caught up with Baagii and Naraa, a young couple who exemplify the best in Mongolian church planters. Baagii was one of the original 14 teen girl disciples in Jesus' Assembly. Naraa, her husband, had been in prison while we were in Mongolia. He had come to faith through a Mongolian Bible his mother had sent him. Upon his release, he had come to Erdenet to be discipled in his new walk. Eventually both he and Baagii had gone through the Mongolian Mission Center's (now YWAM Erdenet) Discipleship Training School and SOFM (with me teaching church planting), married and gone off to plant new churches. Their initial target was Darhan, Mongolia's second largest city. The last time I had seen them, I'd been on my way to Erdenet. They had shown up at midnight in my sleeper compartment while the train was parked at the Darhan station. They reported they had been working in Darhan for just a year and had already planted a congregation of 110 and three daughter churches. With all the excitement, I was a long time getting back to sleep after they'd left my sleeper compartment.

Meeting Naraa and Baagii in my train compartment

Not many months later, I received a letter from Baagii with a photograph of them passing a baton to the leaders they had trained in the Darhan church. Actually handling such visible and tangible proof that the movement was now spontaneously reproducing was, for me at least, like touching a holy relic must have been for my ancestors in the Dark Ages.

When Baagii, Naraa and I met again at the conference I asked them about the photo. I mentioned I was surprised they had not stayed on in Darhan as pastors. With surprised looks they responded, "But Brian, we're apostles—and apostles leave."

The model had been seen, understood, and replicated.

Clockwise from top left: 1. Mongol church planters sent out by Karakorum daughter church to Dongxiang of Gansu, China. 2. Author training cross-cultural church planters in SOFM at YWAM Erdenet. 3. Buryat tribal believers, reached by our disciples, requesting missionary training. 4. Author with Baika ('Grieving with Hope'), 2011. 5. Author and son, Peter Magnus, visiting Jedidiah's plane JU-2114. 6. Our disciples worshiping at Jed's grave. 7. Author considering the price paid. Jesus is worthy. 8. Baagii and Naraa (pg. 249), leading the Church of Mongolia, in 2011. 9. Author's son with a Khazakh's eagle at Zaisun Memorial in Ulaanbaatar. 10. Author interviewed on Eagle TV Mongolia upon receiving award at "20 Years of the Gospel in Mongolia." Center: Award given to Brian and Louise Hogan by the Mongolian Church.

Epilogue: Grieving with Hope

On Thanksgiving Day, 1997, Baika and I were staring out over the endless Pacific Ocean when he calmly declared, "Your grief over the death of your son was the most miraculous thing I have ever experienced."

Baika Puntsag, today pastor of Denver's Amazing Grace Church, America's first Mongolian Christian church, had come to spend the Thanksgiving holiday with us in a very strange way. A faithful worker in one of the Korean-led Ulaanbaatar churches, Baika had turned up on a tourist visa at YWAM base in Chico, California. He had been there for several weeks and mentioned to them that he really wanted to connect with the Hogan family who had worked with YWAM in Mongolia and were now said to be living in California. After some tracking and searching by the staff in Chico, we received a call, and I found myself on the line with Baika, whom I'd never met. He said that he hoped he could come south 400 miles (644 km) to our home in Los Osos and stay with us for Thanksgiving. I gathered the YWAM base would be near empty over the long weekend. I wondered what the connection was, but asking would have been rude, so I let him know he was more than welcome. There was one additional detail; I needed to buy tickets for Greyhound. Baika's funds were depleted.

When he arrived in Los Osos, Baika slid into our family life like a hand in a glove. He was a like a younger brother to Louise and me and an incredibly fun older brother to the kids. One of Peter Magnus's first words was "Baika." When I found he'd never laid eyes on an ocean, not uncommon for landlocked Mongolians, I couldn't wait to get him to the nearby Atascadero State Beach.

Baika's dumbfounded awe at the majestic immensity of the Pacific was every bit as satisfying as I'd imagined. As we walked along and he got over being stunned, he began to beach comb and to share his thoughts.

"I think you must be wondering why I wanted to be with you." The twinkle in his eye might have been the afternoon sun glancing off the breakers.

"I didn't want to ask, but yeah, I'm curious. Why us?"

"Even though we never actually met in Mongolia, I know your family." And 'the little brother I'd never had' began to pour out a story that was still very powerful and emotional to him several years after it happened:

> I was saved in the early days of the coming of Christ to Mongolia. My friends and I were so in love with Jesus we wanted to spend all our time worshipping. I began to work in many ministries in my church in Ulaanbaatar. We were all so busy that I didn't even notice when other things slowly began to push my heart away from Jesus. I began a relationship with a girl hoping that she would follow me to Jesus, but it didn't work out that way. She began to criticize my faith and my work at the church. At around the same time, the Korean missionary who was pastoring our church let us know that the path to leadership led through seminary in Korea. I was frustrated that I would be required to learn Korean to lead in a Mongolian church. I lost heart.
>
> Finally, I gave up the struggle. The joy had gone and I just wanted out. I decided to get it over with quickly by going to a New Year's Eve meeting for those in ministry at my church and announcing that I was quitting. I really didn't want to face the pastor, but I felt I had to let my friends hear it from me rather than through gossip. My heart was hard. I wasn't thinking about Jesus anymore.
>
> I went into the meeting determined to say my news quickly at the beginning and then leave at once. It really annoyed me that a girl excitedly spoke out before I could say a word and began to share about her Christmas visit to Erdenet.
>
> This girl was a friend who'd been involved in the church even longer than I had. She had gone up to visit Bayaraa, whom

most of us had known before she left Ulaanbaatar with Magnus and Maria. My friend shared about the horrible shock of the news of Jed's death that came during the Christmas party. She also told us about the gathering at your home after the burial and the memorial service. As she told us what you had shared and how you and Louise had responded to this tragedy, we began to weep. My own hard heart melted as I cried.

"That means a lot to me. We all cried a lot that Christmas," I assured Baika.

"That is not why we were crying though. We were crying at our understanding though your grief."

I was completely confused, "What . . .?'

"Your grief over the death of your son was the most miraculous thing I have ever experienced," Baika explained.

As he said this, the memory of several of the believers in Erdenet saying something very similar when we saying our goodbyes a year and a half earlier came rushing back to me. I had quickly forgotten their statements about our grief being a miracle because it made no sense to me. I had felt that my grief, which I couldn't hide, was a bad advertisement for the Kingdom. I had begged God to allow us to grieve in private in the States with family, and had been completely puzzled when He had made it clear to both of us that we were to stay in Erdenet during the worst months of mourning. I began to get a strange buzzing sensation as if I were about to open a door into a room filled with mystery.

"Could you please explain that for me, Baika?"

"Brian, you can't really understand what it is like for Mongolians. In your country everyone seems to believe in life after death. But in Mongolia no one has any hope for this at all. When loved ones die, they are gone forever! You will never meet or see them again. Mothers in my country sometimes lose their minds when they lose a child. But you were different. You were the first people we had ever seen, or even heard about, who grieved with hope. It came across in what you said about going to where your son is, even if he wasn't returning to you here, in the song you taught during the funeral meal at your flat, and the statement of faith you made at Jed's memorial service. You were being watched, then and over the months that followed. Seeing you and your family grieve *with hope* filled the gaping hole that has always been in every Mongolian heart. When I heard about your grief I *knew* it was all real. The Bible, Jesus, heaven, all of it. That's why we were weeping that New Year's Eve—we had just had our faith confirmed.

I repented before my brother and sisters of what I had been intending to do. I have continued to follow Jesus, and I have come to America to get an education in journalism so that I can start a Christian newspaper and radio station in Mongolia."

I was filled with extreme joy and overwhelmed with love as I realized how far out of His way God had gone to make sure we understood. It was all worth it. God had redeemed even our deepest sorrow and turned it into glory and worshipers. As tears ran down my cheeks, all I could think was "Jesus is worthy."

This thought was carved onto Jed's headstone the next time I visited Erdenet.

Since that day other Mongolians have shared variations on Baika's story, both old friends and strangers, in Mongolia and in the USA. I will never understand like they do, but it is clear that something happened in the hearts of the Mongolian believers as they watched and heard about our grief. At the very point where we felt weakest and doubted God's plan the most, the Father was doing His biggest miracle through us!

Afterword: *Sheep*'s 10th Anniversary

The decade since the publication of There's a Sheep in my Bathtub has provided two opportunities to return to Erdenet, though my global travels have increased my list of visited countries to 70.

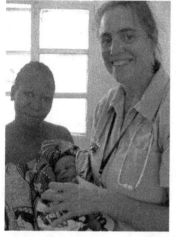

In Spring of 2011, Louise and I, along with our 14-year-old son, Peter Magnus, were on the homestretch of a six month stay in Tanzania. Louise was doing her practical outreach for a Birth Attendant School and Peter and I were along for the year-long ride through Australia, East Africa and India. Even though we were all there for Louise's "baby catching", opportunities to train church planters came along frequently.

On February 1st, I was training Maasai people near Mount Kilamanjaro and made the mistake of checking my email during a break. I found an email from a stranger, the director of Missionary Aviation Fellowship in Mongolia written on January 31st. He was asking my permission to use our son Jedidiah's birthdate as the new registration number of their plane serving Mongolia. They recognized the impact Jed's short life and death had on the Mongolian Church and wanted to memorialize him in this way. My students returned to find their teacher bawling like a baby at the podium. Louise and I told them we'd be honored and the plane was christened JU-2114 for Jedidiah Unforgotten - 2 Nov. 94. I was looking forward to a chance to see Jed's airplane on the trip Peter and I were planning to Mongolia in just three months.

The Mongolian Church was planning a celebration of 20 Years of the Gospel in Mongolia and they were inviting the missionary pioneers to return and tell the story of the Church's beginnings. Louise's training would still be underway in its India portion, but we were determined that at least one of us had to go.

It was not long after training those Maasai leaders that I received a phone call from our daughter telling me that my mother was dying from advanced cancer and I needed to hurry back to the states. I changed my flights and bid Louise and Peter a tearful farewell as we all flew from Africa: me to California and the two of them to Hyderabad. My mother lasted, mostly in the hospital, until July 15th, a week after her 76th birthday. We were thankful that Louise finished her Birth Attendant School in time to say goodbye to the woman she considered "the world's greatest mother-in-law." It was these difficult and portentous times that formed the backdrop to our revisiting Mongolia.

Peter and I arrived in time for the 20th Anniversary celebrations. It was incredible to see the huge crowd of believers from churches across Mongolia gather in the hall in Ulaanbaatar worshipping in unity together and honoring us, the Leatherwoods (with me in pic), and other pioneers who managed the journey to the event. As the churches were introduced in a roll call, I was thrilled to see the largest contingent stand when "Jesus' Assembly in Erdenet" was called.

The high point for the three-day event turned out to be a complete surprise. The pioneers had been drawn back for a "television interview panel" on the morning after we thought things concluded. It turned out to be a ruse so that the Church of Mongolia could give us awards. I didn't see this coming and I broke down in sobs as a boy and girl dressed in royal Mongol regalia reverently handed me a huge spray of flowers and an award reading: "Brian and Louise Hogan For Pioneering in the

Gospel of Jesus Christ in Mongolia. John 4:36. The Church of Mongolia 19.05.2011". I treasure this more than any earthly reward and in my heart, it will only be eclipsed by Jesus saying, "Well done."

The next day, Peter and I visited Jed's plane in the MAF-Blue Sky Aviation hangar, but sadly, they were short a part and we couldn't take a flight. We spent the rest of the trip in Erdenet. Now Peter could put a real place to the family stories he'd heard growing up, yet never experienced himself. We visited his brother's grave with some of our Mongolian disciples and had a meaningful time remembering together on that hillside. Taking Peter through our old

apartment, now a restaurant, provided a fun moment when I mentioned that the dining room we were standing in was where he'd been conceived. He was embarrassed as any teen would be by that announcement, though I doubt any of the diners surrounding us understood my English.

The master bedroom of our old apartment --- now a dining area in a small restaurant.

It was six years before my feet hit Mongolian soil again. Louise and I became "empty-nesters" and moved to northwest Arkansas. She began training village midwifes in African nations and I continued to train church planters and mobilize for missions through teaching in the Perspectives course (averaging 65-70 classes a year). In 2017 we decided it was time to release this book in a fresh edition for new readers on the tenth anniversary of its initial release. I was invited to train workers in Nanjing, China and decided I couldn't resist tagging on a two-week Mongolia trip so I could append an update. As I write this I am still a bit jetlagged from this amazing journey. I was in Mongolia the entire first half of September 2017, most of that time in Erdenet. I spent time teaching in the Mongolian Mission Center (YWAM Erdenet) which has invited Louise and I to return next year for its 20th Anniversary. What a wonder to hear of Mongolian church planting teams laboring among all Mongolian tribes as well as in numerous other peoples and nations (Russia, China, Tibet, Afghanistan, USA, Sweden, etc.). The fact that they have launched movements among formerly unreached peoples --- passed the baton --- and returned home for redeployment gave me the chills and brought tears to my eyes. Both in the Erdenet Church and going from home to home I reconnected with our early believers and the hordes of those who have come in after our departure. Sharing about discerning religion from relationship in the Erdenet mother congregation of our movement was almost as rewarding as frequent shared meals and life with our disciples. Just witnessing their continued faithful obedience and how the movement continues to expand, even to other nations, made everything worthwhile. Jesus is worthy!

Jesus' Assembly in Erdenet has huge outreach goals mapped out and a flag to plant among the nations.

I crossed paths with our Mongolian parents, Ragchaa and Oyuun (now 76 and 75 years old, pictured 22 years ago on pg. 52) leaving the next morning to church plant in the Gobi Desert! My heroes! I was told I'd just missed seeing Odgerel, one of our three original elders and pastor for over 20 years, as he and his family had just set off to be long term missionaries in a huge nation to the east.

During my third day in Erdenet, a group of friends took me out to Jed's grave. I buried a small cedar box containing my mother's ashes

Author with his Mongolian parents, Ragchaa and Oyuun

in the grave of the one grandchild who met her in Heaven. It was so powerful as we each made declarations while standing around this precious plot of earth. I declared that it was worth it as I marveled at the thousands upon thousands in God's Kingdom because of those standing around the grave of that "seed of wheat."

Former teammates, Ruslan and Svetlana

Another evening I enjoyed renewing relationship with our former teammates, Ruslan and Svetlana, and meeting the youngest two of their five kids. They've led another of Erdenet's churches for almost two decades.

Erdenet is home to many churches these days, but I was impressed at the unity and love between these bodies and the way that all look to Jesus' Assembly as model and most successful

— though it's the only church in town without its own building. Surrounded by so many examples of more standard western style churches, our folks often experience a bit of an "Edifice Complex" but as I shared with the elders and leaders they were once again coming back to an awareness of the strength they had in what they assumed was a weakness — meeting in homes. The Disciple Making Movement that God began through weak, untried and young vessels from the USA, Sweden, and Russia continues to defy all expectations (except God's) and reap a harvest from the nations.

My last three days in the country were filled by a surprise invitation to a spare seat on Jed's plane flying charters of hunters and adventure tourists around Mongolia. These trips finance the medical, humanitarian and gospel work of MAF — done with this mighty little nine passenger plane.

My ride turned into three days and two nights of a tour around and across the marvelous land of Mongolia that, although having lived there for three years, I'd seen so little of. We flew east to some sand dunes and dropped passengers off on a temporary runway, then turned around and flew across the country to the western town and province of Khovd, where we spent the night. Our pilots intended to cross the towering Altai mountain range early in the morning to pick up their hunting clients, but gale force winds grounded us until afternoon and we barely had time to retrieve the hunters in the Khazakh lands of the far west before flying south and east to drop them in the Gobi Desert. We were forced to land in Arvaikheer in Övörkhangai Province and stay in another hotel until we could take off for Ulaanbaatar the next morning. What a grand adventure. There are no words to describe the wild and wonderful lands my eyes watched flowing under my son's plane. A sheer unalloyed pleasure to last a lifetime. What a gift!

Appendix: Two Obstacles

As I coach church planters all over the world, I get to evaluate a variety of approaches to this difficult task. God has relentlessly brought two facts to my attention—the two main obstacles to church planting movements across our world.

One: What we are doing is too complex. Even though we stress to those we train that they must reduce the "heavy package" of 'Church As We Know It' to bare New Testament essentials before carrying it to an unreached people group, most church planters are still struggling to strip away the cultural elements that slow or stop reproduction in the new cultural setting. For example, dispensing with the need for a special "holy" building to meet in on Sundays may be easier than modeling active ministry by every believer. The church planter often does so much of the work himself that the fledgling church sees ministry as something only full time religious professionals can accomplish. The movement is stillborn since "qualified leadership" can never reproduce itself rapidly enough. One thing we really need is a simpler and more Biblical view of what "church" actually means. When I speak of "church" in this book; I mean the living organism that corporately forms Jesus' Body and Bride on this planet, not a religious organization. In practical terms: a gathering of any size, committed to one another and to obeying the commands of the Lord Jesus Christ. We have been lugging around a model and definition of "church" that is far too complex and encrusted with layers of nonessential, non-Biblical "barnacles." We need to get radical in simplification.

Two: We don't trust the Holy Spirit in the life of the believer. The biggest reason indigenous churches are continuing, year after year, under foreign direction and control, and why new churches are not even allowed to form in many cases, is a deep distrust of God's ability to work His purposes through others. This is what is behind our reluctance to release our disciples into real responsibility and leadership. We can trust God to work through us, but we think they will mess it up. We need to return to the Bible and take a good look at the Holy Spirit's jobs (conviction of sin, bringing the Word to remembrance, guiding, etc.) and quit trying to do His work for Him. We need to look at Paul's model again. Paul consistently left baby churches for months and even years before appointing elders (or any other leaders beyond Jesus Christ). As he says farewell to the Ephesians' elders in Acts 20, Paul says he knows that they will be attacked from without and within, but he entrusts and commits them to God. He trusts the Holy Spirit to do His job presenting His church in Ephesus as spotless and holy. We must get radical in trusting in God's Spirit in our fellow believers' lives.

In the church planting training we do around the world, we are exposing this pair of obstacles and equipping workers to overcome them. Through the grace of God I continue to learn more all the time about how He wants His Kingdom spread and multiplied. Simplicity and trust in God's Spirit opened the doors of Mongolia to the Kingdom of God.

Keeping it simple at Lake Huvsgul

About the Author

BRIAN HOGAN earned his Master's in Ministry from Hope International University (Fullerton, CA) specializing in World Christian Foundations. He is a sought-after speaker, trainer and coach. Brian serves full time with Church Planting Coaches; a global ministry of Youth With A Mission. He serves YWAM on the Frontier Mission Leadership Team. He enjoys being a catalyst, hanging out, reading books, traveling and trying anything new, novel, and different.

Brian has participated in, led, and started organic expressions of Jesus' Body in the USA, Malta, and Mongolia both inside and outside the traditional wineskin. He coaches those involved in these movements on five continents, especially focusing on where the church isn't.

He is also the author of "An A to Z of Near-Death Adventures" and "Boy Centurions", as well as the article "Distant Thunder: Mongols Follow the Khan of Khans" a case study in *Perspectives on the World Christian Movement: a Reader* (1999; William Carey Library). Brian's training course *Keys to Church Planting Movements* is available and other books, video and audio are available at: www.store.AsteroideaBooks.com

Brian and his wife Louise call the Ozarks home these days, caring for their backyard chickens in Fayetteville, Arkansas, as well as traveling the globe for Brian's teaching and Louise's training of 2/3rds World village midwives.

Enquiries regarding booking Brian and/or Louise for speaking engagements, or regarding translating *There's a Sheep in my Bathtub* or printing outside the USA should be directed to Asteroidea Books.

Also available from

ASTEROIDEA
Books